Gð. Dr. Casp

Ek Einherjar: Hammer of the Gods, 2nd ed.

ISBN: 978-09854760-1-4
Library of Congress Control Number: 2018940547

Also by Gð. Dr. Casper Odinson Cröwell

Vor Forn Siðr
A handbook for the living Einherjar and Valkyrjar
ISBN 978-0-985-47600-7

Ek Einherjar: Hammer of the Gods, 1st ed. 2009©
ISBN: 978-0-615-33074-7

Ek Einherjar:

Hammer of the Gods

2nd ed. Revised and Expanded
By Goði Dr. Casper Odinson Cröwell, Ph.D., DD

Vinland Kindred Publishing
PO Box 630
Kingsburg, CA 93631

Cover Art

Open Source – design Dr. Cröwell

Interior Art

Douglas Heuton
Gð. Harvald Odinson Jones, 1519-CGDC
Gð. Casper Odinson Cröwell, 1519-CCG
Gð. Linda Friggasdóttir Cröwell
Gð. Viðar U. Odinson Harless, 1519-CG (HPS)

Format and Layout

1st ed. Mrs. Linda Cröwell and Ms. Vicky Sharland
2nd ed. Gð. Linda Friggasdóttir Cröwell

"Einherjar" by Douglas Heuton, 2009 CE, Original Cover Acrylic

Dedication

This book is dedicated first and formost to Allfather Odin, and thereafter to to my wife, Linda Friggasdóttir Cröwell, and my sons.

To all Trú Folk walking the Northern Road and Elder ways of the Aryan Tribes. To the Kin and Kith of the Midgard Kindreds of the Sons of Odin, 1519, but especially my Brothers of the Vinland Kindred 1519.

Heil to you All!

<u>IN MEMORY OF</u>

Mein Oma
Mom and Dad
Robert "Animal" Odinson Emery
B.W. Schmidt
Howard "Wolf Odinson" Estacio
Robert Jay Mathews
David E. Lane
Else "Odinsdottír Christensen
Ian Stuart Donaldson
Johnny L.
Justin Thomas Giggy
the Noble wolf himself,
R. Hess
and
All those who died true to the Aryan spirit!

"Vinland Forever,
Forever Vinland!"

The Flag of Vinland

TABLE OF CONTENT

PART II – FAITH

PART III – PROSE AND POETRY

APPENDIX

The Road Home, *Painting by Gð. Harvald Odinson Jones, 1519-CGDC*

FORWARD
To the First Edition

Joseph Campbell, noted authority on mythology stated that unless Western Man can spontaneously create an 'updated' mythology for himself, he will not survive. Fortunately for Western Man (Aryans) we do have great minds who have stepped forward, reached into our Indo-Aryan past and updated the mythology of our Teutonic ancestors to fit the needs of our People in the twenty-first century and beyond. Our Folk Mother, Else Christensen and Heimgest of the Odinic Rite are two such people. Their great minds and spirituality have advanced Odinism (unlike stagnant New Age Ásatrú) beyond the Viking Age and into the modern age. My two mentors who restored me to Wotanism, Jost Turner and Ron McVan are giants when it comes to their work of reaching into our Hyperborean past and updating the Teutonic religion of our ancestors to fit today's and tomorrow's needs of our People. I greatly value what I have learned from each of these four people. The literature they produced and personal correspondence with me helped to guide and shape my path to higher evolution.

In the past few years, we have had another great mind arise and heed the call. I have never met anyone, including the four mentioned above, who I agree with 100 percent of the time and I doubt I ever will. That is one of the great things about the religion of our ancestors; it speaks to each of us in a slightly different way. Be that as it may, when I started reading Dr. Casper Odinson Cröwell's writings, I found much of what he wrote that spoke to me. The book you now hold in your hands is a compilation of Dr. Cröwell's writings. As you read his words, do not be surprised if you feel something stirring within you. What you are feeling is the call of our ancient Gods who live within our Blood. Heed this call. This is a step towards connection with the collective unconscious of our People, our Folk Soul. True spirituality is nothing more than making this connection with our Folk Soul. May Dr. Cröwell's writings speak to you as they have to me, and may this book begin you on the path that restores you to the Myth of the Blood.

14 Words,
Richard Scutari
Kith of HNO and Sons of Odin, 1519

INTRODUCTION

Heil the Order of 1519

Of my thirty-seven years of walking around this world I have been incarcerated for over twenty-one of the last twenty-two years and have been in Fettersgrove for over the last twenty. I have met many, many people and for the most part the typical stereotype of convicts are true, especially here in California. Except for the small handful of individuals, the California convict either use drugs, play with fags, drinks until he's a slobbering idiot or constantly lies and breaks his oaths and tries to justify all this behavior with whatever his pickled brain can come up with.

For these reasons and a few others I have walked alone for pretty much the whole time that I have been incarcerated. For the first eleven years of my sentence I never once uttered the words "brother" or "bro" to another man within these walls until I met Dr. Casper Odinson Cröwell, who is not only my brother, but also chieftain and Gothi. This brotherhood almost didn't come to be, for just as much as I didn't care for and was disgusted by most of the prison population, so was he. Neither one of us was looking to walk alongside anyone else and especially call them "brother." For those who truly believe in the Norns, you know that sometimes we don't always get what we want in this life. I must say that I am very pleased to have been wrong in this case. The first man that I have called "brother" and "bled in the trench" with was Dr. Cröwell and it was a decision that I have never regretted. I am proud and consider it an honor to walk with and be a part of all that he and his wonderful wife Linda have created. Few people have made the sacrifices the Dr. Cröwell has in his life to keep his word, to walk the way that he talks and to promote what he believes in. I can say this for I have been with him, heard his words and witnessed his actions everyday for just about ten years. Just a few of the people whom I believe have made such sacrifices are Bob Matthews, David Lane, Ron McVan, Steve McNallen and Else Christensen. All of these people Dr. Cröwell has a deep love and respect for this reason.

Many people out in the world have read Dr. Cröwell's words, seen him on television and heard his messages on his internet sites and wish that they had a chance to meet him. People here in prison who have had such an opportunity either have the utmost respect for him or can't stand him. You either respect this man or hate him for the very same reasons, what he says he means and means what he says, he loves his Gods and folk and won't stand for the defilement of either, will do what he can to help a good Aryan man/woman as long as they are trying to help themselves and will have nothing to do with self accepted weaknesses. These strengths that Dr. Cröwell possesses are what he looks for in those when bringing someone into the ranks of the Sacred Circle of the Sons of Odin, 1519. For it is the duty of the Sons of Odin to serve in whatever way possible Odin's Holy Nation.

Dr. Cröwell has dedicated his life to the promotion of his/our Gods, first and foremost our father, All-father Odin and to the awakening and advancement of his folk.

So, if you are wondering what Dr. Cröwell is like, as you read his words you will soon find out, for what he writes is what he thinks and believes.

May you all come to know the powerful Gods of your ancestors and enjoy your journey down the
Northern Road.

HAIL ODIN!

Harvald Odinson Jones, 1519-CGDC
Holy Nation of Odin and Sons of Odin, 1519

A NOTE FROM THE AUTHOR

It is an easy thing to learn how to talk Trú North. Yet, it is an entirely different reality to walk that talk. For those who actually do, it can be a very lonely road at times; in some instances, perhaps for many years. For many will harbor animosities against you for a myriad of reasons. For the agents amassed against thee are not always those of the enemies' camps. Far too often they are from within our own. They are the many dissenters and provocateurs who suffer from a host of personality disorders. Counted among them will be immature personalies, halfhearted conviction in their avowed beliefs, the 'You're not the boss of me'; and 'I want to be the leader' syndromes, etc., etc... They will resent you for their own short comings if you refuse to condone them. They will engender slander and lies against you. They will accuse you of being arrogant and elitist because you continue to walk the way you talk.

To be certain, we all have our own idiosyncrasies and personality conflicts with others. This is no crime. It just is the way it is. But the afore stated personalities are the types whom will see that the tide is rising, per se, but will all the same refuse to stand next to those he cares not for or disagrees with, in order to fill and stack the sand bags in a concerted effort to stop the flood, as it were.

Such a selfish disposition is counter-conducive to the common goal of our Faith and Folk's survival. Period!

For the sake of maintaining Frith/Peace, I have invested years with such types in an effort to enrich both Faith and Folk. But the time comes when one must be honest with oneself and see the detriment for what it is, and accept realty. Thereafter, one must alter one's course in service to the greater good.

We, as both a Faith and a Folk, suffer the many maladies which burden our advancement due to our unwillingness to change our heading when we can finally see the rocks ahead. Instead, we more oft than not elect to crash the ship upon the rocks and thereafter struggle to stay afloat. This is what we are essentially doing when we place the welfare of floundering small groups before that of the entire Faith and/or Folk! If a group of Folk do not truly share the same common goal in deed as well as in word, then they have no business together in the first place. Sharing a proximity in locale should not and must not become the determining factor in the endeavor to such formations. For when this occurs not only does said group and its membership suffer, but the Faith and Folk as a whole suffer as well. The survival and advancement of our Faith and our Folk must always assume the station of primacy, lest we forget the sacred mission of the 14 WORDS!

I believe that a great champion and leader of our Folk will arise in the not too distant future. But the path which he/she must travel must be well illuminated and highly visible. Such prerequisites demand selfless and devout torch bearers to keep the flames of that illumination alive. I am but one among many whom have accepted the great and awesome burden of that all sacred responsibility. Though I did not seek such a responsibility, I did not shirk or seek to selfishly shrug it off when it was hoisted upon my shoulders. I have accepted the torch of the sacred fire of the Aryan Tribes which our ancestors had held in their outstretched hands, awaiting those both willing and fit to bear the burden. And with pride and genuine purpose, I shall hold it ever high to light the way for he/she who is to come! Or to pass it on to the next bearer, that the flame may never die.

Were my own convictions in this not stalwart, then what an expensive and futile exercise in forfeiture of a great deal of money, time, effort and my own personal liberty, this all would have been!

Fortunately, for both myself as well as those whom have placed their trust in my efforts, my noble convictions remain inexorable.

As for the loneliness associated with traveling the road less taken, such has been a great engine wherefore motivation is in regard. The fruit of said motivation awaits your perusal on the pages which follow. My contribution to keeping the flame alive for the next link in a great and mighty chain... the next awaiting torch bearer.

Fetter Grove, Lower West Vinland
For the 14 WORDS

"Cattle die, kinsmen die,
the self must also die;
but glory never dies,
for the one who is able to achieve it."[1]

- The Hávamál; Stanza 76[1]

---

[1] 1. Larrington, Carolyne, ed. The Poetic Edda, trans. Oxford University Press, 1996 ISBN 0-19-283946-2

"Victory or Valhalla" by Gð. Viðar U. Odinson Harless, 1519-CG (HPS)

FORWARD
To the 2nd Edition

The subtitle of this book, 'Hammer of the Gods', is indeed apt. It obviously relates to the instrumentality of the Einherjar, who dedicate our eternal lives to serving the Will of the Allfather Odin, who is 'Wotan' (the Will Of The Aryan Nations). The Einherjar are devoted to Truth and Order, for we are the Vanguard of the Host; the rocks upon which the tidal wave of death and destruction must break. As we are all comprised of a Spirit, Soul and Body, it must stand to reason that there must be a Greater Body, a Host, a 'Hammer', for the Warrior Spirit to wield, in the service of the Eternal Soul; the flame from which all Sparks derive. For the Aryan people our instrumentality is a given, as is our creative nature, albeit Goethe poses the quintessential paradigm: "We are either the anvil, or the hammer". The Honorable Herjan, Goði Dr. Casper Odinson Cröwell, herein provides us with our very own "hammer"; our theological instrument, with which we may re-forge our faith into a comprehensive way of life, or Vor Forn Siðr (our ancient religion). Just as Asa-Thor must wield His hammer, Mjöllnir, so too must we wield our own hammers. This requires us to gird ourselves with fortitude and discipline, as Thor is girded by His belt of power, Meginjörð, and with a firm grip on reality, as embodied in His iron gauntlet, Járngreipr.

As the Father of what has come to be Fundamental Odinism, Goði Dr. Cröwell has led the way in both identifying, and elucidating the truly essential tenets of our faith. From many of the theological essays in 'Ek Einherjar', fundamental doctrines have been established. In the chapters titled "Fundamental Odinism" and "Odinism vs. Asatru", we come to realize the divergence of modem Ásatrú from our ancient religion of Odinism, by it's adoption of "new-ageism" maladies, such as hedonism, relativism, and individualism, to name but a few. The most glaring and blasphemous aspect of this emerging dichotomy is the relegation of the Allfather Odin to an "equal" status with all the other Goðanum (Gods and Goddesses). This theology clearly contradicts the Gylfaginning (first book of Prose Edda), wherein it states: "Odin is called Allfather because He is the Father of all Gods" and, "Mighty as the other Gods are, yet They submit to Him like Children to the Father" (Gylf.3 & 20; see also the chapter "Odin as Allfather".) This is the quintessential doctrine of Fundamental Odinism, and I have not personally seen it posited by anyone before Goði Dr. Cröwell. Another doctrine not found elsewhere is explained in the chapter titled, "The Loki Factor". For the longest time I was vehemently opposed to, and even nauseous at the prospect of, anyone offering anything to Loki, in the way of religious worship (giving due honor). Truth be told, I still blanch at the idea, but I was won over by the honest logic of Goði Dr. Cröwell's position. "How can we offer anything unto Odin, as Odinists, while ignoring His Word?" he said, laying the proverbial gauntlet at my feet, "For does He not affirm in the 'Lokasenna' that He oathed never to accept a draught not also offered to Loki?" Needless to say, I was forced to admit that this was a reasonable position, and founded in the Eddas. It was a matter of common sense. More importantly however, this lesson illuminated the necessity, for those who are sincere in our faith, to both know and adhere to the wisdom of the Eddas, and that honor, or a lack of it, is not transitory, but eternal. In honoring the Word of our Allfather Odin, painful as this one might be, we remind ourselves of the power, and heavy burden that our own word carries. The primary theological paradigm, or custom of thought here is that we must both know and live our faith, not simply as our ancestors lived it, but certainly in the light of the same wisdom. Fundamental Odinism is not about hedonism, or doing what you want, but wanting to do what is Odinic; ours is a living Siðr.

Through his sermons, or "Hof Services" as they are called, Goði Dr. Cröwell has been able to reach out, and touch the lives of a great many of our Folk. In the darkest holes of solitary confinement, to the loneliest souls surrounded by teeming throngs, in and out of prisons, these sermons found fertile soil, and took root. I remember the early years of a simple typewritten page, being passed around and photocopied; read and discussed. There was always a moral message, or sermon, a suggested blót (ceremonial communion with the Divine), and runes to meditate on, each and every month. I for one felt connected, and a part of something greater. There was a need among the Odinist community, for a strong moral, unyielding, constant and persistent voice; thus Odin chose His vessel. Little did Goði Dr. Cröwell know that these sermons would take flight, on the wings of Huginn and Muninn (Odin' s mythological ravens; representing Mind and Memory), no less. His only thought was to simply fulfill his oath of service to the Goðanum (Gods and Goddesses) and our Folk, but the reality was so much greater. These sermons were the seeds which would give rise to the Holy Nation of Odin, not as an ethereal idea, but as a formative Community, via the vehicle of a fundamentalist Outreach Ministry. The format of Hof Services expanded into "Gungnir", the original and official publication of the Holy Nation of Odin. This expanded medium did not, and does not, supersede it's progenitor, often including new Hof Services, but opens new doors, and gives rise to new voices. In this way, the Message which began millennia ago, with the birth of the Aryan people, and which was reborn in a simple typewritten sermon, gains the momentum of a rolling thundercloud , reverberating throughout Miðgarð. Who could have foreseen this? Indeed, who? Thus, some of the early Hof Services are reproduced herein; soul-shaking and timeless.

Some might wonder why poetry would be included in a theological instrument; especially one called a "Hammer". It seems to me that great men, in the service of the Allfather Odin, and our Folk, almost invariably are poets; .touched by, or with a share of Oðrærir, and the ability to stir passions. Egil Skallagrimsson, Adolf Hitler, David Lane; all of them great men, and poets. Much of the content of 'Ek Einherjar' is hard and painful; a thorn or an elk sedge, according to one's nature. The truth hurts, as is often said, but it is given lightness in prose and poetry. The blood of Ymir runs shallow and deep, salty and sweet, but whatever our need, there we meet.

All in all, and for the same reason that the 'Hávamál' (the Sayings of the High One) is included herein, the Word is our primary instrument for unification with, and on behalf of the Divine Spirit. The Allfather Odin lives within all of Aryanity in our breath, and in our blood; Þa nam ek frævask ok fróðr vera ok vaxa ok vel hafask; Orð mér af Orði Orðs leitaði, Verk mér af Verki Verks leitaði ('Hávamál' st. 141).

The Word is the precursor to the Work, as expressed in this stanza of the ' Hávamál ', and it is my prayer that this work aids in the resurgence of our Folk living Vor Forn Siðr (our ancient religion).

Goði Viðar U. Odinson Harless, 1519-CG (HPS)
Court Goði of the Sons of Odin 1519
and Private Secretary to the Honorable Herjan

PART I

"Thor" by Gð. Viðar U. Odinson Harless, 1519-CG (HPS)

The Road North

WALKING THE NORTHERN ROAD
(The Road North: A Revolution in Thought)

What do you suppose mortally wounded Renaissance man? Might contemporary man be discounted wherefore, such an inquiry is A pais? I think not! As sure as Nietzsche's Zarathustra descried loathsome contempt residing in the minds and hearts of contemporary man of his day, wherefore Ascension is in regard, we too may spy this very same abhorrence in Contemporary man of today.

Renaissance man of old built and repaired his own home. He hunted and grew his own food with which to provide for his family. He taught and educated his own children. He was lawyer, physician and statesman, all in one. The very virtues of "Self Reliance", "perseverance" and "industriousness" all come to mind here. Why, the mere notion that Renaissance man depend upon some other man to tend to "his" needs, would have rendered him ill to his stomach. Any such suggestion that he do so may have brought him to bear arms against such a whelp of a man!

So then, what happened to Renaissance man? Where did he go? And just when did he recede into the memory of a yesterday so far gone now?

Diminished desire for excellence as the standard by which we mark achievement and pronounced interest in supply and demand are the engines which both propelled economic growth at a rapid pace and, there in concert with said stimuli, corrupted the majority of man! Money/gold solves every malady, became the new mantra.

Got a sore throat? Don't bother gathering and mixing some lemon, eucalyptus, honey and Sage into a tea. No, call a doctor and pay him to do it. Oh, and be sure that he's a specialist, because specialists killed Renaissance man! Where Renaissance man once tended to all of his own needs, there is a specialist for everything. You know; "the guy"!

Leaky roof? No problem, friend. Just call the roof guy. Car acting up? Hey, don't want to get those shiny tools in the garage dirty. No Way, dude! Call the car guy. Satellite dish not getting your favorite channel? Call the dish guy. Kids acting up? Call some one else to deal with it. Sure, just pay some specialists to deal with it. We've become a society of "call the guy", folks! With the exception of the farmer, we've lost our connection with the soil of Mother Jord. That is to say Mother Earth. All our food comes from the market, so far as we are concerned. We have no respect for our resources! The supermarket will always have food. Right? Right? Why should anyone today, in our morally bankrupt society seek out the arts and sciences when they can just buy this, or that, or pay "some guy" to do it, build it, or provide it for them. Why here in 21st century Vinland we have gone from a nation of manufactures and builders only 30 years ago, to a nation of packagers and assemblers, all of the goods that used to be produced here, now are produced elsewhere. The corporate moguls get richer cause they don't have to pay an American workforce any longer. They just use third world slave labor and pocket the difference. And the more you buy, the more they make. We are "dumbing down" contemporary man!

Do you realize that the number one industry in America is pharmaceuticals? And the largest sector in that industry is "antidepressants"? That's right. We as an unconcerned society pimp and pander legalized dope to our citizens via an elaborate conspiracy! Big business financers, lawmakers, pharmaceutical laboratories and the American Medical Association and their shrinks, all promote and profit from anti-depressants sales. Further exasperating a "deliberately cultivated" mentally ill society! All for profit! But a guy growing and consuming a little bit of the green Goddess (marijuana) for medicinal purposes is arrested and imprisoned. Dope is dope, legal or not!

So what's the answer, right? A revolution in the way we think is the answer. We must alter our perception of socially accepted behavior and see it for the pernicious and self defeating reality that it is. We must relearn how to think in terms of healthy behavior and deploy reason and logic, not television commercials and mono culture corporate mogul ads, to arrive at sound decisions on behalf of ourselves and our loved ones.

I'm certainly not even close to being the inventor of the concept for a revolution in thought. Though, I am most certainly, without a doubt, an ardent proponent. And I shall remain adamant that such is the way out of a stupor that so many suffer.

All peoples have traditions, cultures and a heritage which are indigenous to them. Regardless of what folk a person comes from, the indigenous ways of one's own ancestors, up to the point of corruption, had kept their entire lineage healthy and progressing towards ascension. Only when mono-culture ideology enters the equation does the calamity begin to unfold. The introduction of foreign and alien concepts usurp their own indigenous way of life that has been familiar to one's family and kept it flourishing generation after generation, and universalism supplants what was an indigenous plan by the design of nature's laws. The result is the mono-culture in which we live. It has replaced all indigenous faiths and heritages with a sick one size fits all, universal religion and way of life. And anyone who resists and defies this is branded a racist, a bigot and an anti-social outcast. And sure, such heroic men and women, whatever their folk be are a valid threat to the current promoters of a morally ill society. Smear campaigns and tactics are employed against them. Spin doctors weave their unjust lies to discredit them and turn public opinion against them and in their own favor.

There is a way to correct this malady which is offensive to natural order on so many levels!

For the descendants of the Germanic tribes, of the Aryan people, it is the northern road. It's the same road which our noble ancestors trod prior to the advent of Christianity. For the American Indian, it is the Red Road of their ancestors. It is Shinto for the Japanese and for the West African folk - it is Ifa, Yoruba with its Orishas (Gods-spiritual forces) such as Osun, the Goddess of love and marriage. Elegba is the guardian god of the road between the worlds. Oya, is the goddess of wind, justice and the dead. Obatala - God of Mercy, Purity and spirituality. Sango, God of thunder and fire, the warrior king who is said to be the lion in the bush!

These and other Gods belong exclusively to the West African tribes people and their descendents. It is their indigenous birth right to know and honor their noble ancestral faith, free of any interloper's corruption. Just as it is our inherent right as Aryan folk of the Germanic tribes to commune with our ancient Gods of our noble ancestors without being labeled bigots and racists! The only bigots and racists are those who point the accusatory finger of such at us! It is our birthright to know Odin, AllFather and God of wisdom and victory, to say the least. Frigga, AllMother , mother earth by some accounts and Goddess of marriage and family; Thor, God of thunder and strength, Tyr, God of self sacrifice for the good of all and just action. Also, there is Freya, Goddess of love, beauty, joy, lust and harmony. This is by no means a full account of these Gods functions nor a complete catalog of our beloved Gods. I merely seek to illustrate their very reality and nature, albeit rather concisely so, so as to afford a conscious awareness of their reality to you. They have been there near you your entire life and they are now even as you read this. The very notion that the Gods of the North have somehow forgotten or abandon us is altogether absurd! Abandonment is a symptom of the human condition and it is an ill quality attached thereto. Our Gods have always been around, awaiting their folk's returned desire to know the true and elder ways. They await your companionship on the northern road. They can heal your sick spirit, your empty and lonely heart and they can teach you how to right a wrong which was perpetrated against you, prior to your own birth!

They will restore the balance and replace the chaos in your life, the unnatural, with the harmony of natural order. They seek no slaves for they are no masters over us. They ask not that we bend our knee and bow our head before them. Instead, they seek only to know those whom have descended from them so long ago. They demand no blind faith, for they are everywhere in our lives to see in this lifetime! No waiting till we die to know them, or see and experience their presence, glory and reality in our own lives. All they ask of us is that we assume accountability for our own life and affairs; that we shun weakness of the mind and spirit. That we exercise reason and logic to render our decisions as opposed to following the herd or abandoning our lives to some pie-in-the-sky blind faith which demands we do not pursue life's joys in the here and now, for some promise of a better "next" life! Get a grip on reality and embrace the revolution in thought. Place your feet on the road north and start walking brothers and sisters. There is nothing at the old watering hole, except stagnation and disease. Leave the herd and follow the river's flowing current north...

For there you will quench your thirst and find life renewed, and the rebirth of a new renaissance man.

WALKING THE NORTHERN ROAD
(Gjallarhorn: Answering the call)

Political correctness rarely exhibits any respect for the laws of natural order. I therefore submit that any religion which observes the constrictions of political correctness must be spiritually vacant and completely devoid of any validity regarding that which is divine. For certainly that which is divine must exist within the breadth of natural order.

For roughly the past one and a half millennia, Christianity has sought to eradicate and supplant any and every indigenous Tribal religion, wherever they have been known to exist. To be sure, these conversions were anything other than benign in the early days of the advent of the Christ faith. Indeed, the contrary is more the instance. The overwhelming majority of them were very violent and even fatal for those who declined the gift of the new faith. The sheer magnitude of brutality, in fact, dwarfed any of that committed by the Barbarians the Christian Missionaries sought to convert!

Children of those who refused conversion were given unto the Church as mere orphans as though they had been wandering the streets abandoned and alone. This seemingly kind act of benevolent charity is belied by the harsh reality however. These children were little more than chattel and thralls to the church. They were worked to the point far beyond any Third World child slave labor we may descry in the late twentieth and twenty-first centuries. In addition to this deliberate and otherwise criminal lack of welfare, these children, 'Our Ancestors', were often raped by the very servants of the Lord Almighty! They were pimped as child prostitutes by the church's own clerics. After these kinder's parents were either imprisoned, or executed, their property and land was stolen by the church and in some instances, given unto the neighbor of good Christian morals, whom had turned in the barbaric, idol-worshiping heathens. This of course was not a reward, but more an 'Appointment Officialis', as it were, by the church whereby, the informant... er, I mean, the good Christian citizen, was charged with the duty to cultivate and harvest the Lord's new land and prosper from his benevolence as a reward for keeping the faith, as it were.

Truth is however, in all fairness, every people of every faith in days of auld, have committed atrocities in the name of their God(s) and nothing has changed in the past millennia. For it continues today in several guises as I commit these very words to print upon this paper. Nor is this essay an indictment against the Christian faith. I've known many a good Christian in my lifetime and still do. In fact, if any indictment merits validity against anyone, then it must surly rest with our own folk, those of Germanic descent! For such an egregious crime perpetrated against our beloved faith could never have occurred were it not for our faith suffering a corrupt spiritual breakdown at the hands of late eleventh century ancestors, whose very greed ushered in the new religious era which nearly annihilated our ancient and indigenous faith. However, though these ancestors of ours may have begun and contributed to this plight, they are in no way to be held accountable for the current state of spiritual poverty and moral bankruptcy the Germanic people suffer. That mantle is one which we today must assume. For the truth and its accompanying facts, have long since existed and been available to any seeker of the truth, courageous enough to seek it out. We all did! Those with a sincere desire to unearth the uncorrupted facts of history and the details of their ancestral culture, heritage and traditions needn't look very hard at all. Nor must they accept the inaccurate, revised, politically correct accounts which are not only lax in form wherefore facts are in regard, they are outright lies!

The Watchman of Asgard, the God Heimdall, has been sounding the Gjallarhorn for quite some time now. He has been calling our folk to return to the elder ways of our ancestors. Pointing out the way back home to us like a compass which never fails... Revealing to us, the Northern Road!

The Gjallarhorn is so mighty that its sound may reach into the depths of all worlds and pierce all time. Listen! Can you not hear its mighty blast? Summoning the holy folk to return home and heed what the old Gods of our noble and hearty ancestors have to say to us today. "ODIN LIVES !" And His sacred wisdom, so hard won, is just as valid today as it was 40,000 years ago:

Orð Mér af orði   Orðz leitaði
Verk Mér af verki   Verks leitaði

One word from a word   led me to another word

One work from a work led me to another work
- Allfather Odin, the Hávamál 141

We hear tell quite oft in the Odinist and Ásatrú community at large, the world over, of the "Great reawakening, or Revival of the Elder ways of the North', which in its current incarnation here in Vinland (North America) may be traced back to the late 1960's and early 1970's to Stephan A. McNallen. A man to which we in the Odinist and Ásatrú community, all owe a great debt of respect to. He is but one sound example of the Gjallarhorn's call penetrating the twentieth century. This reality of Odin and the other Gods/Goddesses' existence made manifest by the very word and work of Mr. McNallen which have led others to the word and work of Allfather Odin. But the mighty Gjallarhorn's call was heard long before Mr. McNallen first heard it in the latter part of the 1960's. Scholars and students alike agree on when and where the Gjallarhorn was initially heard in regards to the great reawakening, in some instances and yet they disagree in others. Was it von List, Löns, Rudd-Mills, the Brothers Grimm, Dumézil, Evola? Truth is, no one can say with a complete certainty. Oh sure, we may date the earliest known, but we cannot be certain that he was in fact the first to answer the call and thereafter, endeavor to reawaken the folk to our indigenous Gods and faith. So much has been destroyed and lost to the very ebb and flow of time. All of the aforementioned men have been instrumental in answering the call of the mighty Gjallarhorn and resolving to incite a renewed desire in our folk towards the end of rekindling the sacred flames which leads us back whence we have come: the Northern Road.

So many among us now, including Christensen, McNallen, Thorsson (Flowers), Holley, McVan, Aswynn, Gundarsson, Britta-Titchnell, Moynihan, Wolff and far too many others to catalog in the scope of this space, have all contributed significantly to the great reawakening. Who was first or most recognized now is a moot issue. What is of paramount import is that the great horn continues to sound and that the holy folk which hear it continue to answer it! The morrow will reveal new minds touched by Odin, and new voices and souls to reinforce the ranks of the Living Einherjar. Those ready to divulge truths long hidden, concealed by liars and cowards. Someone perusing these very words will emerge as the next generation's voice. Yes you, quiet and content men and women of today. You shall grow weary and exasperated of the moral decay, lies and spiritual poverty! And you shall hear the mighty blast as its call reaches your inner ear and stirs your soul. Having journeyed some 40,000 years, it will pierce the very barrier which technology has erected between you and the majestic honor of the past. And from you, possessor of stalwart character, will the restless Gods stir within your soul, encouraging, "NO!" Imploring you, to take up your place in service to the Gods and folk of the North. You courageous brothers and sisters of the new dawn, lurking just beyond the Northern horizon. You will lead our children's children down the Northern Road the way our fathers' fathers once before us did, and we today do. Against all tyranny and all adversaries who would so gaily deprive you and deny you what is yours by birth!

Strength, courage, honor, integrity, nobility and self respect which all accompany the man, or woman strong enough to command one's self and one's life. The ones strong enough to be self reliant and accountable to one's self. The ones strong enough and brave enough to live independent of the mass/herd! “Independence is a privilege reserved for the strong!", so scribed Friedrich Nietzsche. If you would command thy self, then you must wield the Hammer of Thor and swing it justly, devoid of the guilt, or the yoke of oppression and remorse associated with the ill devised concepts of political correctness. The very vices of misplaced guilt and temporal, albeit, instant gratification are designed to rob you of your birthright, or even harboring any interest in it at all! Leave the herd and think for yourselves... More so, think for the future of your descendants.

TODAY is the day! If you have not already answered the call and begun to walk the Northern Road, then today is the day. Begin right this instance. Within your very blood resides the Folk Soul of our Gods and Ancestors... Everyone whom ever lived before you and everyone who will live after you, in your family lineage. You have it within your DNA, the might and fortitude to ascend the fetters of gray slavery and the thralldom of guilt. Leave behind the Bedouin faith. Leave it in the dry and dusty sands whence it emerged from to enslave Fjorgyn's population! It will never speak to your Northern soul, not truly. It will only fetter your mind with misplaced guilt. That is not living, my brothers and sisters. That is existing. Odinism says "YES" to life!!!

It teaches one to excel and rise up to meet life's challenges, to embrace all of life's joys and hardships and to address them with grit, courage and determination. It is all about the majesty of life and participating in it, not being a mere spectator in your own life. It is about you and me walking the Northern Road in the company of

Allfather Odin and the Gods/Goddesses of the Æsir and Vanir. It is about listening to the voice of our Ancestors and honoring the ancient traditions which they left us, by affording our heritage and culture the deference of respect and appreciation which they warrant, devoid of any misplaced guilt placed at our feet by the agents of alien faiths and the spiritually broken minions of political correctness.

Say yes to life and yes to a bright tomorrow for our future the way that it was intended for us by those whom paved the road North with their precious blood and efforts, so that we may walk it today and our kinder tomorrow. Answer the call and Fara með Odin (Go with Odin)!

"Without the Gods, a soul wanders, but is not free." – An Odinist Proverb

WALKING THE NORTHERN ROAD
(Love Thy Neighbor: A genuine call for diversity)

Today's monoculture in the Western world not only robs the people who comprise its society of their own indigenous cultures, but it has many who seek to connect with their indigenous cultures often apologizing for it as well. This nonsense is unacceptable to those walking the northern road. We do not offer any apologies for honoring the traditions and Gods of our own ancestors. In fact, to my way of thinking, if anyone owes anyone an apology, at all, it is owed to me and my folk walking the northern road.

"By whom," you query? How about the United States government to begin with! For systematically raping any folk of their indigenous culture and heritage whether they are native European (Aryan), American Indian, African, Asian, etc. There are laws and amendments in theory and doctrine which protect every individual's right to freedom of religion and speech, etc., but in the reality of things as they occur, people are discriminated against and persecuted if they don't "go with the flow," as it were. This government, along with the fundamentalist Christian right, has been waging a cultural war on people who subscribe to non-mainstream faiths and philosophies for quite sometime now. I guarantee that if you go into the American prison system you will see a large chasm in the parity of prisoners' rights between those of mainstream faiths and those of non-mainstream faiths; with very rare exception. This is the case in fact!

Yet - the Religious Land Use and Institutionalized Persons Act of 2000, also known as RLUIPA, guarantees parity and protection of religious accommodation to all. The reality is this, a monoculture society or melting pot is much easier for a government to control, profit from and sustain an economy with, then a society of multiple cultures. As we go through life residing in western civilized society, we're systematically cut off from nature's laws and our own natural desire to function within the parameters of natural order. We are taught to place our trust and support into the inferior laws of man and technology, erroneous though they may be and not into the superior laws of natural order. Thus, we cut ourselves off from our true selves. We have been robbed via this unnatural process of so much of who we could and should be. The voices of our ancestors and Gods that our fathers' fathers were able to descry with ease, are but a jumble of confusing emotional conflictions which are more often than not, contrary to what we have been indoctrinated to believe.

We've been taught to view Goddesses and our women folk as whores and inferior to ourselves rather than as equals. If you think our female ancestors resemble the fair sex of today, you would be sorely incorrect. Some of our ancestral sisters were more able to efficiently wield knife and sword than many men today would be. Most men have an ego that demands that they discount such a fact. Such is a prime example of being less than aware and disconnected from the self one should be aquainted with, and would be if one observed and respected the laws of nature.

Nature's laws dictate that there are no favorites, and no equals among men. The simplicity of nature's decree is that the strong excel and survive, while the weak perish. Yet man's inferior laws would deprive folks of their true and natural peer groups; placing the strong and weak together in the same peer groups and then demanding by some constitutional decree, that the strong respect the weak as their equal. This is pernicious ideology and unnaturally absurd. Even more so, it is more often than not exasperated by the fact that most of the weak elect to be so by their own volition. Or they have within themselves the ability to excel to a greater and naturally more desirable level of strength, whereby fortitude and will constitute said strength. They simply elect to remain weak, for their desire has been corrupted in their true nature of self and replaced with a revulsion for the strong individuals, strong enough to stand erect and proud, resisting that which is unnatural in order to survive and thrive.

It is a down breeding technique. And it has succeeded in the main. The detriment of this egregious and systematic state sponsored de-evolution is evident in nearly every quarter of Western civilization today. What happened to the community our elders once knew? They became targets of mass consumerism. Taught to believe that every other natural experience, was, as we encountered them, a traumatic one. Hey, don't worry they have a pill for that. Little Jimmy won't settle down in school and apply himself to his lessons, give him a pill. Traffic accident you witnessed on the way home from work today just too upsetting to get on with your life and out of your mind, don't worry there's a pill for that too! Feeling less then your self today? No problem. There's a pill for that. In fact, there's a magic pill for everything in today's Western society, instead of just assuming accountability for yourself and command over your emotions. This is just one of the many agents responsible for the breakdown in our family units today. It's the lack of accountability and responsibility for one's own family affairs. When was the last time you sat down to a meal with the entire family? Been a while, huh? If we do not elicit and encourage stronger and more responsible family ties at home, then why should we expect the members of such families to be assets and contributors to the community in which they live? A community is after all, an extension of family comprised by the sum of collective families which reside within said community. If the overwhelming majority of households in any given community are not healthy in morals and civic duty ethics, then the community as a whole will suffer.

Ah, but the corporate moguls get rich. Pharmaceutical magnets profit most of all, and the economy of the nation can always depend upon consumerism to save the day and stimulate the depressed economy. The notion of any true community is repulsive to business moguls and the government. How many of your neighbors do you really know? Where were you when the fellow down the street was robbed and killed last week? Or when the next-door neighbor's 16-year-old daughter was raped? How aware were you when the car was stolen 30 yards away from your front door? Community? Indeed!

And all the while, the problem continues with no corrected antidote being offered to future generations. The critics of such realities continue to promote such journalistic slogans such as, "bridging the gap between communities," or "building the communities of tomorrow, one home at a time," and my personal favorite "love thy neighbor".

First of all, in order to bridge any two communities together you must first have two communities. Next, I shudder at the idea of what the community of tomorrow might resemble in lieu of the communities of yesterday. And finally, love thy neighbor? What in helheim does that mean any how?

While it would seem to infer a call for diversity, surely that is not the case in fact at all. While today's Western society may make much fanfare about a multicultural and diverse society, I can assure you that it is much to do about nothing. Nothing more than a falsehood anyway. Diversity requires the healthy promotion of unique and diverse cultures and heritages. That is just not the reality of western society's agenda today, which promotes the destruction of any one racial group along with their respective culture and heritage, and seeks to replace it with the universal one; A one race fits all monoculture.

Love thy neighbor - indeed! We must first learn to love our own folk, and respect our own culture and heritage before we can ever consider the notion of respecting another. For none among us may afford any respect to any other if we cannot initially respect ourselves and the inherited ways and traditions of our own ancestors.

ORIGINAL SIN

We all know the story of original sin... Or, do we? Well, let's see. As we are told, the story goes something like this.... God (Yahweh) created man (Adam), and woman (Eve) from his rib, to people the Garden of Eden. He pointed out two trees which he informed them were sacred, the tree of life and the tree of knowledge. Both being fruit bearing trees, God told the couple to "freely eat of the tree of life, and ye shall never grow old and die. However, eat not of the tree of knowledge for I forbid it! If you violate my law ye shall know death and all of man after you as well; For ye will introduce sin into the world." So spoke God. Of course, Eve was tempted by a snake (Satan) in the tree of knowledge, who told her to taste an apple which she did and from this act, all of mankind is condemned as a consequence. Ergo, Original Sin a la Old Testament.

The first thing any sane person of average, or above intellect, should ask themselves is; "What kind of God forbids you, his children, from gaining in knowledge and then thereafter, punishes you and your entire line of descendants for seeking said knowledge? Moreover, what kind of sane person who has considered this, would elect to follow such a God? And blindly at that! A slave who has no confidence in him/herself. That's who. Just consider the gravity of the situation for a minute. A man wrote this story about 1,680 years ago, just as I am now writing the words which you rest you very eyes upon today. A MAN! And for nearly two thousand years since then, an overwhelming portion of the world's population has subjected itself to this form of bondage associated with original sin while they lift their hands empyrean, singing about God's love. What strange love this is! First of all, I contest this notion of original sin. If anything constitutes original sin, how about the fact that so many intelligent people have been duped into forsaking their indigenous traditions and cultures in exchange for the trappings and enslavement of a Bedouin faith conceived and chronicled by Canaanites, AKA Jews. That's who wrote the Bible, the Torah and the Koran. Or how about giving birth to the very conception of 'Woman' being the root of all evil for mankind? This is not only ludicrous it is evil in and of itself. For it laid the very foundation, one might even say of Biblical proportion, to treat women as an inferior species. Think about it for a moment. The very gifts of our Gods are our women! Holding within them, the very hope for the next generation of our family and tribal line. They have been made to suffer inequality until just about 50 to 70 years ago here in Vinland (U.S. & Canada) and still continue to be persecuted in many places in the world! The very promise of humanity's continuity resides within our women, and still, intelligent men and women would place their trust and faith in this God who has placed the burden of original sin upon her tired shoulders? I'll tell you what a sin is. It's weak men from an era nearly two thousand years ago, while seeking accountability for poor crops, failure to produce a male heir, or any and all woes which besieged them, assigning the blame for ill fortune in their lives and land, to their women via the vehicle of the 'Fable' of Adam and Eve. Another sin is with that crime against women, man began a tradition which continues to this day... Shifting accountability and reassigning blame where it is not warranted, simply because it is convenient.

This work is not designed as an attack upon any religious philosophy, nor is it intended as a slight upon anyone who subscribes to a given theology. It is a study in facts and perspective in an effort to arm intelligent men and women with the factual information to render an informed decision regarding their own spiritual welfare and thereafter, the growth and advancement thereof.

So then, let's examine the scope of what most refer to today, albeit erroneously so, as traditional religion. Traditional would actually imply a thing's origin to be rooted both within the means of antiquity and indigenous culture and heritage. Ergo, we shall simply address this subject by its legitimate genus; the Abrahamic Faith. Or more accurately, plurally; faiths. Christianity actually has its roots within Judaism. Abraham, born 2000 BCE in Mesopotamia (Iraq today), heard the voice of God (Yahweh) which commanded him to take his family and relocate to Canaan (later called Palestine and now called Israel), so he did. But after many bad years of drought Abraham once again, packed up his family and tribe, now called the people of the land of Canaan, or Canaanites, later called the Israelites and today's Jews claim to be descended from this tribe of Bedouin

Semites otherwise known as the Hebrews; though no validity may be afforded to such a claim. Of all the world's Jews today, less than 1/2 of one percent would actually carry the genetic DNA marker which a genuine Hebrew of four thousand years ago would possess. The reality is that the overwhelming majority of those whom call themselves Jews today, are actually descendants of the Khazars, or even outright Caucasians whose ancestors, at some point in their lineage, converted to Judaism to become "God's Chosen People," as it were. But getting back to Abraham, he moved his people yet again, as earlier I had mentioned. This time from Canaan to Egypt which is how the Hebrews came into bondage under the dynasty of the Pharaohs. We all know the story of Moses which follows thereafter. Abraham died at the age of 175 in 1825 BCE and this is when Judaism begins to congeal. As an actual theology it would not institute a Rabbinical Priesthood until after Moses led the Hebrews out of Egypt and died himself, and Joshua led them back into Canaan.

Christianity may arguably begin with the martyrdom of the Jewish prophet, Jesus. Jesus, born in the year between 8 to 4 BCE, was considered by his followers to be the Christ (Greek - Anointed One / Christos), or the "Messiah" as it were. He was crucified around the year 27 or 30 CE. Upon his death, his first twelve disciples became the Apostles of Christ, all Jews, and they began to spread his teachings, or what they claimed were his teachings. But the legitimate founding of the Christian church has its origin in the fourth century Common Era (CE), when in 324 CE the Emperor Constantine, by official decree, declared Christianity the official state religion of the Roman Empire.

Islam begins with Mohammad (also sp. Muhammad) (570 CE - 632 CE), who had a vision in approximately 590 CE, while he was praying in a cave in Mecca. It is written that while praying in this cave, the angel Gabriel appeared to Mohammad and informed him that he was to correct the perversions which had occurred within Judaism and Christianity at the hands of their respective earlier prophets. And that he was to complete the divine revelation of God (Allah) which had begun with those religions. Or more historically correct, which had begun with Ibrahim (Abraham) hearing the voice of Allah (God) approximately 1985 to 1980 BCE, as it is portrayed in the second Sura of the Qur'an (Koran).

Abraham is credited as the father of Judaism, Christianity and Islam by the adherents of all three faiths. The story of creation, as it were, is the same in all three faiths and their respective holy writs.

The Book of Genesis is the first book of both the Jewish Torah and the Christian Bible (Old Test.) and may be found in the Second Sura of the Islamic Qur'an (Koran). These three faiths all have their origins in what was once called Mesopotamia but is today called Iraq. Further more, all three are based solely upon blind faith and obedience in an unseen God. The eldest among the three is Judaism which begins when Abraham hears the voice of God sometime after 2000 BCE, approximately 4,000 years ago.

Conversely, the indigenous religious / Spiritual beliefs of every race of people on earth had existed in one form or another since the very beginning of their respective Ancestral lineages. For those of us of White-European ancestry and heritage, that origin is in the religions / spiritual paths of that which we today call Odinism/Wotanism and Ásatrú.

The Gods, "Our Gods", of these Norse-Teutonic religions, as they exist today, had also existed , unmolested, in Europe for at the least (recorded history) six thousand years contra the 'Less than' one thousand years in which Christianity has existed in Northern Europe to date (2008 CE). However, artifacts excavated from caves and dig sites as well as megaliths spanning the breadth of Europe, are overwhelmingly indicative of the presence of our Gods, with their same attributes, as far back as Cro-Magnon (Proto-Nordic) man, some 40,000 years. Clearly ours is one of the oldest religions on the face of the earth (Midgard), in one context, or another. The history of the White-Aryan race is seated in the late Paleolithic period. Additionally, it is an absolute at 37,000 to 40,000 years! Though it has been argued by scholars as possibly dating as far back as 50,000 years. However, as a barometer I shall follow the rule of inexorable credibility and stand by the historical fixture of 37,000 years and leave the debate thereof older estimates, to those so inclined to posit thus within the scope of their own works. The late Paleolithic period is fixed at 35,000 BCE.

The old Testament Bible was in fact created in 325 CE by the Council of Nicaea. It was of course and is an inexorable fact, created one hundred and twenty-five years "AFTER" the New Testament Bible, which was developed by the Church in 200 CE, 1,808 years ago.

In 724 CE, Boniface (St. Boniface) the Christian Missionary, cut down "Thor's Sacred Tree" (a sacred Oak) of Geismar, in Hess, Germany, in an effort to destroy the old Heathen/Pagan religion.

Charlemagne murdered tens of thousands of Odinists during his reign. Refusing to be baptized as a Christian, eating meat during

Lent, Cremation (the funerary rite dedicated to Odin) and pretending to be baptized, were all offenses punishable by death! According to Arthur Kemp, ("March of the Titans"), in 768 CE Charlemagne began a 32 year long campaign of genocidal evangelism against the Heathen/Pagan Saxons (Germans) in Western Germany. This campaign began with the cutting down of the Irmunsul at the Externesteine. The Irmunsul is symbolic of Yggdrasil, the World Tree which supports the heavens and all worlds, including our own 'Midgard'.

In 772 CE, in the name of Christ, he ordered the death of every Saxon man, woman and child who refused to forsake their own Gods and accept Jesus Christ. Christian Priests served as the executioners. In 782 CE, at Verden, he ordered the beheading of 4,500 Saxons in a single day!

This theme repeated itself the world over where Christian Missionaries found savage Pagans in their journeys.

The tactic of brutal conversion to Christianity by threat of death had continued in Europe until the year 1,000 CE when Europe was declared by the church as fully Christian. Some of the last hold outs were the people known to history as, the Vikings. While less significant raids had already occurred, the 'Official' beginning of the "Viking Age", as it has come to be known, occurred on June 8, 793 CE with the raid upon Lindisfarne located on the coast of Britain. There is much speculation as to whether or not the forced conversion to Christianity and murderous Christian torment of Pagans was the reason why the Norse raiders chose the Christian monastery targets or if it was solely based upon the wealth which they possessed.

What is not speculation but rather, fact, is that no matter what one may present in the way of facts, to a believer of one of the Abrhamic Faiths, they are not going to believe anything contrary to what they had been taught and built their whole life's foundation upon. For many people today, it is easier to continue living a lie than to reorganize the way they live their lives, based upon what they now know is the truth.

The truth is really simple. Jesus was a Bedouin Semite; a Jew. All three Abrahamic Faiths are indigenous to the Bedouin peoples of the Middle East. Were it not for the forced conversions and imported Bedouin faiths, the world would not be so Christian, Jewish and Islamic today. All of those Bedouin peoples still have their indigenous cultures and heritage. Think about that, because the truth is in the telling here folks. The reason why they still have their indigenous ways about them is because they never forfeited them, their indigenous religion, or their ancient homelands. In fact, they have fought war after war believing that it is worth dying for if need be. Because they understand that without that loyalty to which they owe their very existence to, they would be forced to assimilate and watch the ways of their ancestors perish. It is easy for them to descry, you understand. For they have witnessed its very occurrence with the Nordic peoples of the world. Where Aryans (and other races as well) have been forced to convert, or did so of their own volition, they have forfeited nearly all that is indigenous to them in lieu of the desert God's promise of a better next life in some paradise/heaven. Because of this detrimental theology, people have shunned the ways and traditions of their own indigenous ancestors. They have been told that they are of no account in the next and eternal life, so why bother with such trappings here? But ask yourself this... How many poor Clergy members of the Abrahamic faiths have you seen? More so, how many poor or run down houses of the holy have you ever seen where the clerical hierarchy hold their court. None! That's how many. If these wealthy and nice trappings are so unnecessary, then why are all the main Cathedrals, Mosques and Synagogues so lavish and wealthy?

I'll tell you what friends. If there is an after life, it will be based upon what you did with this life and how you lived it. Did you honor and respect the very traditions that your own ancestors fought and died for to pass onto you? Or did you forfeit them in lieu of adopting some strange and foreign ways? You would be well served to consider such queries, friends. Cause to my way of believing, we will all answer to our own ancestors, all the way back to their beginning, more than we will answer to any Gods! You see, to them, the original sin won't be about some fable out of the Bedouin's desert Faith. No, no. To them, Original Sin will be all about the day that their descendants shunned them and turned their backs on the traditions, customs and beliefs which they killed for and laid down their own lives for just to pass onto us!

We should "all" endeavor to respect "all" others right to subscribe to whatever religious/spiritual views each person feels so inclined to pursue. For it is an individual pursuit, first and foremost, prior to the seeker ever arriving at the doors of any physical Temple of "any" faith. But we should never forget just how those faiths came to be, nor should we ever forget whence we have come from.

May Allfather Odin touch your mind. May Allmother Frigga touch your heart. May Tyr touch your soul. And may Thor teach you how to wield your own Hammer and smash the chaotic forces which threaten your return to the ways of our ancestors.

"Sympathy, the thing itself, is always coveted by the undeserving. For those souls whom warrant it, seldom desire it."

- Hon. Herjan, Casper Odinson Cröwell, Ph.D., DD

SLIGHTED BY OUR OWN HANDS

For several years now I have often marveled at the high degree of intellect within the prison population, and it has always amazed me just how it is possible to keep so many sophisticated and intelligent men from escaping the bonds of this ill society which we call corrections!

I mean, consider for a moment, that there are several cons in here with various degrees in law, mathematics, engineering & psychology to highlight but a few fields of academia. There are cons with Ph.D.'s, your writer included in the latter, and yet, recidivism is at an all time high.

Well, it needn't require a scholar to understand the cause of the afore stated effect. The primary cause is substance abuse/addiction. However, no less accountable is one's penchant for prison politics. Why, the latter alone is largely responsible for the institutionalization of so many minds and that is what I wish to address with this article as it pertains to our folk behind the walls/wire.

First of all, it is an inexorable fact that institutionalization, a by product of prison politics, does indeed account for the high rate of recidivism every bit as much as substance abuse/addiction, if not more so. When we cultivate and espouse the yard/prison politics to which we are exposed upon entry or return to the prison environment, we are actively committing ourselves to a vicious cycle that serves as a revolving door, in and out and back into prison! We are virtually retarding our chances for success in a free world environment. Slighted by our own hands, we subject ourselves to an unrealistic perspective. One, that is motivated by aspirations that are in concert with and governed by prison politics, and two, behavior which is not conducive to anything other than prison living conditions dictated by the politics attached thereto. This arrested development will most certainly ensure your return trip back to the joint before you ever raise up and reach the gate!

In addition to this non-productive demeanor one adopts, this sword cuts two ways to be sure. Where the Kindred/Group is in regard, prison politics taint our holy faith! Hence, these perversions and manipulations of our faith not only stymie our advancements in here, but we sever our most valuable assets and resources as well by doing thus... 1) the development of healthy and responsible kinsmen as well as the healthy/positive advancement of our holy faith, both inside and out of prison! 2) we discourage outside supporters from wanting to get involved, or help us when they witness negative stereotypes being confirmed. This will inevitably result in poor or no funding support to the only organizations dedicated to serving our needs. No funds equals no help for us! Not to mention the total lack of respect for those fine folks whom put so much of their own personal affairs on hold to assist and serve you, or don't you suppose they have other matters of importance in their lives that they could tend to rather than spend all of their own time trying to help us in here. Only to have their hard and tireless efforts negated by the consequences of prison politics?!!!

In addition to being contrary and counter-productive to our Nine Noble Virtues, and our Holy Rede of Honor, prison politics is a one way ticket back to the pen for life on the installment plan, until that one day the door slams shut behind you for the last time. Remember always; "In all that you do, consider the benefit or harm upon yourself, your children and your folk!"

Two paradigms from the Eddas and myths come to mind, wherein our daily struggle of self mastery is to be regarded. Let me first remind all that it is the teaching of Odin that "Without struggle there will be no victory."

So bear in mind that pearl of wisdom when next you fall victim to one of your unwarranted fits of anger, or when the effects of attrition are bearing down on you! My attention is initially directed towards the tale of Thor's fishing trip, wherefore Asa-Thor seeks to conquer and slay Jórmungandr, the Midgard serpent. In this example we see Thor in a state of constant struggle with the monster until the day of Ragnarok at which time he will finally slay the serpent. Alas, it will also cost our dear brother Thor his own life as well. Theosophically and metaphysically speaking, this adventure of constant struggle can be equated with our own struggles on a continuum. Hence, the greater lesson to be gleaned here is this: If we await too long to slay our own dragons, it may very well cost us our own lives.

The other illustration I'd like to share comes to us in the form of Harbard's Saga. Here we are privy to a battle of wit vs. might. In Harbard's Saga, Odin is disguised as a ferryman on a large waterway which Thor desires to cross. Not recognizing the ferryman to be his own father, Thor greets him with an insult (the arrogance of strength), by hailing the ferryman as a "Pipsqueak." Henceforth, the game is on. A duel of hurling insults to and fro ensues, and continues for quite some time, until Thor is thoroughly enraged! In the end, Thor is forced to skirt the entire measure of shoreline to gain the other side... wit will always beat might when properly applied and employed.

And so, the metaphysical equation breaks down thusly: in this instance, Thor may be viewed as our uncontrolled anger and our desire to deal with that anger in a physical manner; with shear might and main. All the while, Odin (Harbard) never relinquishing his command of the situation, easily remains in control over all Thor's awesome might and main, by retaining his wit.

Our hardships and struggles in this environment are many, and at times intense, to say the least. Albeit, if we learn to wield and employ All-Father's gift to us, wit and wisdom, no obstacle will be insurmountable on the Trú path. Overall we can learn to control our Thor-self by employing our Odin-self; our own might will begin to serve us through the vehicle of wit and wisdom. Lest we go on slighting ourselves by our own hands, and continue to embrace the politics of a sick environment.

I find it rather curious that most prison politics concerning our folk are disseminated via the vehicle of prison gangs, with names which include the word "Aryan". This is a severe misnomer, in as much as the very word itself means "Noble" in the Sanskrit language, and there is certainly nothing Noble about any group of men which employs drug use and sales as one of its chief components, whereby they poison our folk and then turn us against one another, often killing and maiming our folk while destroying the lives of our folk with lifelong and sometimes life ending addictions! There is nothing noble about any of it, no matter what banner they herald themselves beneath. If you would truly be an Aryan man, or woman, an Aethling motivated by noble endeavors, then shun the poison of prison politics and begin to edify our folk!

And for those of you in free society...you too are the company which you keep an associate yourself with. If you are at the local bar every day/night, you will be a fellow in the hall of drunkards. If you hang out in a social circle of drug addicts, then the

hardships associated therewith shall be attendant to your life. Better off are you, and our Folk thereafter, by seeking commune with our Gods, and Folk whom abide by their laws.
Oðinn Með Oss (Odin with us)!!!

HAMMER OF THE GODS

"Mjöllnir", that mighty Hammer which has protected both Gods and the Folk from time immemorial, wielded by the great defender, Thor himself and forged by the dwarfs Sindri and Brokkr at the behest of the ever cunning Loki, is mythically accountable for the production of both thunder and lightening as a direct result of big brother Thor smashing some Jótun (giant) in his noble effort to defend both Asgard and Midgard!

Of course, the aforementioned is of rudimentary nature wherein the followers of the old heathen religion, or the student of Northern mythology are concerned, and serve only as a mere primer for which to initiate the content of this essay with. For while our myths certainly occupy an essential and valid role within our faith, it is not my intention to address the mythological role, or importance said vehicle imparts to us, the adherents of the Elder Faith; but rather, it is the literal role which the Hammer of the Gods can and does play in our everyday lives.

You see, the Hammer is made manifest in the reality of our daily lives in the metaphysical form of our will which we employ in an endeavor to overcome the metaphysical Jótuns (the forces of chaos.) The wondrous God Thor does indeed reside within each one of us, and we are the mighty Hammer wielders whenever we exercise the might of our will, whether it is individually, or collectively as a Folk!

Göthe once penned that; "You must conquer and rule, or lose and serve... suffer, or triumph, and become either the anvil, or the hammer!" No doubt Göthe well understood the conceptual hammer as "will" analogy, as well as the power his words may wield and elicit in those whom possess the Germanic soul and spirit.

We all, whether free-worlders, or prisoners, encounter a myriad of chaotic forces amassed against us, some seemingly unnoticeable, ergo easily dealt with, while others may become overwhelming and unleash the affects of attrition in what may only be perceived as an all out assault upon us from the realm of the unseen!

As Odinists/Wotanists, it has become a commonality to don and wear daily an amulet of Thor's Hammer around our necks both as an outward statement for all to see that the wearer openly professes his/her return to the indigenous faith of our noble ancestors prior to the advent of Christianity. And secondly, but no less important, as a daily reminder to the wearer that he/she does indeed wield the power, might and authority of Asa-Thor and his mighty Hammer. To smash and defeat the forces of chaos which we encounter on a daily and routine basis, which would seek to besiege and overwhelm us, thus denying us our victories over the negatives of our lives. And yet, in so many of these times of despair we often neglect or become absent of mind to just merely touch the hammer's about our neck's so as to remind ourselves of the might within us, or the fact the big brother Thor is always by our side to encourage us on to victory over the minions of chaos and self accepted weakness. Albeit, this is of no concern to fret over, for you see I have noticed with great delight just how ample our every day environments are in fact filled with the very images of the holy hammer! Yes, they are everywhere in our society, whether in subtle form which only one of us would readily recognize, to the loudly obvious incarnations which may adorn an ad, or a bottle of Armor All, or to the local hardware store sign. Upon nascent consideration, it appears that these copious embodiments of the hammer are little more than random; Though, I would posit that of course they are not! They are, to my way of thinking, Thor himself providing me with discreet yet ample visual confirmation that he is always near, and as a reminder that I always posses the power to face and overcome that which would oppose my will, and stand between myself and the victory which All-Father Odin promises shall always be mine, as long as I have the strength and courage to face the Jótuns in my life!

However you may elect to view this somewhat phenomenal occurrence of hammers and hammer images all about us, is of little importance really. What is of paramount importance is that whenever we do see one of these signs, we are immediately reminded of our own courage, might and fortitude to address and overcome that which would otherwise reek havoc upon our well being and our lives!

So then, live bravely and embrace the adversity in our lives, for no matter how one may go about dealing with it, for better, or worse, no one is exempt from it, save for the final hour... For every hour wounds, but the final one kills!

Hail Thor!!! And hail the mighty gift of fortitude which he imparts to us. May you all wield your might well, and may your hammers always strike Trú.

VALHALLA TODAY
(A 21st Century Perspective)

Val-hall-a, Val-hall, (ON Vall-hall); Valhalla, the hall of the slain. Odin's home in Asgard where he gathers the souls of warriors slain in battle. Valhalla is located in the quadrant of Asgard called 'Gladsheim' (Bright home, or Joy home), the magnificent hall is thatched with silver spears and golden shields and its benches are bedecked with the finest armor! Of course, the description exceeds the bounds of the aforementioned, and lavishly so. Albeit, thus is a moot issue wherefore this essay is A pais. In fact, assigning too much ado to the mythological description of Valhalla by either the Skalds, or chroniclers of the past, is the very premise for which we shall go hitherto from this point forward.

I am amazed at just how many of our folk still view our faith and its sacred institutions, with the tired eyes of yesterday as opposed to the fresh vision of tomorrow. I cannot tell you just how many times in the past years I have had some Kinsman or another approach me with sincere dismay in their heart over the quandary of their potential disbarment from entering All-father's hall should they fail to leave this world without a sword in their hand, or die a 'straw death' (old age, or illness). They bring their books to me to show me the descriptions of the great hall, which I have read myself time and time again over the years. They point out the clear description of the prerequisite for entry to Hár's hall, with deep concern etched upon their faces! Well, it is long since due that we bring about a modern, albeit educated knowledge and understanding of Valhalla today.

First of all, I've said a thousand times if I've said it once; "Let us employ the past as a guidepost, not a hitching post!" With that said, I must submit that our faith is not more appealing to our folk in mainstream society in large part due to the manner in which our faith is portrayed and presented to the folk at large in terms of yesterday's mythological conceptions. I shall endeavor hereafter, to afford a modern perspective, while remaining within context of the sacred concept of afterlife, as it applies to Valhalla.

To begin with let us examine with honest eyes, both the authors of our myths and their motives and designs in preserving and advancing them. While many actually believe that our myths appear today in print in the same, or exact fashion in which our Skaldic Ancestors sang/recited them, of course, this is an absurd notion to say the least. Chief among the reasons against such a notion is that the chroniclers of our myths were all Christians whom up to the point of recording the myths, were very driven and bent on eradicating the heathen, indigenous customs and practices of our ancestors.

Even where they found a favorable hand to pen them, if only for ancestral posterity; such an author would have been both influenced and educated by a Christian institution all the same! Next, and just as important to consider is the fact that hundreds of years had elapsed between the end of the hero Viking age/era and the time of any author's chronicles of the myths. Then, there is the difference in tribal/clannish location and perspective in the recital of the Skald's rendition of accounts as they may have occurred. Geographical location and timeline play a significant role in addition to the aforementioned as well. So many factors must be accounted for and added to the equation for any honest consideration as well.

Then there are the myriad of harsh realities and circumstances surrounding our ancestors during the period in which these myths were engendered and the events for which they are attributed, occurred. Hardships abounded en force, to say the least. An honorable death in battle bestowed prestige and glory upon not only the warrior, but his surviving Kin and their descendants. This no doubt is chief among the reason of appealability for such a hall of honor for the souls of the dead, a hall of the slain and their war God!

Let us jettison forward a millennia. Today we must approach the concept of Valhalla from a modern day perspective which fits within our own period, the 21st Century. Sure enough, the concept of a hall of honor for the souls of the noble and honorable dead is timeless, albeit the conceptual route for which one may gain entry to said afterlife world is not!

Whether one's idea of Valhalla is literal or figurative is a moot issue and in fact, a matter of personal choice in concert with one's ideas, be they metaphysical, metaphorical or theological. For one individual Valhalla may exist as a literal place while to another it may indeed be a final state of mind wherein one's own conscience in concert with how one lived one's life, will serve as the guide as to whether one's soul returns to the greater folk soul (Valhalla), or not based upon how one lived one's life.

This brings us to the battle dead and dying, with sword in hand. The metaphysical equation to such plays out as follows...Life is a constant battle for each and every one of us, to a greater, or lesser degree on any given day in our lives. Should we fail to aspire and act to overcome the myriad of struggles which constitute our lives, then we allow for life to live us, rather than we live our lives. This is the modern equation of a straw death! But if we rise up to meet our challenges and overcome them, we are fighting the battle. If we live our lives in accordance to/with the Nine Noble Virtues, the Æsirean Code of Nine, the Rede of Honor and the virtuous archetypes our Gods and ancestors have left us in the form of our myths, lore and sagas, as they apply to our environment today, then we have taken up the sword and the Hammer. Should we leave this plane we call Midgard having espoused these honorable principals right up till the Gods gather us up to them, well then, we have died with our proverbial swords in our hands and we enter Valhalla in a state of grace before the Gods we love and honor!

We are the progeny of our Gods, and therefore should endeavor to follow their examples and employ such in our own pursuit towards greater evolution and advancement of our noble folk, the majesty our ancestors left us, and our descendants thus warrant! Let us not get stuck in yesterday's frame of mind. See the past for what it is, and travel the road of today while we aspire to tread the highway of tomorrow together as a folk. Lest we forget that the Dinosaurs were incapable of adapting, hence they perished! We are more than capable of adapting and the morrow can belong to our children and their descendants if only we are bold enough to light their way into the future.

May your hammers and swords strike Trú...and may we all of noble soul meet in Valhalla!

A CALL FOR HOLY WAR

The many guises of Holy War may be witnessed on several fronts and in several locations all about Midgard. Whether they constitute a corpus of atrocities or righteous reckonings is a matter of heated debate, as all parties ensnared in any campaign will assume the mantle of either 'Patriot', or 'Terrorist'. Which one is merely a matter of perspective, for such may not be measured by the quantity of pain and suffering. To be sure, no one side in any conflict may lay siege to such a dubious monopoly.

But are all Holy Wars to be enacted upon the physical Theatre of Operation? Let us consider this query on a deeper level and equally so, let us afford it the deference of an honest examination.

The object of primacy for any military campaign is to contain, neutralize and eliminate the perceived threat to the welfare of the folk involved. So then, let us endeavor to examine and consider some of the very legitimate adversaries we as a faith, folk and tribe are posed with. To begin, we must establish just what constitutes a genuine threat to our survival, welfare and advancement as both a faith and folk. I would submit that we may all concur that any such agent which is counter productive to our welfare and progress, may constitute a legitimate threat and therefore warrant the mantle of "Foe Profane!" Thus do I stipulate upon the afore cited presumptions.

So then, in concordance with the afore stated, lets examine the catalog of agents amassed against us as members of our sacred and beloved faith/folk community...

VICES: Vices are any number of undesirable behaviors, often habitual and morally derelict in concert with depraved states of self accepted weaknesses. These will vary from person to person, though some will share several of the same, and chief among them is 'lack of accountability'. This of course is followed closely by substance abuse, gambling, sex addictions which lead one astray from one's own mate, or any activity which one knows to be selfish, detrimental and places one's own desires over and above the needs and safety of one's family and folk, are all categorized as vices.

SELF ACCEPTED WEAKNESS: Self accepted weaknesses are any moral, spiritual, psychological, or physical weaknesses which one seeks to justify as opposed to endeavor to correct. Any state of mind which goes with the flow of what appears to be harmless, albeit is a detrimental current. That is to say, one has identified less than desirable elements residing in one's life, yet one merely resigns one's self to accept it as a non factor, semantics, or a non threat to one's progress. Institutionalization is a self accepted weakness!

INSTITUTIONALIZATION: Institutionalization is the espousing of a totally pernicious ideology on every front of self defeat. This encompasses components from vice to faith/folk destruction for the sake of not only accepting but willfully embracing the destructive and morally retarded prison culture. Drugs, gambling, homosexuality, extortion, racketeering and fratricidal prison gangs all contribute so greatly to the decay of the Aryan Tribal ideal and thereafter, the very destruction of our faith and folk community. Does no one find it ironic and absurd that so many white men and women come into these dungeons, learn about white pride, mark their bodies with tattoos of racial distinction and honor, yet all the while so many act in counter productive and non-conducive ways toward building and strengthening our folk! What is so horribly wrong with this picture?

Folk proudly dawning and wearing the marks of what they deem to be equated with Aryan honor, while acting out in very dishonorable ways which will inevitably destroy the very thing we claim to love so much... Our Race! This is not, however, an indictment against anyone. Rather, it is a call to you all to take a positive stand in the name of our Gods/Goddesses, Ancestors and Aryan Tribal pride, this very day. It is within our means and devices to remedy the far reaching maladies cited herein, which we face as a faith and folk.

The most concrete manner to assure the endurance and longevity of a thing is to construct it from the most durable and indestructible stock available. For when this measure is employed, it, the thing itself, becomes impervious to the assaults of all others. If such a desirable stock does not exist, then one must endeavor to devise and establish such a stock. By seeking to place total accountability within ourselves, as a faith and folk, rather than shifting the blame for our short comings to others, we may address these short comings and thereby create that desirable and impervious stock. In fact, we shall become that stock and in concert with becoming thus, we may truly control our own destiny as a faith and folk! There are no revolutionary fantasies to be had in the reality of Vinland (North America) today. The revolution must be in the way we think! There are no quick and immediate fixes!!!!

Vinland, with its government institutions will be here a hundred and fifty years from now. The question is; "Will we as a faith and folk be here then?" The only viable fix is a long term one. We must rid ourselves, our faith and folk of all the pernicious habits and short comings we suffer from. We must breed and raise intelligent Kinder (children) in the ways of our faith and folk and replace the erroneous shame which has been hoisted upon our backs, with pride. We must send them to college to earn degrees and insert them into the government and its institutions so that one day we too will have a voice and representation to defend our faith and folk and reverse the racist labels so erroneously placed upon us! This is our best and most immediate, valid option. We must cease tossing about some old tired clichés as though it were mere sport and reclaim our bona fide grandeur. This will only be accomplished by becoming the very Hammers we don around our necks which tell the world who and what we are... Children of the Hammer. Within our veins flows the thunder and lightning of Mjollnir. It is hard wired into our very DNA, this desire to return to the height of our Ancestral lineage, the Gods themselves. Only the hammers of this life shall pound out and shape their own destinies, while the anvils will forever be destined to receive one beating after another! The choice is yours alone to make.

Therefore, in light of the afore stated; I issue this challenge to you all... Declare Holy War against these agents of chaos and destruction which threaten the majesty of our faith and folk.

Legitimate honor may be found in genuine service to our Gods and Folk and denied to none whom remain Trú and loyal to the end. Let this be our Holy and Sacred resolve as we seek to pass our ancient tribal ways and our beloved faith onto our Kinder of tomorrow as we assume our stations in the light of victory as holy Sunna smiles on the House of Odin, and those whom have earned the right to reside within. Heil Allfather Odin!

> "You must conquer and rule, or lose and serve. Suffer, or triumph, and become either the anvil or the Hammer!"– Göthe

RESIST AND DEFY

Resist and defy! Well, that certainly infers a great deal of chaos wherefore directed focus is lacking. But we are Odinists, not anarchists and therefore the call for resistance and defiance is not an anthem of anarchy but rather, it is a call for restoration of order, strength, unity and majesty on all fronts of Aryan Tribalism.

We cannot hope to achieve any meaningful gains if we do not first resist and defy the deleterious influences of a morally bankrupt society. We must resist capricious urges which may seem innocuous enough upon their initial inception. For when we glance back whence we have come, most of us, if honest about it, will be able to discern the damage which we have inflicted not only in our own personal lives, but in the lives of our loved ones and our folk community overall, in concert with our previous impulsive and capricious actions.

The majority of you perusing this right now are incarcerated. Residents of the 51st state! Why the 51st state, some may query? While others entering their 20th year, or better behind the walls and wire are all too familiar with the term. Today in Vinland (the U.S. part) there are in fact enough people incarcerated to constitute a 51st state! And while we are technically still citizens of the U.S., we are no longer citizens of the states from which we either hail from, or find ourselves incarcerated in. We are now residents of the 51st state called "Corrections", and sadly so. Enough of us assisted in the formation process of this 51st state, resplendent with its perverse and ill social order. A mere by-product of a larger socially ill and morally bankrupt country and its government.

"Corrections" is a multi-billion dollar business annually in the U.S. and it is not sustainable by corporate, local and federal government greed alone. NO, not at all. It further requires that "WE" participate in the process. Recidivism is the chief component of the economic engine which powers and promotes the corrections industry. With the end of the "Cold War" with Eastern Europe, the U.S. economy suffered a devastating blow. No where was it more immediately felt than in California which was home to the overwhelming majority of the nation's Aerospace Industry. California quickly realized that it desperately required a major economic engine which it could stimulate its dying economy with. Corrections became that engine which would provide the fiscal infusion California so critically required to fill the economic vacuum it had inherited with the fall of the Berlin Wall and the erosion of the Communist threat which ceased in the latter part of the 1980's.

As the economic woes spread across the U.S., other states followed California's lead and new prison construction exploded. New laws were established to fill those new prisons to maximum capacity and the prison industry of America changed its name to the more socially acceptable mantle of the Corrections Industry.

Consider the absurdity for just a brief moment. When a guard, which are no longer referred to as Screws, Bulls, or Hacks, but rather as, "Correctional Officers", feeds a prisoner his/her meal, is he correcting the meal? How about distributing prisoner's mail. Is he correcting the mail? The answer is of course not. That is because no social, or moral ills are being corrected within the U.S. prison systems wherefore genuine rehabilitation is in regard. Such genuine rehabilitation is absent in its entirety. In fact, the only thing that the corrections industry has corrected is a large portion of the nation's economic system which incurred a state of arrested development in the late 198O's. The entire corrections facade with its "Corrections Officers" is intelligently designed so as to afford a sense of normalcy to unassuming citizens whom continue to foot the bill for their continued day to day operations as opposed to investing in an authentic rehabilitation program to immerse the offender in prior to his release back into society. This is not the equivalency of re-integration of a functionally developed individual back into society! It is tantamount to turning lose an angry man whom has been warehoused for years of his life much in the same manner as a living room set of furniture at the local "U-store it" facility! But enough with the history and social studies lessons and finger pointing. Let us endeavor to assume accountability as opposed to shifting the blame. This corrections business would not be so very prosperous if not for our willful and voluntary participation. And no one is going to alter our attitudes and perspective of the current state of circumstances in our lives, but ourselves alone!

I'm not referring to the initial crimes which landed us in prison; in so much as I am referring to our helping the system prosper by going with the flow of its current. There is an entire socially retarded culture which could not exist in these dungeons without our consent. Example: Upon one's initial exposure to this environment, most endeavor to hold fast to the ties which connect them to their home, families and society from which they had come. But the repetitive indoctrination which one is exposed to on a continuum in prison renders it nearly impossible to hold onto tight enough. The prison/corrections' deliberate agenda promotes an ill design wherein a prisoner is encouraged to forfeit any sound and civilian social skills in exchange for the promoted diet of a morally derelict prison culture resplendent with substance abuse, homosexuality, dishonor, betrayal, fratricidal prison gangs, lack of any authentic self respect, or esteem, etc., etc., etc.. This breakdown, once total and complete, constitutes a state of institutionalization. This is the key contributor of recidivism and is indeed tantamount to total failure as far as a functioning human with any productive living and social skills are in regard.

I implore you all to resist and defy this state and federally sponsored sickness! Do not accept it when some guard refers to the cell which you occupy as your home, or house, for it is not your home. It is a cage which you are forced to occupy. Identify it as such. Your home is wherever your family or loved ones reside... Not in some cage which when occupied the state, or government makes a few dollars off of! We forfeit our dignity, self respect and identity when we willfully embrace the ill social etiquette of the penitentiary culture. We've been taught to think in this erroneous manner and now we must resist and defy this pernicious thinking!

Odinism is about self accountability and taking control of our lives. By living the Nine Noble Virtues, the Rede of Honor, the Æsirian Code of Nine, we may reconnect with the majesty our noble ancestors and our Gods have lovingly preserved, fought for and died for so that we could inherit them. We must restore a sense of fraternal love and solidarity amongst ourselves and then openly exhibit it for all to see the love and respect we seek to restore to our faith/folk community both within and without the prison systems of this nation. We must shun the behavior and attitudes which are not conducive to the welfare of our faith/folk community if ever we would recapture the genuine nobility and strength which once, so very long ago, constituted the Aryan Tribes. This we must embrace, cultivate and teach in the name of our Allfather Odin and the rest of the Æsir and Vanir. And we must resist and defy any agenda which is not in concert with our healthy advancement. As we seize yet another year in our lives, let us edify our faith and folk as we endeavor to walk the Northern Road.

ODINISM vs. ÁSATRÚ, A Clarification

There is an erroneous perception going around these days, like a bad flu bug infecting our faith/folk community. In fact, it has been a malady which has beset upon and burdened us for nearly the past thirty eight years that I've been an Odinist. I am, of course, referring to the misconception that Odinism and Ásatrú are one in the same faith/religion. In fact, there are many whom share the common view that there is but one Northern Faith with several names ascribed thereto including, but not limited to: Odinism, Ásatrú, the Troth, the Way, Irminism, Theodism, Norse Wicca, Vanatru, Northern Dawn Revivalists, etc., etc.. Indeed, some of these are very much the same Theology/Philosophy while others are not. Odinism is most certainly not one and the same with any other denomination within the Northern Tradition. If you are one of the many whom believed this to be the instance, it is not your fault. Most have been erroneously taught this by another who was taught this way and another before him/her! Much in the same way we have been taught, or exposed to Christianity by those whom believed it to be so, and we in turn believed in them. Be that as it may, it is long overdue to correct this long standing error. No other faith or individual will ever take us seriously if we do not take ourselves seriously and seek to establish a liturgy of our own within the Northern Faith, which sets us apart from all other denominations. This does not render Odinists as elitists, nor should it. What it does do is allow us the space to practice our faith with like minded folk devoid of the cancer of back biting which so commonly exists within the Northern Faith community today! This exists because so many insist that we are all following the same faith with different names all the while, excluding those we don't care for. This leads to a great deal of back biting, which in turn contributes to our faith's arrested development. Acceptance of this reality is the key element required here in order to cease this self defeating nature we exhibit. If ever we would escape the fetters of retarded growth and ascend beyond 'cult' status, then we must face the inexorable facts.

Does Odinism share similarities with Ásatrú and other denominations of the Northern Tradition? The answer is a resounding 'Yes'. But to what degree? To some minor extent, mostly of mythological proportion and equivalency and deities, Odinism shares some basic similarities with all of the afore mentioned denominations within the Northern Tradition. And yes, more so it shares its greatest similarities with Ásatrú, albeit, the two are not the same.

Let us consider the realities predicated upon the facts: The dawn of our race may be traced back some forty-thousand years to date. In all of that time, Allfather Odin, has been either worshiped, prayed to, or honored in one form/name, or another, consistent with the qualities, attributes and archetypal concepts which we to this day can and do attribute to Allfather Odin as the primordial consciousness of the racial lineage otherwise discerned as the Aryan Tribes. All that we may descry in the echoes of nature's laws, including the personae of the other Gods and Goddesses, are manifestations of his divine will and thereafter his conscious thought 'to be'! And as such, the spark of that divinity resides within each one of us, whether we elect to acknowledge thus, or not.

On the other hand, Ásatrú is a relatively new entity in the history of the Aryan Tribes. Ásatrú is an Old Norse word which translates to "Troth, or loyal to the Æsir (ON Sky Gods)". Rooted in the (probable) century leading up to the era we today know as the Viking Age (Approximately 789 to 1100 Common Era). So too, do many of the Gods/Goddesses have their beginnings in the Scandinavia countries during this era. Along with the Vanir, these deities of the Old Norse Æsir constitute the corpus of the Northern Gods and Goddesses of Ásatrú today. Whether the Aryan Tribes migrated from Asia Minor is a matter of ongoing debate among scholars today. It certainly exceeds the allotted space afforded this essay. I merely raise the issue as it has been posited by scholars that the origin of the very word/name: Æsir, is of Asian origin and as thus, were we able to substantiate such a claim, then we would further thus be able to fix the origin of the Æsirian deities to that locale and the period of the inhabitants thereof as well. Yet, the Æsir came to be known as such in the Scandinavian countries only, in their infancy, and not in the Teutonic countries whose inhabitants (i.e. Germanic Tribes) would have most certainly made the same migration journey out of Asia Minor to Europe via the Caucasus

Mountains. Though, the Æsir as they were/are known, would have been foreign to them beyond Wotan (Odin), Donar (Thor), Frija (Frigga), Paltar (Baldur) and Tiu (Tyr). They would not have known them to belong to the family of Gods known as the Æsir, or even what the Æsir were. Were this not the case in fact, then Cornelius Tacitus (56 CE - 115 CE), when composing his treatise: the Germania, surly would have named, or identified the Æsir, and/or other deities beyond those cited in his chronicle which predates the Viking Age by over six centuries. In fact he does wherefore Nerthus/Erde/Erda/Ertha/Erce, and Isis are concerned, and not more!

The knowledge of Odin as Allfather, or as "Thee" Allfather, predates the knowledge of the Æsir and Vanir within the memory of our race, by millennia.

So then, we whom profess ourselves as avowed Odinists, identify Allfather Odin as the primordial consciousness of creation and the progenitor of the race of people which constitute the Aryan Tribes and their descendants today. Furthermore, with all due respect to Dr. S. Flowers (Edred Thorsson) whom posits within many of his published works that the difference between an Odinist and an Odian, is that the Odinist worships Odin while the Odian seeks to emulate him. This I see and denounce as a preposterous employment of semantics in an effort by Dr. Flowers to create and employ verbiage created by himself and used by adherents of the esteemed Rune Gild. I must assert that I have been an Odinist for nearly thirty eight years and it has been my own experience, as I believe it to be the natural progression, that any and all whom profess themselves to be Odinist, will begin their own journey as I myself did, somewhere near the bottom end of comprehending Odin, initially via the vehicle of worship and then evolving through self transformation on a continuum until one ascends to the place where one gives one self to one self and thereafter seeks to honor Odin by emulating him and his own holy quest for wisdom. Anyone who would lay claim to just instantly and fully comprehending the divine consciousness that is Odin, from the beginning of their journey, is either severely confused, or suffering the delusions of some grand illusion! One thing is for certain, no such person truly knows Odin!!!

In concert with our theology, nothing else would be possible without Odin first, all else follows thereafter. And as thus, Odin warrants our supreme respect and honor as we ourselves seek to emulate his own quest for Ascension via the vehicle of self transformation on a continuum. Do we still honor the Æsir and the

Vanir? Absolutely! They too are our beloved Gods/Goddesses as well as our ancestors and friends. Albeit, they would not "be", anymore than we would "be", save for Allfather Odin`s desire and will thereafter.

I know of no Ásatrúar who perceives walking the road North in the same manner. For them, **ALL** Gods within the Northern pantheon are equal, non greater than the other. And there is nothing wrong with that at all. It's just not who we are, or the way we do it. Even more, I am a fundamentalist Odinist, as are all of the members of the SONS OF ODIN, 1519 and the overwhelming majority of the HOLY NATION OF ODIN. That is to say, we live, eat and breath our beloved faith in Allfather Odin, to the extreme wherefore troth/loyalty is in regard. The mantle of zealot quickly comes to mind, and for me - rightly so.

That this issue has up till now, not been addressed within our faith/folk community only further solidifies the sad evidence that we incur too much unacceptable squabbling and fail to enjoy the solidarity we so desperately need to survive, let alone, progress. Too many get and remain confused by the myriad of differences within what they were led to believe was all one faith with only one denomination. Hence the origin of so many lingering confusions wherefore learning about a Northern Path is in regards.

We of the HOLY NATION OF ODIN, are seeking to remedy this ailment which has required correction for way too long now. By removing some of that confusion and replacing it with some sound understanding, we hope to achieve just that. Because the past should be a guidepost, not a hitching post. And the road North in the 21st century and beyond should not be fraught with confusion wherein one's source of solace and stability is in regard. It should be illuminating in addition to being a source of righteous might!

Providing a sound vehicle, to attain such a state of genuine spirituality and strength is what Odinism is all about!!!

"That which is open to all, is respected by none."

- Stephen McNallen

"Folk Mother"
by Vidar U. Odinson Harless, 1519-CG

PRISON BREAK
In Memory of Else Odinsdottir Christensen

The twenty-first day of Merrymoon fell on a Laugardagr... I won't forget that because it is the day that Vor Trú, Issue No#70 arrived at my prison cage. I opened the envelope where prison mail inspectors had taped it shut, and I withdrew the magazine from the manila envelope. As I did so, I noticed a picture of woman quite familiar to me. Well, I suspect... quite familiar to many among our folk really. It was none other than Else Christensen and her likeness was adorning the back cover of the latest issue of Vor Trú. As I went on to read the caption beneath her image, both eternal & fast in print, my mind went numb as it sought to comprehend the caption's message. My eyes began to well with tears as the realization set in that the Gods had called Else home on Merrymoon 4th, 2255 RE. I am not too proud to concede that I was shattered and must have looked a sight to my Kinsman & Celly (cell mate) as I stood there and openly wept, consumed with grief. I was 220 lbs. of completely tattooed mean, reduced to a sobbing knave.

I realized that many in our Folk community knew Else, and probably more so and better than I. Why, I wouldn't even be so audacious as to dispute that fact. Albeit, I'd appreciate the latitude to share my story with you all and in doing so, share a part of Else with you as well. For I have something to say, something about one of the richest treasures our folk was blessed with in the twentieth century... Else Odinsdottir Christensen.

Else entered my life in 1984 CE. An Odinist in Glendale Arizona, named "Torch", gave me her address in Crystal River Florida. I wrote to Else, who was at the time, 70 or 71 already, with a braggart's arrogance about how I'd been a Heathen on the path of Odin since I was sixteen. She wrote me back with a barrage of questions regarding our faith, which I could not even begin to answer. I was ashamed to write her back and while I was contemplating what to write her back, she wrote me again, as three weeks had elapsed without a reply to her letter. She told me it was rude of me to not reply to her letter and that if that was who I was, not to waste her time with anymore junk mail.

I had no idea how old she was at the time and my ego was a bit bruised. Be that as it may, I wrote her back with an apology and told her that I would very much like to learn about the true faith of my ancestors.

For the next few years, Else personally wrote to me about twice a month with lessons, booklets, current and back issues of "The Odinist" and she sent me several books on Norse-Teutonic mythology & the Sagas. She also helped to advance my lacking academic education by encouraging me to enroll in college courses, she even advised me about grants which were available at the time. Else was my very accomplished teacher. In 2236 RE (1986 CE) I professed through her and the Odinist Fellowship which I became a proud member of. On the back of the membership card were words to the effect that; "I will defend Kith & Kin, home & hearth and that only the blood of my ancestors will flow through the veins of my descendants."

I began my first genuine self transformation through the tutelage of Else. And I stayed in touch with her until she was set up by some Nithlings and sent to prison! I never directly heard from her or wrote to her after that, though I had sent several messages to her via several members of our folk community over the years.

I suppose about this time the average reader may be concluding that while this may be a nice story, what's so special about it from anyone else's memories of Else, what makes my story so unique?

Right then - In 1984 CE when the Norns elected to weave Else into my life, I was a twenty-two year old on my way to prison. I had nothing to show who I was in life other than a birth certificate and an Honorable discharge from the Army. Having suffered severely from ADHD/ADD, dyslexia and a host of other maladies, as a youth, I had no high school diploma, as I had quit to enlist on my 17th birthday. I went to prison and got caught up in the gangster life and up to the point when I had met Else, I was a drug addict, a liar, a schemer, a whoremonger and a womanizer - with little or no true self respect, let alone any genuine respect for my ancestors or folk!

But all of that changed over the past twenty-one years. Today I am an educated man with a healthy dose of self respect and sincere love & respect for my ancestors & folk. I am a Gothi and teacher and I live everyday of my life in service to the Gods & folk! I haven't touched drugs in many years, nor have I been involved with gang life for several years now. I have educated literally hundreds to the ways of our ancestors and I continue to do so. I have co-founded the Vinland Kindred of the Sons of Odin, 1519. I am now the Chief Court Gothi. And while I am serving life in prison, I am no prisoner - Else taught me how to achieve a prison break long ago and I in turn remain free and teach others how to free themselves! I am the Hofgothi of our faith here at this facility, and I find myself constantly battling with the prison administration over our rights. It is an endless struggle! And just when attrition seems to overwhelm me, it is Else's words & lessons to me which drive me on like a Valkyrie prompts her hero. And now, she has gone to take her place among the Disir. No doubt she will attach herself to the worthy and guide them, just as she did tirelessly and without complaint all the days that she lived. I feel it is a safe assumption to make, that while others worthy of note had contributed to educating our incarnated folk, and still do, none have done so en masse as had Else. For literally thousands throughout Vinland's prison systems had returned to the ways of our ancestors and achieved their own prison breaks either through Else's direct mentoring, or the teachings of her many students over the years. Where knowledge of our ancestral faith is concerned, throughout the prison world, the guiding hand of a folk mother named Else Odinsdottir Christensen has been ever present. And it will always be present and living on in the deeds of those of us, who were so blessed to have drank from the horn that she held out to us!

Now it is our turn to raise our horns to her...

Fara meth Othinn, Else!!!

I remain in service to the Gods & Folk of the Holy Nation of Odin.
Member of the Odinist Fellowship, circa 2236 RE/1986 CE

REMEMBERING DAVID...

Dateline June 1, 2007 CE

Only this afternoon my wife Linda had informed me that our kinsman Ron McVan had contacted her to inform her that David Lane had passed away earlier this week on Memorial Day.
How David passed is not nearly as important as how he lived or the severe consequences he had incurred in concert with his noble convictions and principles. More so, with David's passing both the Aryan folk and Odinist/Wotanist faith have lost a champion. The battalions of Zionists and their misinformed sympathizers are most assuredly overjoyed at our faith and folk community's great loss. Albeit, one hundred perhaps two hundred years from now, history will be rewritten to reflect the reality of the role genuine Patriotism played in late 20th century Vinland (USA) where European folk, heritage and cultures were to come under siege and remain so today. And where such history shall be chronicled, the name of David Lane will appear upon the Patriot's Roll of Honor.

David Lane was born in Woden, Iowa, Vinland on Wednesday – (Odin's day), November 2, 1938 CE and he was a life long folk patriot; Whom on many occasions disregarded his own comfort and personal safety in service to that which he most loved and remained stalwartly committed to; "His Folk". David now leaves us to join Allfather Odin and the myriad of heroes whom await him in Valhalla.

The piper's song is mournful, as it wends its way across our Odal lands, and I fear that many "Armchair Patriots" will seek to capitalize off his honorable name and memory. The deluge of poetry, essays and songs will now begin, and were they are proffered by the legitimate Folk Patriots, such fame of sound praise is always appropriate. But where the Aryan man or woman lacks even the desire to abhor the many maladies which plague our Race, all the while singing the praise of David Lane, an even a greater disservice our foes could not afford his valiant memory.

For David, just as all true Folk Patriots, despised the Aryan man or woman in name only; those who refuse to acknowledge the damage that drugs, vice, prison politics and fratricidal behaviors destroys our people with. It was David Lane who gave us the 14 words, "We must secure the existence of our people and the future for white children".

As surely as we honor the memory of this kinsmen, who now joins the ranks of our honored ancestors, others will come to fill our ranks where the fallen once stood. The only question that remains is this, "Will those who come along honor or deface the memory of David Lane with their actions?"

Cattle die; Kinsman die
and so each one must die;
One thing I know shall never die,
the deeds of a good man.
– Hávamál - 77

David Lane was 68. We shall miss him sorely. But we shall never forget him, or his selfless and tireless efforts. Fara meth Odin, David!

FUNDAMENTAL ODINISM

There are many among our folk today in what constitutes the western world, whom subscribe to one form or another, of what may loosely be regarded as Paganism, or Northern Heathenry. Arguably, the best known among such spiritual paths, one would find Odinism and its next of kin, Ásatrú. While the two paths are indeed nearly hard to discern at times, and even argued by some to be one in the same, they **ARE** in fact, two separate paths. More so, many who define their spiritual path as Odinism, bears very little resemblance to that which Fundamental Odinists adhere to in their spiritual endeavors.

Fundamental Odinists harbor the belief that there is an all pervading divine spirit which manifests itself throughout the cosmos and the laws of nature and is therefore self-evident within the realm of nature. For us, that divine spirit is the Allfather Odin, whom without, all else would fail to be possible. The Allfather Odin **IS** pure spirit and the primordial conscious thought of the Aryan people. He too is thereafter, the very will of that first thought. Our Gods and Goddesses are therefore manifestations of the spirit that is the Allfather Odin.

We do not bow our heads or bend our knees before our Gods. We do not worship them as our masters. We honor them as children should their parents. We seek to emulate their noble qualities and conduct ourselves and live our lives with a great degree of personal strength, honor and courage, just as our noble ancestors did prior to the advent of Christianity and their forced conversion thereto said faith! Our Gods are our kin and friends. We are their descendants...their living folk.

We advocate and promote the Germanic Tribal system as opposed to the minute, albeit not discounted, Viking Era model which is so popular within the Ásatrú community at large the world over. We acknowledge that while the Viking Era had indeed made vast contributions to the overall corpus of what constitutes the history of the Aryan people, it too was that very era's corruption of our indigenous religious beliefs which ushered in the alien and Bedouin Christian faith among our unsuspecting ancestors. It must further be asserted that it was during that era that the noble virtue of loyalty to one's kin/folk, became bankrupt in lieu of the enticing lures of non-folk fornications in foreign lands. Whereas the Germanic Tribal system may be traced back in time for millennia prior to the Viking Era and for all that time, by what was chronicled by the likes of both Herodotus and Tacitus, our ancestors possessed a great love and respect for the virtue of loyalty to their native culture and heritage. Such remained inexorably in tact up to the latter part of the Viking Era!

We believe that nothing is more sacred than our blood! For therein lies the complete entirety of our ancestry, both Gods and Folk. We promote a genuine respect for our spiritual leadership and Elders and we recognize the full merits of structure, hierarchy and the ordained Gothard (Priesthood). We hold that tradition does not seek to store the cold ashes of the past, but rather, seeks to keep the flame alive for future generations.

We hold that our holy and sacred Rites and Ceremonies **ARE NOT** open to the general public, for either scrutiny or criticisms. And that only those of our folk may bear witness to, or participate in our holy Rites, or those of our folk whom are sincerely seeking to learn about the noble spiritual beliefs of our ancestors.

We fully acknowledge that the Groves are indeed sacred and play a major role in outdoor Rites. But we hold that the Hof (Temple) is equally as sacred and indeed, to the HOLY NATION OF ODIN, our Hofs are as they once were in elder days, and now are once again, our houses of the holy.

We hold that the Eddas, Sagas, Lore and myths are all certainly valid learning texts wherefore discovery and comprehension of our spiritual beliefs are in regard. They are filled with hidden mysteries and knowledge and wisdom designed by elder skalds and chroniclers to be rediscovered by their descendants one day(us today and future generations to come) and to be merely tales of entertainment to the unintended peruser throughout the ages. Albeit, we further fully accept that these chronicles, for all their value, have long since been tainted with the corruption of Christian scholars and a myriad of interlopers with deliberate designs to cast an unfavorable light upon the noble spiritual path which our ancestors both followed and left to us. Furthermore, we hold that what constitutes the corpus of literary works of the Aryan people from antiquity to the present time, warrants both the respect and study of our folk, and we vigorously promote the study of these critical works of history, philosophy, art and all intellectual medium as a valid means of restoring our own unique indigenous culture and heritage. We promote fraternal solidarity among the Aryan people, both within and without our particular spiritual community.

We firmly believe in the genuine concept of fate/destiny as predetermined by the Norns (the Goddesses which govern all of our fates, including the Gods!) There is an Old Norse saying; "If you are meant to hang, you won't drown!" This is not to infer that we are without control over our own lives; for we do indeed harbor an honest belief in self determination. That is to say that, the destination and time of departure from this life to the next may reside in the hands of the Norns (Skuld, more pointedly), but the journey is ours to control through the vehicle of our own will and self determination. We are extremely Pro Life! We constitute the world's minority due to low birth rates and abortions. This is tantamount to self induced genocide... The family unit requires a family!

We are unapologetically Folk oriented, which is to say that we are anti-universalist. We fully comprehend the inevitable destruction of all unique racial groups and sub groups and their innate heritages and cultures that the seeds of multi-culturism will one day reap if they are not met with even greater resistance in accordance with the first law of natural order; the will of any given species/race, to survive!

This is neither an endorsement nor license for anyone to disrespect anyone else. It is merely an undisputable fact of nature! As Fundamental Odinists, we shall always be respectful and considerate to all whom extend the same to us, no matter their race, creed, or color.

Furthermore, we are truly conservative in nature and character. While we place an immense value upon the qualities of personal freedom and liberty, we equally insist that full accountability for one's choices and actions must accompany free will.

We are protective of our kin and folk. This includes our DNA (blood, tissue and organs). While any and all are certainly free to do as they please, a genuine Fundamental Odinist will not donate his/her blood, organs or tissues. Being protective of, and accountable for one's DNA (blood, organs & tissue), one must responsibly take into consideration that when one donates their DNA, it may go to anyone! You may not choose who will get it, unless it is specific to a friend or family member's surgery and you are a living donor. In which case, it would certainly be permissible and a family duty in addition thereto. Albeit, when one signs an Organ/Tissue Donor card, or you donate blood at a blood drive, or blood bank, you have no control as to whom will receive your DNA. One of the problems which plague the advance of both our folk and faith today is that so many who claim to adhere to our sacred precepts do so in word only. Our proverbs and axioms of ethical and moral behavior become little more than mere clichés and catchy phrases to far too many. Actions noble in word most certainly do not equate with actions noble in deed. I assure you!

If we claim to fully comprehend that every ancestor whom has ever lived in our entire line, does indeed live in the blood coursing through our very veins, pumping through our hearts, if we accept this to be the factual reality then how or why would we give it away so freely and without a care as to whom will receive it? The answer, of course, is that we would not if we truly believed in the power of our DNA/Blood.

Once more regarding the myriad of cliché hurlers... Why is it that so many view the host of struggles and hardships we all must face, from a 'victim's' point of view, when they are all but grand opportunities to rise above the pale. Every day of the true Fundamental Odinist's life, is pregnant with potential! It is a component required in the exercising of one's will. It is the process of overcoming weakness and asserting one's will to survive and excel. Yet so many, who claim the path of our Allfather Odin take the perspective of life's struggles as something that has befallen, or plagued them. Such simpering are the weak rantings of the clueless wherefore genuine Fundamental Odinism is in regard!

While we do believe in an afterlife, we don't waste our lives awaiting it. We live each day in the here and now with vigor, all the while remaining aware of our solemn responsibility for our future kin. Regarding the conceptual Odinist afterlife, see "Valhalla Today" (also in this book). While everyday of our lives are holy, as life is a sacred and holy event, we hold that Odinsdagr (Odin's day = Wednesday) is the high holy day of the week. We value the wisdom in sound leadership and organization as a means of tribal survival, advancement and longevity. We do not submit to oppressive or ego-maniac whims in our leadership! Lack of personal accountability for one's actions should never be confused as, nor pass for freedom/liberty. Nor should sound Rede (counsel) or respect for leadership structure and standards, be confused as oppression.

We recognize the timeless wisdom and worth of loyalty to family, kindred and folk, as nature's imperative and therefore, our Gods' wisdom.

We recognize the inexorable fact that we are a part of nature and natural order as opposed to being apart from it! And as such, we further recognize that the laws of nature are superior to the inferior laws of man. Taking this into account, we temper such a reality by realizing that while this is so, it is necessary, in order to maintain a society of order and just laws, to abide by the laws of man and society where they either further, or complement the laws of natural order. Where they do not, we resist and remain defiant for survival sake; which once again returns us to the law of natural order and the will to survive.

We hold that our ancestral past is a valuable compass for our future survival, albeit, we must take care to apply that wisdom and knowledge to the here and now if ever we as a folk/people are to have a future at all. Our illustrious past is intended to be a Guidepost... NOT a Hitching Post!

We honor the Æsirian Code of Nine, the Nine Noble Virtues, the Rede of Honor, the 14 Codes of Aryan Ethic and all wise doctrine which is conducive to the survival and advancement of our Faith and Folk.

Fundamental Odinism is an ethnic religion which is indigenous to the native European people of the Aryan Tribes i.e. Germanic Tribes (e.g. Norse, Teutonic, Celtic, Baltic and Slavic Tribes).

We do not promote, practice or preach hate, bigotry or racism. We are racially aware and proudly so, as should all people be of their respective Folk/people. We afford due respect and consideration to all people who return the gesture. We do not promote or endorse any political program or agenda. We do not endorse, espouse or condone any gang activity! We do not condone or accept homosexuality as a legitimate component of the laws of natural order. In this our official position, we are not alone, as the Catholic, Orthodox Jews and Islamic faiths all have prohibitions against homosexuality as well. Homosexuality defies the natural order of family procreation and therefore, our Gods.

For us, the genuine Fundamental Odinists, we acknowledge that for far too long now, there has existed a severe lack among our people for self reliance, self determination, industriousness, respect for the plight of our folk and indigenous faith and the future of both, honor (both personal & Kindred), loyalty to one's own, strength/fortitude and rectitude, hospitality and perseverance to catalog but a few. Many of those whom exhibit said lack of respect for the afore stated, wear a Thor's Hammer or other symbol indicative of our noble way, around their necks! Too many toss about what amounts to mere clichés that are memorized, but far too few live by them anymore. So many... Too many, fail to pay their own way, or pull their own weight when they are in a position to do so. They elect not to and then justify to themselves and others why it is so. These folks always have their hands out looking for something for nothing. They do not constructively participate in the process of productivity but they are quick to participate in the process of levying a host of ill accusations about others whom have towed the line. They expend their energy and others associated with them, cultivating problems like they are the spawn of Loki, rather than seek solutions to the problems which face us as a faith and folk, as would befit the offspring of our Gods!

Too many desire and even demand equality and respect among the folk when they have not done a thing to warrant such as a peer who positively participates in any beneficial activity. Everyone wants to ride on the Longship, but far too few are willing to man the oars and pull their weight. They want their portion of the plunder, but they don't want to get their hands dirty in the pillage. They all want a free meal, but they don't want to slaughter the beast and bloody their hands in the killing, cleaning or cooking of it! Even among those who do pull their own weight today, so many have lost our ancestor's spirit of yore... Instead of complaining that you pulled your weight and you are not going to pull Svein's too! You do just that! You resolve to pull Svein's weight too, fully comprehending that we all make shore together, or we perish in the storm together. When you do make shore, you get at ol' Svein and unless the reason he slacked off was because he suddenly took ill, or the like. You explain to him, "If you've no intention to pull your own weight, don't try to get back on the boat!" The moral lesson is simple; the Fundamental Odinist will resolve to do what needs doing in order to succeed both individually and collectively. While the others either complain, quit, or fall short of the mark!

The genuine Fundamental Odinist says "YES" to life and he/she lives by the old German proverb which exemplifies so well the noble virtues of self reliance, perseverance, courage, self discipline, industriousness, and honor above all others; " Lerne zu leiden ohne klagen ", (Learn to suffer without complaint).

I could go on and on about what constitutes Fundamental Odinism and what does not, and indeed, I shall at a later date compose a handbook on such. But for now I shall leave you with this content for your own consideration. May Odin bless you all and may your Hammer's strike Trú.

I leave you then with the following meditation:"No man may levy a valid indictment against thee, save for thy own conscience! Then all shall know in time through thy own actions."

ALL ABOARD THE SHIP OF FOOLS

Long ago in the Land of the Midnight Sun, whence came our Fathers' fathers, and their fathers afore them. The Folk had assembled around the hearth in many a' hall when did Sköll chase Sunna with a fierceness. And the cold dark of Nótt reigned for half of the Jera (year). Enthralled, they sat about hall and hearth and hung upon every word which had escaped the Skald of the moment's lips, as he masterfully weaved a colorful tapestry of the olden lore with expertise.

Of life's creation and end would he sing. And of great and mighty Gods and Goddesses too! And the awful and awesome feats of battle and the truly brave souls whom they gathered up to their holy halls, upon their passing over the Bifrost Bridge, from Midgard to Asgard. Such tales of heroics and adventure swelled many chests with Norse-Teutonic pride and emboldened many to shun the quiet and content life in lieu of great and often peril filled adventure, too rich with reward to be recounted here. Such a career of romantic adventure would no doubt be brutal and vicious more oft than not and life itself could be counted on to be cut harshly short just as oft. Such were the welcomed risks and hazards, and such rich accounts of these adventurous feats would captivate the attention and ignite the souls of our folk without end. And so it remains today, among us, their descendants. And Gods, Norns and Ourselves willing, it shall remain thus for millennia yet to come!

Several, if not nearly all of our beloved myths and lore, exhibit a reoccurring nature. What I mean to say is that while these tales are set within a given timeline and geographical locale, the very crux of the tale is yet a rendition of a moral or ethical lesson in the offing. Each one is so much more than a mere vehicle in which to advance an enthralling tale. And just as with the moral lesson of our Ancestors' day, were encrypted into the myths, they were designed as such and remain just as valid today, in concert with the very virtues which our Ancestors held to be so necessary to their sense of community, society, civic and social duty and responsibility.

You see, more oft than not, our Faith/Religion/Lifestyle this day seems to attract a large amount of folks whom view it as "The Viking" religion whereby its Thew (virtue) of 'Freedom', to their way of thinking, seems to imply that life is just a big party of drunkenness and fighting! Where one may live a life of reckless abandon devoid of guilt, or concern for one's own actions or the consequences attached thereto said actions.

But a glance at reality as it truly existed and continues to exist today, will illuminate the genuine concerns which face our Faith, Folk and Future. To begin with, while the Viking Age (ca. 793 CE to 1100 CE) certainly provides us with a window into a very romantic and adventurous period of our Ancestral history, which indeed blazed new trails across both land and sea and left their indelible fingerprints upon new world settlements and colonies as well as modern social inventions and reform, we cannot, "Must Not", dismiss the fact that it was the latter part of this era and our very own Ancestors whom peopled it, which began miscegenation (Race Mixing) in foreign lands, disregarding the sound compacts of Norse-Teutonic Law and ushered in the complete and near total breakdown of our Ancestral Faith/Religion, which up till that age had endured for millennia past! By selling out to the church in Rome, our indigenous Gods and Faith were nearly lost to us for evermore! In contrast with the Viking Age, the Germanic Tribal Era, often referred to as the Barbaric Age (ca. 300 BCE to 400 CE) had flourished with morality and accountability as the order of the day. Teutonic-Norse chivalry ruled the roost and the notion of betraying one's own people/folk or that which they as a folk/people, owed their very existence to (their Gods and the laws of natural order), would have been absurd, unnatural and sacrilege to say the least. The bloodline, Odal Lands and Gods of our folk at this time were held in the highest esteem and wielded the most paramount importance!

These hearty ancestors abhorred the Romans and their whoredom of an Empire even centuries prior to the birth of the Jew, Jesus and the advent of Christianity in his name. Let us not forget the stalwart Cheruskan Chieftain, Herman and the epic battle of Teutoburgerwald, wherein Herman and his host of German Tribesmen whom were gravely outnumbered by three Roman Legions, had soundly defeated Varus and his entire host at Kalkriese in the year 9 Common Era; Ever saving both Faith and Folk from the moral corruption of Rome. Sadly so, our own ancestors in positions of power over the Tribes and Clans of our folk, sold out both our faith and our folk to the church in Rome in the 11th Century Common Era, which history has otherwise afforded the dubious distinction of being the end of the "Viking Age", as it were.

What had led to such social breakdowns, en mass, that such a good and noble way of life could be purchased by the church and sold out by our ancestors? Disregard for honorable virtue, lack of accountability, unchecked substance abuses (alcoholism) of the day and plain ol' greed... That's what! The living became the living dead. Aryan souls were bought and sold with a frequency. The Gods were replaced with greed for outland gold, power and lust for that which was foreign to their indigenous nature and lifestyle.

The old lore tells us that upon the death of a loved one, the family has a duty to cut the dead's nails upon his/her fingers and toes so that the ship Naglfar (ON: Nail ship, or Ship of the dead) could not be completed any time soon, and thereby staving off Ragnarok! Naglfar is made from the finger and toe nails of the recently departed dead and that this ship will ferry the Sons of Múspell (the Brood of the damned) to Vigrid Plain for the great and final battle 'twixt the forces of good and evil (Christian interpretation) or chaos and order (Norse-Teutonic interpretation). The Battle to end all battles pitting the Gods, Einherjar (Dead & Living) against the Army of the Damned, led by Loki.

Upon this ship of fools traitors, race traitors and those whom sought to kill off our faith and folkways and traditions. Those oath breakers whom swore to protect and defend both our faith and folk. This hideous army of the damned will face the Gods and their host of noble and virtuous Einherjar and Valkyrjar. Those who follow with pleasure, Loki and his brood, shall find their selves upon this ship of fools. Those who said; "All for me!", and "Me first and damned the consequences!" Their reservations await.

And those wretched souls shall be gathered from all eras ever more, including the 2lst Century and beyond, right up to the time of Ragnarok.

Ragnarok occurs, in miniature, on a continuum throughout our lives. Any whom are destined for Valhalla at this point, may find themselves boarding Naglfar, if they fail to keep their feet upon the Northern Road and continue to honor their sacred oaths. And any bound for Naglefar at this point, still may correct their pernicious attitudes and behavior and alter their reservations for the ship of fools and instead, board Skidbladnir (Frey's ship - the very best of ships) which may ferry the souls of the good hearted and virtuous, to the great battle, those whom are not destined to assume their place, upon death, among the Eihnherjar and Valkyrjar. The point is, it is never too late to cease negative, selfish and irresponsible behavior while one is alive... One may always find the Road North, atone, and secure one's own place among one's own folk.

Assume an attitude of service to your faith and folk, before you seek to serve your own desires. Consider the cost and consequences of your actions upon yourself, your family and your folk. Always inquire of yourself; "Is this a noble act?" "Will it bring rewards or consequences to myself, my faith and my folk?" These are queries which should always be predominant in every Odinist's mind.

Just because a man, or woman wears a Hammer around their neck does not make them an "Atheling" (a Noble person), merely because they call themselves Odinist, or Ásatrúar. There are plenty of "Níthlings" (Ignoble) out there with Hammers around their necks and claiming our sacred and beloved Gods as there own as well. Believe me when I attest that I have made the acquaintance of more than a few in my years upon Midgard!

Decisions regarding one's life, faith and one's responsibilities in concert with family, faith and folk, should be arrived at freely and with a sound and open mind, heart and soul. One would indeed be wise to consider all harm or benefit regarding thus.

Conversely, one should not stave off what one knows to be just and noble in lieu of doing what pleases or feels good for one, at the expense of one's family, faith and folk. And then seeking to justify such behavior as the virtue of "Freedom", while historically, albeit erroneously so, pointing to the Viking Age; or equally as erroneous, believing that they have plenty of time to change later. For one can never know before hand just when the Gods will gather them up to them, or when the thin thread of the Norns will break! Gods forbid, that upon such a reckoning the first words one hears be; "All aboard the Naglfar!"

Study the old lore: the myths, sagas and chronicles, for they are indeed ripe with morals, ethics and virtues which sustained our Ancestors in harsh and trying times. They are the voices of both Gods and Ancestors which have traveled millennia to us today, and their wisdom and wit is ever a blueprint and repository of righteousness which we, their descendants, may employ in this current Wolf's Age. Just as our forbearers had intended each following generation to employ them. Honor them by visiting them often and taking measures to ensure that our faith and folk will survive yet another millennium!

And don't forget to clip the nails of our dearly departed prior to burning, or burial. For every bit as important to staving off Ragnarok, is the honoring of our ancient ancestral traditions. When a folk/people honors and respects their heritage and cultural traditions, their folk continues to live on no matter whom endeavors to destroy us.

> *"Striking a blow for justice is the way of Thor, Tyr and Forseti. Albeit, deliberately striking the wrong designation is the providence of tyranny!"*
>
> the Hon. Herjan, Casper Odinson Cröwell, Ph.D., DD

"Fetter Grove", photograph by Mrs. Linda Cröwell

FOLK af FJOTURLUND
(Folk of Fetter Grove)

1 vs. 100

"Let no man become overconfident in his bearing that he fails to remain ever vigilant and prepared to battle the forces of chaos amassed against him. For they offer neither truce nor reprieve."
- Casper Odinson Cröwell, Ph.D., DD

Some realities are best faced head on, so-to-speak, if ever they are to be confronted and overcome. Especially wherefore "Will" is in regard. One such reality, however unpleasant it may be, is the 1 vs. 100. Oh sure, in and of itself, it is innocuous enough. But when you consider these odds in conjunction with the incarcerated Folk walking the Northern Road, the reality is not a pleasant, nor conducive one wherefore our Faith, Folk and Families are concerned. You see, for every one hundred prisoners whom become adherents of any particular religion while incarcerated, only one is expected to either continue adhering to said religion, or succeed at remaining free, once they are released from prison.

Where Odinists/Wotanists and Ásatrúars are in regard, we are no exception to the rule. In fact, some would say, quite the contrary is the instance. I must concede that I have certainly known many

Odinist/Wotanist and Ásatrú prisoners whom upon their release from prison, either immediately or not long after, returned to a life of crime and vice. In fact, I myself am guilty of such an assertion. Though I believed at the time, that because I had consecrated some land to our Gods in the mountains and desert and I visited the Hörgs (Alters} there often, that my own transgressions were acceptable. They, of course, were not!

This did not render me an insincere Odinist by any means. For I have always been very devout if nothing else. Albeit, it did most assuredly mean that I was counterproductive to both my family and faith... Point blank! Fortunately I was able to exercise enough will to straighten myself out so as to become a productive member and contributor of our Faith and Folk community. But this did not occur until I finally took the Oath of the Gothar. Don't get me wrong, I had always contributed to our Faith and Folk community in many positive manners. It is just that those positive contributions meant little in light of my negative actions and the consequences and repercussions which accompanied my actions.

Just imagine, with what my wife, myself and a few Kinsmen have accomplished with this ministry thus far, how much greater those accomplishments would be were I free. For one, we would have an actual Hof/Temple and a Sacred Grove with weekly services. No question about it! Alas, this is one of those consequences which I alluded to earlier in this article. Such are the ramifications associated with our negative actions. What might have been as opposed to what is; We must find a way to convert those "might have beens", into "the way that it is".

Now, I have employed myself as the example herein in an effort to disarm those souls whom may otherwise become defiant and disregard the worth of this content, had I pointed the imaginary accusatory finger at others. Though, Gods in Asgard know, there are many whom fit the bill all the same. I was once a liar, thief, drug addict, killer, whore monger, womanizer, bank robber and brutal problem fixer for wealthy, albeit unsavory types. I freely admit that I was all of these things. If anyone reading this feels that they too fit the bill for one or more of the above, there is no need to fret. You can change. I did. And you can too. There is nothing shameful about admitting that I was once any or all of these things.

The only great shame is if I had to look at myself in honest light and say that I am "still" these things. That would indeed be a genuine shame! Life is not about what you did yesterday, be it good or bad. It is about what you are doing today and what you elect to do on the morrow. "Good or Bad". The choice is 'ALWAYS' yours and yours alone to make.

Folk whom continue to use drugs, drink and embrace vice while incarcerated are doing themselves and their families, our faith and folk a grave disservice whether they elect to admit it to themselves or not. Does this mean that they are insincere in their being an Odinist/Wotanist or Ásatrúar? No! No, it does not. For only such a man or woman may truly answer that question themselves. What it does mean is that whatever positive contributions they may provide are more oft than not negated by their pernicious behavior and the consequences associated with them.

It further must be asserted that the reality is if one is espousing such deleterious habits while inside the walls and wire, they will most certainly continue it upon their release.

Recently, I had a Kinsman whom for nearly eight years remained clean and productive after I helped him get straight. He went home over a year and a half ago, to a .large family whom all of supported him in every way possible so as to assist him in the cultivation of a positive and successful lifestyle. He appeared to be doing well for nearly eight months to a year before he began to reach into his old bag of tricks, as it were. Though in reality, he began his sneaky and manipulative behavior about ninety days out of the gate. Needless to say, things are not well between him and those whom once believed in him and held out a hand to help him. In fact, he continues to place several of his family members in deliberate harm's way without regard for their safety and welfare. He had everything at his disposal to succeed except the two things required to make it, once paroled. 1) The honest self examination of one's reality, on a continuum. And 2) the will to succeed. Without these two components, failure is inevitable. How long one may last is a matter of mere conjecture. But failure is both imminent and inevitable, no matter who is on one's side, or how badly they want you to succeed.

Another equally important thing to consider is 'Freedom of Association'. Or more pointedly, 'Desire' to associate! When one embraces a non-conducive lifestyle, it does not matter that one wears a Thor's Hammer around one's neck. Or that one may even harbor a genuine penchant for Vór Forn Siðr (Our Faith). Folk who seek to promote our Faith and Folk community in a constructive fashion, whether in prison or the free world have little or no desire to associate with those whom do not share their positive view and collective goals. And of course, no one acting in a negative manner has any credible or valid argument to levy, in suggestion or support thereof, their desire to be taken seriously by those fighting for our religion's parity within the greater religious community both in and out of prison.

This is a "Free" religion. True enough. But the dictum of Freedom of Association reserves the rights of our folk to determine whom we elect to assemble and associate with and whom we have no desire to include within our sacred Vés and Hofs (Enclosures/spaces & Temples).

Every time one goes back out to the free world claiming to be of the Gods they will be scrutinized thoroughly by our free folk, be they of our faith, or not. And more oft than not, they will be laying in wait for the 'Fuck up', to appear. Now I know that this does not seem right. But so many of our folk have been burnt before or know someone who has. It renders them, for the most part, and for their own survival sake, skeptics as opposed to believers in rehabilitation.

And if one sets about to prove them wrong solely for that purpose, they will likely fail. For the motive is impure. On the other hand, if one sets about to simply live their life in the free world (Or in prison) as a true Odinist/Wotanist they will eventually earn the trust and respect of our free folk simply by virtue of the manner in which they conduct them self.

I am a Holy Man. I am therefore going to make myself available to the service of any of our folk whether they use dope or not, as long as they demonstrate an outward and honest profession of our faith. But let me be perfectly clear about my own ideas and defense of the right of freedom of association... I will always make my services available to those whom seek them out. But I will not seek out people to serve, nor would I allow any drug addict or non-productive/conducive person to assemble with either myself, my family or those kinfolk whom place their trust in me to serve their needs and safeguard their welfare, with the decisions which I arrive at. I will not ever purposely or deliberately expose any under my care or whom place their trust in me, to any potential and foreseeable harm!

So then, while freedom of association may indeed be a right we all enjoy. It too must be asserted that it is equally a privilege as well. One which must be earned. One should not entertain notions that one will be openly embraced or welcomed by any group of folk, if one acts in any manner contrary to that group's positive designs and goals. Nor should this be a surprise to any reasonable thinking person.

Your success or failure depends upon your will to succeed. Not some odds or statistics. The Gods stand with us always. That is a fact! Not an odd or statistic. If only we could learn to fully exercise our wills and descry what our Gods seek to teach us, we too then could shift the odds in our collective favor.

To a day when 1 vs. 100 will assume a positive connotation to reflect that for every one hundred paroled Odinists back to the free world, only one will ever fail and return to prison!

For now, this remains an elusive fantasy. Whether it ever becomes a reality remains up to us. Both individually and collectively overall.

REGARDING HONOR

Recently I perused a letter posted by someone whom I have long since considered to meet the criteria of Kith and Kin. Albeit, this brother had written about something which I feel he had omitted to afford any honest consideration to prior to his committing his thoughts to paper and mailing said communiqué.

In an effort to shed a degree of light upon the matter at hand, though, at the same time protect both the identity and integrity of this brother, I will offer only that circumstances as of late have not been gentle, nor kind, he has been the target of vindictive prison officials due to his tireless campaign to secure parity rights for Odinist and Ásatrú prisoners. He was recently transferred as a direct result thereof and subsequently thereafter, he incurred the rape of his personal property, to illustrate the least. Indeed, many of us are in fact veterans of the state sponsored war against our 'Lawful' religious rights.

So then, what has this to do in conjunction with honor? Right? Right then. This brother had made a rather disparaging comment, alluding to the acceptance of an ignoble and dishonorable act committed by another, which in his alluding, he was fine with.

Now I certainly am not without any sympathy for his current plight, or the effects of attrition attached thereto. Albeit, I must contend that "Sympathy" may be located in any dictionary within the distinct parameters of SHIT and SYPHILIS! I must further assert that I am reminded of two of Nietzsche's gems. The first is the well used and oft quoted cliché; "That which does not kill me, makes me stronger." And the other is a paradigm wherefore he had penned to some end; "Drink not from the same well as the Rabble, my brothers. For their lips do poison the water and weakness breeds weakness! If you want to be a star, then you must avoid the Rabble and shine all of the time. Not merely when it is either convenient or fashionable, but especially when you are down and the Rabble are kicking dust in your face! It is then that you must shine the most, if you would be a star."

Not exactly his word for word exclamation, but it is never the less the conceptual root of the wisdom which Friedrich Nietzsche sought to impart to his reading audience.

While this brother may currently be experiencing hardship and difficulties, to which I can indeed sympathize with. They are by no means unique to his own situation, nor do they grant one leave from one's sense of honor, either in word, or deed!

At the risk of presenting redundant journalism, I feel compelled to impress upon one and all that the very virtues which we profess to live by must staunchly be adhered to with a certain tenacious resolve if in fact and deed, we would be genuine Trú Folk. Otherwise, it all becomes naught more than a pedestrian exercise in marking time, while employing the corpus of a noble path and its symbols and traditions - Nothing more. And none among us should confuse such as the equivalent of the genuine article, for I can assure you all that is not! A spider web is but a spider web. It is only feared by the fly until he has discerned at some length, that, the web's owner has long since perished. And in time, the web too will succumb to the elements in which it sits, and perish itself.

Without any legitimate honor, one is but a web without a spider... An empty nest of sorts! The very environment which most of us find ourselves confined to is rife with dishonorable people and decay of integrity on all fronts, whether they wear a prison number, or a badge! These places are truly rampant with ill characters whom espouse and promote dishonor. It then becomes an exercise in personal will, fortitude and courage to defy and resist the lure of this cultivated and promoted moral bankruptcy if honor you would know and entice to remain a permanent resident in the Hof/Temple that is your soul.

Do not look upon these words with despair in your hearts and minds, thinking that it is too late for you to alter your destiny. For surly it is not!

If you conduct an honest examination of your life and your current behavior, and you arrive at the uncomfortable truth that your deeds and your perspective are in fact detrimental to yourself, your family, your faith and your folk... Well then, resolve to do something about it right now! Right in this very moment! That's right, assume command of, and responsibility for your character, your actions and thereby, your soul. Identify all outside influences which have been holding you down in your life; Embracing prison culture, substance abuse, gangs that promote vices and fratricidal behavior... Anything which does not serve the best interests of our faith and folk community (This includes one's immediate blood kin), and wrest from these pernicious and chaotic influences/forces, the power over you which they wield and take control of your own destiny and contribute greatly to that of our faith and folk! Do it right now, in this very moment if you have not yet. Look at your hand and arm. Look at it and know that just below its fleshy, structured surface, exists the very soul of your ancestors, coursing through your veins and arteries right this moment and know they are every bit as real as the hand and arm you now gaze upon. Reconnect with those ancestors and their Gods..."Your Gods "! Do it right now if ever you would truly espouse and merge with the genuine honor that is the Aryan soul which you share with your ancestors and our Gods! Our faith and folk's future are incumbent upon it. Make no mistake about it.

In your moments of despair and darkness, seek to embrace the Goddesses of the shades. When you find yourself in the realm of the shadows, harness the anger and might of Thor. Embrace the honor of Tyr as your own. Merge and become one with Allfather Odin! Let these be your loyal sources of inspiration, your motivation to show the Rabble just who "YOU" are. And then, dare them all, dare them all, to kick the dust in your face when they believe that you are down and at some disadvantage, so that you may show them just how you shine as one with the glory of those in command of their honor yet, and elect to employ that honor as the compass which it is. For it will lead you back to the soul of our ancestors past, our descendants unborn and our rightful place in our Father's house; "VALHALLA!"

"Do not capitulate to the minions of honor's theft! For they cannot wrest this gift from the Gods from thy soul. Only thou may forfeit that which your mighty ancestor's hath passed on to thee. With your life's risk, hold fast and dear to your heart this gift of honor. For a life devoid of this gift is merely slavery. Perhaps even, existence at best!"

-The Hon. Herjan, Casper Odinson Cröwell, Ph.D., DD

ODIN'S OATH: The Loki Factor

Many have been the times when I have either witnessed folk debate the circumstances surrounding Allfather's oath of blood brotherhood to Loki, or been approached by seekers walking the Northern Road as to what constitutes appropriate etiquette wherefore offering Blót or Sumble to Odin is in regard. "Why would Odin swear such an oath to Loki?" "Must we offer Loki a draught as well?" "What if I don't want to offer Loki a draught?" "What's the big deal, anyhow?" And, "Isn't offering Loki a draught the same as honoring him, or inviting his chaos and mischief into our lives?" These are just some of the most common queries I am posed with by these folk. Their concern is just as valid as the questions which they posit.

Let's begin with the first query, "WHY WOULD ODIN SWEAR SUCH AN OATH TO LOKI?" If one takes stock of the Northern myths and lore, one may descry that in the early days of the Gods "being", the heavens and worlds were yet becoming and progressing. In this beginning, Loki is merely the personification of a major component in that "becoming". He is the necessary chaos from which order will evolve. Hávamál, stanza 47 has Allfather telling us;

> I was once young, I traveled alone,
> then I found myself going astray;
> rich I thought myself when I met someone else, for
> man is the joy of man.
>
> (Poetic Edda Larrington trans.)

The above stanza speaks to Odin's frame of mind regarding a traveling companion, perhaps, Loki. Loki was indeed instrumental in large part in Odin's early travels as was Thor. In fact, Loki figures so prominently, that in the creation of man, it is Loki whom imbues

Ask, the primordial ancestor, (and Embla as well) with circulating blood and the emotion of passion.

In consideration of the early days of the Gods in our myths, Loki is no bad guy at all. In fact, just the opposite. His every action leads to the very cause and effect of creation. His behavior is nothing less than advantageous to both the Æsir and early man. This is a probable causation as to why Allfather would enter into an oath of blood brotherhood with Loki at such a time in the evolution of the Gods.

Further on in the Hávamál, stanza 51, Odin alludes to a friendship turning sour;

> Hotter than fire between bad friends
> burns affection for five days;
> but it dies down when the sixth day comes,
> and all that friendship goes to the bad.
> (Poetic Edda Larrington trans.)

Once again, could Odin be referring to Loki and his increased antics evolving as no longer beneficial to the Gods and Man, but rather, a liability now? Might this allude to Odin's exhibiting regret for having sworn a sacred oath with Loki?

So then, here we have a possibility as viable as any as to why Allfather would enter into such an oath with the likes of Loki, in addition to whatever regrets he might have assumed later on, for having done so.

MUST WE OFFER LOKI A DRAUGHT AS WELL? WHAT IF I DON'T WANT TO OFFER LOKI A DRAUGHT? WHAT'S THE BIG DEAL, ANYHOW? Certainly no one must do anything which they do not feel comfortable with. And that would include offering Loki a draught, as well. However, here's the big deal, as it were, and something to consider. The concept of what we call the NINE NOBLE VIRTUES, in all of their carnations, are culled from our myths, by our ancestors. That is to say, that if we are going to draw upon an example of say, Svein's reputation for adhering to his word and oath with an iron grip, circa 975 Common Era, we too then should illustrate how Svein had learned about such honor for that and the other virtues, as a boy by listening to the heroic tales of our Gods in what we today call the myths. That considered, one of the paradigms for the virtue of honoring an oath, and in all probability, the most predominant paradigm at that for this virtue, would be that of the shared oath twixt Allfather and his blood brother, Loki. The lesson of primacy being twofold in my educated opinion. First, that one would do well to consider the future, not just the moment, when one is considering entering into a sacred oath. One should consider years into the future. After all, it is the very gift of Loki himself, the emotion of passion, which plays havoc with the moment, when one is feeling all warm and fuzzy inside, which will nearly always become the agent which blinds one to the further considerations of weighing the common sense factors and the ramifications that may be attached to hasty decisions and such oaths sworn. An oath should always be fully weighed and considered prior to swearing it and assuming the long term burden of responsibility associated with said oath!

Two, that the power of the oath sworn should not, must not be forgotten nor abandoned! Unless the two (or more) avowed parties to the oath agree to come together and consent to mutually dissolve the oath between them, the power of that oath must not be disregarded, lest they become oath breakers! The oath was sworn with the participant's blood, and so too must the mutual dissolution be consummated with their blood. This was/is done by both parties washing their hands with their own blood before a Gothi/Gythia. Ergo the old phrase: "I'm washing my hands of you."

Short of such a mutual dissolution, the power of the oath remains in tact and the one whom disregards it is the oath breaker.

Let's consider the oath between Odin and Loki;

> Odin! dost thou remember
> when we in early days
> blended our blood together?
> When to taste beer
> thou did'st constantly refuse
> unless to both 'twas offered?
> (Saemund's Edda, Thorpe trans.)

And from Lokasenna (Loki's Quarrel), stanza 9, Loki said:

> Do you remember, Odin, when in bygone days
> we mixed our blood together?
> You said you would never drink ale
> unless it were brought to both of us.

And in stanza 10, Odin said:

'Get up then, Vidar, and let the wolf's father
sit at the feast,
lest Loki speak words of blame to us
in Ægir's hall.'
(both stanzas Poetic Edda, Larrington trans.)

No matter how distraught with Loki Odin may be, he honors his Oath with Loki! From this tale, our ancestors gleaned the power of an oath as exhibited by our Allfather Odin, and it has survived to set the tone of Aryan man adhering to the bond of his word. This is why it is so important to offer Loki a draught when making an offering to our Allfather. It is not in honor Loki. It is in honor of Allfather's oath and to constantly serve as a reminder to us, his descendants, just how sacred an oath is and what it means to honor, or violate that oath!

To say otherwise is not a simple matter of semantics. It is an unwillingness to accept the standard which Odin has passed down to us. How and why would any among us expect Odin to accept our offering to him if we will not respect and honor his oath? Of course, we cannot expect him to either accept our offering, or afford us his blessing, when we would, by proxy, encourage and promote oath breaking!

On the other hand, to reiterate, as earlier stated, one should never be persuaded to do something one is not comfortable with. On the other side of that same coin, such differences among associating folk should always be taken into account wherefore assembling to conduct Blót and Sumble are in regard. For example, if one espouses an aversion to offering Loki a draught while making an offering to Odin, it should be made known to all expected participants prior to assembling so as to avoid embarrassments or hard feelings among folk. For just as one's rights must be respected if one elects to omit any offering to Loki as part of the offering to Odin, one who does make such a gesture in an endeavor to honor Odin's oath and the power of honoring oaths, should not and cannot very well be expected to attend services with others who do not share in the common beliefs of our ancestors, in one's own perspective.

On a more metaphysical and Theosophical level, the Loki draught portion of an offering to Odin, may be viewed as reminder that while one is offering Blót or Sumble to the 'Higher' self, one must also remain vigilant and aware of one's 'Lower or Base' self. And that the mastery of one's self only occurs via the acknowledgement of the lower self (Loki) by the Higher self (Odin) and the balance or Dagaz, between the two and thereafter synthesized by the Eihwaz which each of us are wherefore our polar opposites are in regard. In the teachings of my own mentor, the late and beloved Folk Mother, Else Christensen, Loki's Quarrel/Flyting is anti-Odinist based upon the afore asserted postulation.

It is understood that there will always be those, 'Devil's Advocate arguments against this position, and that I do not espouse them does not render them invalid, nor totally without merit. Albeit, to afford such any consideration would most certainly leave the door ajar, per se, for further such considerations in the future wherefore our rules, regulations and liturgy are in regards. Say, like for instance the validity of homosexuality, or the like. And that, I can assure you, will never happen so long as any among our current spiritual and administrative bodies, are alive!

I hope to have illuminated some of the shadowy confusions surrounding this subject. Always remember when all has been considered at the end of the day, your personal spiritual growth advances our faith and folk community as a whole. Promoting and serving that ideal is the mission of the HNO, no matter where you may reside at this leg of your holy journey back home to the Gods from whence we have descended.

> *"But what measure might we calibrate the strength of a man's character, if not initially by the iron bond of his word?"*
>
> *-The Hon. Herjan, Casper Odinson Cröwell, Ph.D., DD*

ODIN AS ALLFATHER

Recently we received an email from a reader whom, while he supports our efforts, insists that we are not 'true' Odinists, as he himself is. The premise for his assertion is that we at the Holy Nation of Odin (HNO) are monotheists as opposed polytheists, due to our position that Allfather Odin is the primordial divine spirit/Godhead.

This essay is both an illustration of chronicled points of authority wherefore this matter is in regard, and an offering towards genuine spiritual enlightenment. Toward such ends, I posit and submit the following...

Initially I wish to express that we at the HNO are most definitely NOT monotheists! We are in fact polytheists, or more correctly asserted, we are polytheists whom are pantheists. That is to say, that we subscribe to the Northern Theology/Philosophy that our Gods and Goddesses are synonymous with the forces of the universe and the laws of natural order; Just as our Ancestors of the Aryan Tribes did.

Furthermore, that Odin is the Allfather and thereby the primordial divine spirit/Godhead, is not only the HNO's position, but rather it is the consensus more so than not, among the authorities on the subject, both living and past.

It must be stressed at this point that there are only two directives of authority as put forth by Odin in the Havamal, regarding the mandates of our religion, as it were, that is to know and use the Runes and to know how to sacrifice. And beyond this, in chapter eight of the Ynglinga Saga in the Heimskringla, Odin ordains that the dead should be burned and their ashes dispersed at sea or buried in the ground, and that sacrifice (Blót) is to be made at the beginning of winter, midwinter and a third one in summer. Beyond these, ours is a free way of life and honoring they which are divine. There are none among us whom are charged with the authority to dictate to any, save for those whom place their spiritual welfare in the hands of their ministry's clergy/leadership, for what may constitute the rules and regulations of any given Hof/ministry to which they belong.

One's relationship with the divine is truly a personal one and accommodates no room for interlopers with designs on placing restrictions or encroachments upon such a sacred and personal relationship! It is up to each one to decide how best to exercise or pursue that relationship. Whether or not they desire membership with any given Hof/ministry/order, or simply elect to remain a solitary practitioner is entirely up to the individual. Members of any given Hof/ministry/order become thus as an espousal of doctrine and shared kinship exists among the collective membership thereof. What is right for this Hof or kindred may not and will not always be what is right for others. For any among us to exclaim that this person or that is not a true believer of any religion, or less than another, is as ludicrous as any mortal telling any other you can't worship my God(s)!

There exists a great deal of elusive and or politically correct language within the heathen religious community as to whom may or may not be an Odinist. Race and sexual orientation are often hotly debated topics. Let me be perfectly candid regarding the HNO and this uncomfortable subject. Neither I nor any other member of our religious administration may tell a non-Aryan, or homosexual that he or she may not honor/worship our Gods or practice our religion.

I/we, may however, say that such individuals may not and will not be permitted to do so with us or within our religious institutions, and that is exactly my/our position at the HNO! We are exclusively Folk oriented, non-universalist and we will in no way or fashion whatsoever condone homosexuality. Such is our express right to freedom of association. All others enjoy the same said fundamental right as well and will always be best served by seeking out like minded individuals with which they may assemble and congregate with.

Furthermore, how one may perceive our Gods and Goddesses will vary among Odinists, both within and without the HNO. Some will subscribe to the belief that our Gods are just as the myths describe them, resplendent with their flawed human qualities and all. Others will lend them a metaphorical quality. And yet others will espouse the concept of the Jungian school of thought regarding thus. For many among us, it may be a complex combination of any/all of the above. And no school of thought negates or renders invalid any one over the others. Ours truly is a free religion and way of life and there in concert with, did our ancestors assign such a highly prized value upon said concept of freedom.

Regardless of what position one may assume, all continue to exist within the scope of metaphysics and are resigned to the authority of the laws of natural order and the outward expression of Allfather Odin's will "to be!" And his divine desire to thereafter create both the pantheon of Northern Gods and man. For nothing is born or created, from nothing!

From the Myths of the Norsemen by H.A. Guerber (1909 CE), we may read in chapter I: In the Beginning / Myths of Creation - page 2; "In the beginning, when there was yet no earth, nor sea, nor air; when darkness rested over all, there existed a powerful being called **Allfather**, whom they dimly conceived as uncreated as well as unseen, and that whatever he willed came to pass." Chapter II: The Father of the Gods and Men - page 16; "Odin is highest and holiest of the Northern Races. He is the all-pervading spirit of the universe, the personification of the air, the God of universal wisdom and victory and the leader and protector of princes and heroes. As **all the Gods are descended from him, he is surnamed All-Father**, and as eldest and chief among them he occupies the highest seat in Asgard."

The Dictionary of Northern Mythology by Rudolf Simek (2000 CE) says on page 240; "**ODIN** - the chief God of Eddic mythology", and that, "He is father of the Gods."

The Oxford Icelandic Dictionary says this about Odin; "Odin's name bears an allusion to mind or thought, and breathing; it is the quickening, creating powers; **it denotes the all-pervading spiritual Godhead**."

In the Prose Edda by Snorri Sturlusson, it is written in Gylfaginning 19; "Odin is highest and oldest of all the Gods; he rules over everything and however mighty the other Gods might be, **they all** serve him like children serve their father. Odin is called Allfather, because he is the father of all the Gods."

Adam of Bremen wrote about sacrifices (animal and human) which occurred every nine years. While he did not say that they were dedicated to Odin, Snori Sturlusson's Heimskringla says in chapters 25 and 43 of Ynglinga Saga, that human sacrifices among the Gods was exclusive to Odin! And Germania by Tacitus also reflects thus in chapter 9.

Carl Gustav Jung postulated in his 1936 essay, "Wotan" (Odin), the following;

"Wotan disappeared when his oaks fell and appeared again when the Christian God proved too weak to save Christiandom from fratricidal slaughter." And further on he writes; "It seems to me that Wotan hits the mark as an hypothesis. Apparently he really was only asleep in the Kyffhäuser Mountain until the ravens called him and announced the break of day. He is a fundamental attribute of the German psyche, and irrational psyche factor which acts on the high pressure of civilization like a cyclone and blows it away. Despite their crankiness, the Wotan worshippers seemed to have judged things more correctly than the worshippers of reason. Apparently everyone had forgotten that Wotan is the Germanic datum of first importance, the truest expression and unsurpassed personification of a fundamental quality that is particularly characteristic of the Germans."

Still further on in his essay, Jung goes on to say that; "There are people in the German Faith Movement who are intelligent enough not only to believe, but to know, that the god of the Germans is Wotan and not the Christian God."

The late Odinist and revolutionary, David Lane, wrote; "Odin on the other hand is the exclusive God of the Aryan Folk. He is an expression of the Will Of The Aryan Nation, an archetype, a repository of wisdom and an ancestor, deeply ingrained within our genetic memory."

Stephen A. McNallen, in his work, The Lessons of Asgard, wrote; "The Gods and Goddess of Ásatrú are many things to us - forces in the universe, symbols in the unconscious mind, friends and role models."

Then there are the words of Ron McVan, from his books 'Creed of Iron' and 'Temple of Wotan: Holy Book of the Aryan Tribes' comes this remarkably undeniable insight; "Odin symbolizes the true ethnic, quintessential figure, the cosmic life force and essential soul and spirit of the Aryan Folk made manifest." / "The evolved and perfected folk archetype known as Odin, the Allfather of the Aryan Race, has long been revered as the high God of our ancient ancestors." / "The God Odin is supreme among the Aryan Gods and man, all-powerful in his own right, the Lord of Life and Death." / "The lesser Gods of the Odin pantheon represent for the most part nature and the planetary forces, and the drama of man writ large. The soul of man is conceived as a center of energies which requires appropriate fields of expression. These expressions are mirrored back to us through our folk Gods." / "Central to Wotanism (Odinism) are the Euro-ethnic sky-god pantheon known as the Æsir, and the more earth-based, agricultural and fertility-centric Vanir. Chief of all the Aryan high deities is the archetype sky-god Wotan, the immortal root and essence of Aryan being."

And finally, from 'Blue Rúna' (1994-1998) by Edred Thorsson (aka: Dr. S. Flowers), we get the following; "Odin is not only considered the high God of the Germanic Peoples, but he is also known as "**All-Father**", for he, along with other aspects of himself, imparted this gift (life & spirituality) to humanity." / "Odin: the Living God - the will to power and self knowledge embodied in Odin must be recognized, understood and directed -for it will not be denied - if the future is to hold out any promise for us." / "The mythology shows Odin to be the highest God of the Germanic pantheon, the Allfather of the Gods and humanity, (the archetype of Odin)." / "The archetype of Odin, once again; He is **Allfather**, progenitor of Gods, demigods and human society." And finally; "The way of Odin is a timeless path. Those who follow it rightly do not look to the past as such for their models, but rather to those paradigms preserved from bygone ages which are in and of themselves outside the measure of time. Taking into account what Jung and others have written about Odin, it might be said that he is, and has been for ages past, the true hidden God of the west."

In sum, I feel as though I must point out the obvious. For it may not be all that obvious to some folk, after all. And that is that while Odinism is indeed a way in which we may serve our descendants while we honor our ancestors and respect the very traditions which we have inherited from them, we are more than a mere link in the great chain, we are more than a mere conduit for which the line may continue through. We are 'NOW'. We are today! And there must be a purpose for today. And of course, there is: Self transformation on a continuum and thereby, the constant evolution of the Odic Force. Such is the power which allows us to convert the ebb and flow of time's swift hands, into positive growth, as opposed to the melancholy erosion of our time upon Midgard, for thereby shall we arrive at our most majestic purpose. Not serve as just a bridge between yesterday and tomorrow.

But as a beacon which never dimmed, but grew ever brighter! That tomorrow might safely find today, as we ourselves found yesterday.

This is all an evolutionary process from inception to culmination. It would serve neither our folk or religion, to belittle those whom are not on the same page as we may believe ourselves to be at any given time in our transformative state of being. Better, I opine that we, our Gods and our Folk community may well be served, that we simply allow for others to stumble, fall and grow at their own pace; For such are the prerequisites of self transformation and ergo the word "self", preceding that of transformation.

We might simply remain near enough to offer support, insight an encouragement where it is warranted, or requested.

And when we are fortunate enough to meet up with those rare examples which are not only willing to listen to a bit of sound wisdom, but actually grasp it and make it their own... Well then, we may yet again rejoice in the knowledge that Odin Lives!

> *"I may not be counted among the league of intellectual minds of our times, nor might I wield the golden quill of the eloquent writers. But this can I own; where the assembly meets of those who gather their facts quite fastidiously, I shall always be present and warmly received."*
>
> *-The Hon. Herjan, Casper Odinson Cröwell, Ph.D., DD*

THE CELTIC CONNECTION

It is a sad reality that our Celtic heritage, more oft than not, is reduced to some sort of second class heritage next to our Norse/Teutonic heritage wherefore our beloved religion is in regards. In fact, next to the Viking age, all else seems to recede into obscurity. What accounts for this historical and religious malady? I would submit that more so than any other reason is probably that when Folk first learn of our religion, whether it be to merely study it, or to adhere to it as a spiritual way of life, most submerge themselves in the literature which is inundated with the old lore pertaining to our Gods, heroes and our ancestors who chronicled or sang the old sagas (Skalds & Scribes).

This is not only unfortunate, it too is erroneous, for any number of reasons. This has led to some of our folk whom are seeking a spiritual connection with both their ancestors and the Gods they honored, to look elsewhere rather than Odinism. Often I have had some young man or another say to me; "Odinism is an awesome Aryan religion and way of life, but I have no Aryan or Viking blood... I'm Irish (or Scottish, Welsh, etc.)"

While it is not my intention to sound condescending or as if I am ridiculing, this is a ridiculous assertion!

To begin with, the word 'Aryan' is of Sanskrit origin and it means 'Noble or the Noble People'. It is descriptive of the original Indo-European Tribes/ Peoples which includes the Celts, Germans, Balts and Slavs. Its twentieth century employment seemed to afford the Germans exclusivity, albeit an erroneous and dubious one.

Then there is the knowledge that the Celts had not always been in the lands which we have come to know today as Ireland, Scotland, Wales and Britain (now England). They had begun their migration from their original homeland in the Caucasus between 4000 BC and 500 BC. They eventually settled in what is today Southern Germany and Northern Austria where they spent more time in than any of the lands which they currently reside within, by thousands of years. It was from there that they migrated further to the British Isles. The Roman conquest of the Celts in the British Isles is responsible for severing the Celts from their pagan past.

Next, one must consider the Viking Age, indeed. For the Norsemen did in fact raid Ireland beginning in 795 CE when they raided a small, albeit somewhat wealthy church on Lambey Island, just north of Dublin. Dublin itself was originally a Viking fortress from which they launched their raids and forays. It was established in 841 CE. The name Dublin means 'Black Water'. The Initial Viking raids had occurred twixt 795 CE and 873 CE, which resulted in large parts of Ireland being raided and falling under Norse rule. Viking rule, wherever it had existed in Ireland, had ceased in 1014 with Irish King, Brian Boru's victory at the battle of Clontarf. Boru himself had perished in the battle and many of the Norsemen had remained in Ireland permanently. Though their assimilation there was not the end of their journey.

In 795 CE the Vikings raided and sacked a monastery at Iona. Their terrifying raids would plague the west coast of Scotland for the next fifty years. Eventually they began to settle on the west coast and numerous islands of Scotland. The Islands included the Hebrides, the Orkney and Shetland Isles. Their descendants remain there to this day.

Of course, the Viking age began with the raid on England's East coast in 793 CE when the monastery at Lindisfarne was raided. But lesser known raids had in fact occurred as early as the late 780's. The catalog of raids, battles and Norse rule in England are far too numerous to list in this essay. Suffice it to say, they lasted from the late 780's until 1066 at the battle of Stamford Bridge. In 840 CE Charles the Bald had assumed the throne of Western Europe in Francia (today's France), though this did not go down well with his two brothers Lothar and Louis the German, and while the three brothers argued over the throne's inheritance, the Norsemen were quick to see the opportunities created by the brothers disunity and their Kingdom's vulnerability. The Kingdom was divided twixt the three brothers. Charles the Bald would keep the West of Francia. Lothar would take the Rhineland and Frisia and Louis the German assumed rule over a large part of what is today Germany. This divided rule of the Frankish Empire was complete by 843 CE. But Francia's problems had only begun and they arrived beneath the standard of the Raven from the North!

Charles' Kingdom was hardest hit as it was ideally located for the Northmen's taste due to the lengthy coastal access and many rivers which accommodated their longboats. Lothar, on the other hand, had employed a bit of tact with the Norsemen, he granted them land holdings with the provision that they not raid in his land and they loosely ally themselves with him. In 911 CE, Frankish King Charles the Simple had opted for peace with Rollo and his Norsemen when he granted him rule over a territory which would be named for the famed Norsemen, 'Normandy'. The particulars of this negotiated peace and land and title grant? Rollo and his merry marauders would no longer raid in France, but defend the coast and rivers from other raiding Norsemen. Oh yeah, and they had to convert to Christianity.

In all of the afore discussed lands inhabited by the Celts, the Norse (and even Teutonic) had settled, assimilated and bread and their descendants remain to this day; Ergo, the Celtic Connection to our ancestral religion.

Odinism is the original religion of the Aryan Tribes and the Celts **are** one of those Tribes. Yes, indeed I shall be the first to concede that the Germanic peoples of the Aryan Tribes are what come to mind in most people's initial idea of which heritage constitutes the Odinist way of life. But the Celts, Balts and Slavs have the same valid inherited ancestral **right**.

Two Sagas which quickly come to mind are Njal's Saga and Grettir's Saga regarding accounts of Norse adventures in the lands of the Celts. And then there is this to consider where DNA is concerned; Iceland is the last Norse land to convert from the old religion and one of the first to legally recognize it once again in the twentieth century. Iceland's people are said to be the purest Aryan people left on Midgard (Earth), genetically speaking. They are a mixture of Norwegian and Irish people! I myself, am German, Irish and Rús, Russian from today's Ukrain.

So then, the next time someone of Celtic heritage says to you that they are not of the right ancestry to be an Odinist, you tell them; " That is Balderdash! " And then educate them to the Celtic Connection.[2]

> *"Seek not to assign fault to others. Rather, seek inspiration from their faults to correct your own."*
>
> *- The Hon. Herjan, Casper Odinson Cröwell, Ph.D., DD*

---

[2]* For additional research of the Celtic Connection, peruse "Orkneyinga Saga" And good reading to you all.

WHEN THE WELL RUNS DRY

Civilization is man's hallmark achievement. For it is what sets us apart from all other earthly life forms; that is to say, the very quality of possessing the gift of intellect and thereafter employing it in service to the advancement of higher idealism and our successful and industrious evolution. Alas, often has been the instance, especially as of late, whereby civilization has become every bit the bane of humanity as has it been our wondrous boon.

For we have become "too" civilized equally as oft as not here in the late 20th and early 21st centuries. We have become so complacent, spoiled, lazy and greedy. All too often anymore, we fail to recognize the very gifts and necessities which our Gods have delivered unto us. Or, the ancient wisdom which our ancestors seek to impart to us from beyond the grave and millennia past seems nearly impossible to descry for many, if not most. The constant assault upon our senses, from the man made 'Over Civilized' societies in which we live have caused great discord and detrimental blockages to occur, regarding our innate sensibilities. To say the least, this has thus far had devastating consequences. Soon, these consequences will evolve to catastrophic levels and then ultimately, they will result in an extinction level event for our race and religion! This, however, will not only have damning consequences for us North Folk, but all other peoples as well, which have not yet been mongrelized.

For those of us whom walk the Northern Road, we all eventually experience the consequence which I allude to. It assumes the quality and/or reality of lack of inspiration wherefore the spiritual and divine presence in our lives is in regard. We may come to describe this experience as the “Well” running dry, as it were. We all have need of the mighty and illuminating draught of inspiration. Alas, when we approach the well of Mimir, we find that the well has run dry for us. We seem to be in a rut which leaves us feeling burnt out and uninspired to a greater degree.

Many have been the occasion whereupon I have been privy to, for lack of a more fitting description, such events occurring within the lives of my Kinsmen. And indeed, more so, I myself have suffered the chaotic un-pleasantry of such an experience, on any number of occasions over my years of walking the Northern Road. I have balled up my fists in fits of anguish and great dismay and within my own mind I have shouted, "Odin, what's wrong with me?!!!"

To be certain, these experiences are quite disheartening. And equally as certain, we shall all come to experience these bouts whereby we find ourselves lacking in divine inspiration every now and again.

Take heart my noble kinfolk; for this is nothing more than the necessary chaos (Hagalaz) required for growth to occur. I can assure you all, the well hath naught run dry at all. Its black waters have merely become pooled and still (Isa), constrained. The water of inspiration (Laguz) has become murky (Ingwaz), as a period of necessary gestation, if you will, or more to the point, the need therefore (Nauthiz).

An arrested state (Thurisaz) has occurred which is also capable of retarding one's ability to even descry any such malady. Remember however, within the greater scheme of the flow (Laguz) wherefore Runic nature is in regard, the ability to break free from the very fetters which bind one's spiritual development and progress, not only exists, it follows the state of restriction (Thurisaz) in the form of pure divine inspiration (Ansuz).

This realized, the great restrictor (Thurisaz), now assumes the quality of the great releaser, (Thurisaz). When one considers the dual quality of the Thurisaz which I have employed in this paradigm, one then may discern the marriage of restriction and release as it transforms itself into a creative force of illumination and divine inspiration which has come forth from the shadows (Dagaz).

Simply put, what is called for when these dry spells occur is self discipline. The self discipline to extricate oneself from the trappings both, mundane and pernicious, of the over civilized society in which we live, if we are to save our source of divine inspiration, our culture, heritage, folk and faith! We must be disciplined enough to sever our proverbial ties to such harmful influences until such a time when the creative force (kenaz) returns to us.

How do we do this?

We might fast and forfeit our voice. We might seek seclusion. Or at the least, we avoid the video games, computer and inform our friends and family that we will not be answering the phone, or email for a short period. The idea is to remove one self from the external, and turn one's self (Manaz) inward, toward the internal (Othala).

If this fails to produce the desired results, then several periods of 'hanging upon the Tree', (fasting, purging, silence, initiation, etc.) may be necessary. Three day periods are best at minimal, for these introspective meditations. The less baggage one takes on the journey, the more likely it is that the results will be favorable.

What appears to us in the form of chaos at times is merely the necessary catalyst required to bring about the desired, or perhaps even, undesired, albeit necessary advances in our journey North. It is, after all, the teaching of Odin, that things are not always as they appear to be.

Is the glassy surface of still and dark water, peace or death? Is it tranquil calm or stagnation? And does the coming tempest herald the impending doom and destruction? Or does it carry forth the necessary seeds of growth and the winds of change? If the waters are still they have become black and such stagnation may lead to an imminent death of the creative flow to be sure. Conversely, the storm tossed waters often churn violently, albeit ever more bringing to the surface that which we are seeking and more so, sometimes, that which we need!

For therein the journey itself, lies the wisdom we often seek and desire. Only when we glean this reality will we come to know that the well may never truly run dry.

RUNIC BIBLIOGRAPHY FOR THIS ARTICLE:

Hagalaz (ᚺ)
Isa (ᛁ)
Laguz (ᛚ)
Ingwaz (ᛜ)
Nauthiz (ᚾ)
Thurisaz (ᚦ)
Ansuz (ᚨ)
Dagaz (ᛞ)
Kenaz (ᚲ)
Mannaz (ᛗ)
Othala (ᛟ)

> *"Is the ripple on the quiet pond an intrusion on peace, or an assault upon stagnation?"*
>
> *- The Honorable Herjan, Casper Odinson Cröwell, PhD., DD*

WHEN ODIN FIRST THOUGHT

"If gray is made of black and white, and darkness is devoid of any guiding light... Then which is the way that shall lead us back to a world that is bright? The Ancestral flame and the Road North. That is the way!"

- The Honorable Herjan, Casper Odinson Cröwell, PhD., DD"

I am often asked by seekers on the Northern Road, "How do you know that the Sál (soul) survives death? And how do you know that all peoples do not go to the same heaven?"

Would not any answer that I postulate merely constitute my own personal opinion? Can any among us here on Midgard (Earth) truly claim to assert any such certainties in regard to such an age old metaphysical query? I have offered you only queries in lieu of the original queries thus far, I know. Yet, does not such a complex issue require an inquiry laden with the weight of many more questions designed to deliver us before the very roots of the tree of life, Yggdrasil? For that is whence the dawn of our own ancestral humanity hails. So then, is such an enigma based wholly upon one's own faith? The answer is of course yes, and surprisingly so, "No".

Of course, there is no scientific evidence of an afterlife. Or is there? Science has in fact demonstrated that electricity may not be destroyed, but merely displaced and transferred about from one host to another; to wit we may stipulate that such a science may indeed infer some evidence, albeit if only circumstantial, of afterlife wherefore the soul survives the death of the physical body (Lyke).

Our heart and brain possess electricity which is why the health care industry employs biomedical machines, EEG and ECG/EKG to measure brain wave and cardio activity. The "E" in the aforementioned acronyms is representative of the energy quality of electricity. For all of the scientific and medical advances which modern technology has produced, the brain remains yet an illusive mystery. Furthermore, the Sál (soul) is an even greater Rúna (mystery). It is this electricity which affords the human Sál its very nature and the quality of the soul/spirit which grants animation to mortals. Though I posit that while we ourselves are human/mortal, our Sál is truly divine. Ergo, it may not be destroyed by mortal death anymore than the very electrical pulse which feeds it throughout our lives will dissipate.

So whither does that electricity within each of us wend upon our mortal deaths? The same place that our Sál goes, I conclude. Back whence we have come from. The greater divine presence which had lent a portion of itself to us upon the passing of our father's seed to our mother and the truly divine miracle of life which begins with that inception. Back to the Folk Soul (Volksál) itself...ODIN! Pure and divine consciousness and being.

Let us look to nature and the law of natural order to better comprehend this reality. Where perhaps the Buddhist might employ "Air" in an effort to illustrate my paradigm, I shall employ "Water", the very blood of Nerthus (Mother Earth). However, of notable consideration is the point that both air and water may conduct an electrical charge from one point to another. That we all require both elements of air and water to live mortal lives, the element of electricity, equal to fire, is also ever present from our brain to our heart. As is, the (Kenaz) fire of creativity and inspiration ever in our minds and the fire of passion in our hearts.

Returning to the example of nature's law, that all must return whence it came from, I ask that you consider a small lake and a mason's jar. The mason's jar is empty. Or is it? Even in the appearance of emptiness, does the secured glass jar not contain air within its confines?

We'll get back to that a bit later.

Consider opening the jar and submerging it beneath the lake's surface until it is filled with water. Replacing the jar's lid, the jar is now secure with its liquid cargo from the lake. It shall remain thus so until it is released from the confines of the jar. The jar of water is analogous to a mortal/human with his/her Sál. The mason's jar is representative of the human corpus (body) while the water within is indicative of the Sál. Now then, returning our attention to the Buddhist example of the jar containing air. If one were to throw the air filled jar to the ground and break it open, what then has become of the air/soul/spirit which was inside? The obvious answer is of course that the previously confined air is now free to return whence it has come from, the air which is all about us! Of course, there is only one air and as the Buddhist example would offer, only "one" soul of humanity/divinity, shared by all in some Utopian and Universal brotherhood. I, however, intend no slight nor disrespect to the Buddhist philosophy in any measure whatsoever. In fact, all things considered, Zen Buddhism and Odinism share various similarities, sans the lack of Folkish concentration within the Buddhist community.

I employed water, the very blood of Nerthus (Mother Earth/Jörd) for my Odinist example to further demonstrate the complexity of nature's self evident truths, as it applies to both, water and our Sál/spirit.

You see, that same mason's jar, albeit filled with water from the lake, is also analogous of the Sál/spirit. However, when the jar is broken, where the water goes is not such a simple affair as it were with the air paradigm. For the air has but only to return to the air. But the water...Well, the water is an entirely different organism. There is not merely one kind of water. Just as there is not only one race of people to share but a single Sál/spirit/divinity. The lake water from the jar is fresh water. Ergo, no matter where the jar is broken, the fresh water inside will one way, or another find its way back to the fresh water source. If broken near the lake where the water was extracted from, the water shall be re-absorbed into the ground, then the water table and then finally the lake whence it has come from. However, if broken by, or even dumped out into the sea's salt water, it would separate and evaporate back into the air, clouds, mist, fog, etc...Once again, the fresh water source! The same may be posited with our Sál/spirit and the Folk Soul whence it came from.

Carl Gustav Jung had postulated that each Folk/People/Race has its own unique Folk Soul. This Jungian Folk Soul wherefore the Aryan people are concerned, is one and the same with the God/Archetype "ODIN". And that this Folk Soul, "Our" Folk Soul, has existed in the form of pure consciousness, long before humanity itself had come into existence! The concept of 'Metagenetics'. Upon our mortal deaths, we shall once more return to our Folk Soul. What this must entail is open to one's perspective based upon a number of components. For myself, chief among such is my relationship with Allfather Odin. For me, the Folk Soul is Valhalla. Albeit, not the literal mythical version. Rather, I entertain the notion/belief that Valhalla is a great and ancient Aryan Folk Soul...A repository of all Racial/Folkish wisdom which the Folk have brought back with them from their life long experiences, to this grand Odinic consciousness.

Imagine this: if you closed your eyes and you heard the voice of your family and friends, you'd still be able to discern who was who from each one's voice, the cadence, tone, rhythm, etc... And your conscious mind would begin to form an image of them from the repository of memories you have of them. They would become as visual to your Hugauga (Mind's eye) as if your open eyed gaze had rested upon them in this reality. It would be like that with the Folk Soul. You would be aware of the presence of these loved ones and know them and they you, in the very same fashion. Only, all other ancestors from the beginning would be there and familiar to you as well. This great Folk Soul also accounts for your intuition, gut feelings and knowing something that you can't comprehend just how you come to know it. This is the wealth of ancestral wisdom and knowledge from the Folk Soul which currently lives on in you, in your blood and in your ancestral memory, where your every ancestor whom has ever lived since Ask and Embla, yet exists! And once we join the great Folk Soul of "Our" ancestors, then we too shall contribute to the constant flow of that amassed wisdom and knowledge to our descendants which have not yet been born.

Needless to say, I could go on about this without limitation as I have afforded many hours and years of dedication to meditations upon it and I so thoroughly believe that it is the reality to come upon my death. It is also due to such that I fully comprehend my righteous sense of duty, while I live upon Midgard, to serve my Gods and Folk.

Each Race/Folk/People have their own indigenous Folk Soul, and each shall one day learn the reality of such a truth, in my opinion. There is NO Universalism which exists within the realm of Natural Order, or the Laws of Nature. Nor is there, in my belief, either an end to life, spiritually speaking, or any one size fits all spirit/divinity, or afterlife.

One arrives at a familiarization with one's Folk Soul and Ancestors by communing with Allfather Odin and the Gods of the Æsir and Vanir, while one is alive and well in this lifetime. For such sacred and Holy Communion lead to wisdom found only at Mimir's and Urd's Wells, rooted in antiquity, and a time when Odin first thought! It awaits there yet, for those bold enough to journey forth on the Northern Road.

The corpus of myths, Sagas, lore, legends, heroic feats, art, music, poetry, architecture and virtues are all but manifestations of "Our" Folk Soul. Very real examples of how our very real Gods and Ancestors continue to reach out to us and speak to us via the medium of that which they share with us, their living folk... Our Folk Soul which was born with Allfather's very first thought.

How any among us can consider what I have postulated herein and still elect to discount the Sál/Soul's survival of the host body's death, should not consume anyone's thoughts. For it would be a waste of one's time. Only what is sensible about what I have presented herein, and more so, how it may serve to enrich your own spiritual quest, should be a point of any genuine concern. And ultimately, how each of us may be of service to our Gods and Folk.

WHEN WE WERE GODS

"To be free, one must follow the way that leads to the place where one dwelt before one was born: The Ancestral Spirit."
-The Code of the Northern Warrior

It would seem these days, that no matter where we cast our gaze, some sort of strife is in evidence wherein religious differences may sum up the heated point of contention... "Holy Wars", either side of the conflict inexorable in one's own, self righteous mind, and no less assured that the very hand of God will favor them, and guide them toward the light of victory; while those who perish in service to this holy endeavor shall reside in God's house of paradise, in the far above heavens!

Indeed, each faction with their respective peoples all have their own concept and name for the aforementioned, all supported by the legends, lore, and sagas of their God(s), and the tribes of folk which supplicate to them.

This position in man's history is not unique to any point, or place in time, for it is an age old bane which has plagued man since his antiquity. Today, in the 21st century, no distinction may be proffered wherefore this troublesome spiritual yoke about man's neck may be considered. One need not conduct a very elaborate survey to discover several nations embroiled in the throes of some holy war, or even on a lesser plane - churches, many of them pledging their allegiance to the same God, in a constant state of disharmony with one another, bordering the very fringes of war, save for the blatant physical violence! In man's search for the Holy Grail, has man lost sight of what is holy, of what God(s) is?

To answer this query, we must travel back to the only true time of innocence. A time when we existed in our purest form, a form devoid of any physical form of matter, where the sexes of male and female were as of yet, absent! Yes, to understand this enigma we must recall to memory a time of pure consciousness. Back must we journey, to a metaphysical time of being, a time when we were Gods.

The Greek philosopher and father of metaphysics, Aristotle (384 -322 B.C.), submits that metaphysics is the branch of philosophy which examines the nature of reality, and the relationship between mind and matter. In layman terms, "meta", is the Greek word which describes that which is beyond, or above. And physics, of course refers to our sense of that which is of a physical nature that which may be seen as constructed of matter, something tangible. Hence, 'Metaphysics' would declare and define a study of all things above and beyond the scope of the physical, in this instance - God(s).

"In the beginning, was the word, and the word was God, and God was the word." (Book of John, the Bible) These words offer one peoples version of the beginning.

The various peoples of the world, throughout the scope of man's existence, all have their own version of 'In the beginning'. One example of this point in case is the Norse/Teutonic peoples. According to the Northern Skalds and Poets, whom were vested with the awesome responsibility of recording, and preserving the lore, sagas, and accounts of Nordic man's beginning, religion, culture, virtues, and lifestyle, it is declared that, ‘In the beginning’ when there was no earth or sea, nor air, when darkness rested over all, there existed a powerful being called "Allfather", and whatever he willed came to pass. In the center of space, there was, in the morning of time, a great abyss called, "Ginnunga-gap", the cleft of all clefts. To be concise in my rendering of this story of creation, as provided by the Elder Edda, to the North of this great gap was a space of ice, while to the South existed a space of fire. Huge blocks of ice filled the yawning gap from these icy streams which flowed forth from the North, all the while, showers of fiery sparks fell upon the blocks of ice, from the South. Steam arose from the gap in great clouds which encountered the prevailing cold, and was transformed into rime, (hoar frost), and layer by layer, it filled and consumed the central space. It is from this matter, that the very first beings were born forth from... A primal frost giant named "Ymir".

Ymir, seeking food groped about the darkness until he found a great cow named "Audhumla", (the nourisher) her udders provided Ymir with an endless supply of milk. Audhumla herself seeking something to eat, began to lick salt from a great block of ice, the more she licked away at the block, a being became visible from within, it was the first God, now set free by the cow's licks. His name was "Buri (the producer). Meanwhile, Ymir, while sleeping, had begotten a son and a daughter from the perspiration beneath his armpit, his feet produced a six headed giant named "Thrudgelmir", who in turn brought about the giant "Bergelmir", from which all the evil Frost Giants are descended from. When these giants became aware of the existence of Buri, and his son "Börr" (born), whom he had immediately produced, they began waging war against the Gods, hence, the foundation is set for the Nordic peoples wherein the primal concept of the war between order and chaos, is in regard, with the Gods representing the forces of order, and the Frost Giants, of course, setting the tone for all of the chaotic forces.

Börr married the giantess "Bestla", the daughter of Bolthorn (the thorn of evil), who bore him three powerful sons, Odin (spirit), Vili (will), and Ve (holy). These three Gods slew their deadliest foe, Ymir and his kin, only Bergelmir and his wife managed to escape to the confines of the world where they reside in a place called Jötunheim (home of the giants), and here they begat a new race.

Meanwhile, the Æsir Gods, of which Odin was now the Allfather, as he himself was 'Spirit', created the earth with the severed body parts of Ymir, and thereafter did these Æsir Gods create the moon, sun, and stars. Finally, they created the first man and woman, "Ask" (Ash), and "Embla" (Elm), named thus for the trees from which the Gods created them from. (from the Poetic Edda).

One must consider that when Aryan man migrated from their original homeland, in the mountain regions of Iran, in South Western Asia, into the rugged terrain of Northern Europe, he encountered a great many difficulties, and was posed with an entire myriad of new hardships dictated by this new geographical homeland and the circumstances surrounding the unforgiving land.

Hence, the very premise for any accounts thereafter, alluding to the ideals, and beliefs, both culture wise, and religiously, are cultivated and passed down to their descendants, (i.e. the Norse/Teutonic peoples).

That the original homeland of these Aryan peoples, was indeed more hospitable to their way of life, as opposed to their new homeland, so entrenched in the vice like grip of snow and ice, so much of the year, we may certainly derive the battle lines being drawn between the forces of order and chaos, (i.e. the Gods from back home, against the Frost Giants of this harsh new land). Anything harsh and non-conducive to their well being was ascribed to the archetype of chaos = Frost Giants, while that which was fair and good to them was viewed as good via the archetype of their

Gods from their more hospitable home land in Southwestern Asia, hence, the Æsir Gods.

I chose these Norse/Teutonic people, and their primal religious views, to chronicle my study, not inasmuch that I, myself am a member of this race of people, or their ancient religious beliefs, but rather, because I believe these people, in their antiquity, possessed a great understanding of the concept of a metaphysical state of being, a God state of being!

Dr. Carl Gustav Jung (1875-1961) a Swiss born German philosopher and psychiatrist, set much of the basis for the understanding of the ancient Norse/ Teutonic religion of Odinism, when he put forth his theory that we as human beings have a unique "racial memory" far older than the human race itself, living in our subconscious minds and memories. He further asserts that through understanding this, we are capable of face to face meetings with our Gods, ancestral, and nature spirits': The name for this conceptual theory is, "Meta-genetics".

Karl Maria Wiligut (1866-1946), set forth his own ideal of this concept which he presented in his composition; "Description of the evolution of humanity from the secret tradition of our Asa-Liana Clan of Uiligotis", (the Secret King, by Dr. S.E. Flowers), in which Wiligut proffers the "Seven Epochs of Humanity".

In the first Human epoch, Aithar - beings, (pure spirits) found themselves in constant struggle with the Water-beings, which were taking shape in this same period. They were without gender, neither male, nor female, they simply were spirit. Through a concentration of their will, they achieved a spiritual union with each other.

In the second Human epoch, we see that a great catastrophe occurred, (an Ice age), which formed an air-entity-belt around the earth. The remaining air and water entities 'Solidified' themselves, while remaining in a constant state of struggle with each other, into bisexual beings, (i.e. beings of both male and female gender),'they lived partly on the earth, partly in the water, and they could fly. They propagated themselves - partly by means of incipient mating of 'homogenous souls' among the air and water entities, and had attained the level of Gods, (i.e. creative consciousness), they evolved into beings of knowledge, and from this point on, they could be characterized as the original hermaphrodites.

In the third Human epoch, we learn that the 2nd Human epoch is destroyed by an all consuming fire, followed by yet, another Ice age, the survivors of the second epoch called themselves the "First humans on earth!"

The fourth Human epoch, is an evolving occurrence giving rise to religion, and ultimately to the fifth Human epoch, which is "Now", and religions as they have come to be in our need, or desire as humans, to label them and identify them with the realities which surround us. (It should be noted here that the fourth epoch elapses over a period of millennia). The 6th and 7th Epochs are yet to come, according to Wiligut.

I would submit that Wiligut's representation of the God, Self, in humanity, is not completely without merit. It is my theory and metaphysical belief, that we all come from a purely spiritual conscious, point of origin, in concert with Dr. Jung's "Meta-genetic" principal; further hence, along that same line of thought, Norse-Teutonic man in his infancy understood all too well, his place within, and, in accordance with the laws of natural order, not as a mere existence outside of, or beyond those laws of nature. And therein the concept of cause and effect did indeed render these folk, Gods... It must have been a truth, which was manifest within the meta-genetic memories of our ancestors, regardless of race, or ethnicity, this would apply to all peoples with regard to their own unique racial memories! Alas, we have long since forfeited that privilege, by perverting what is naturally inherent to us, and our truest understanding of it!

Once the understanding of the divine stream of God(s) consciousness was lost to these people, it became necessary to create gods in the form of matter, the form of man, thus removing God(s) from the truest and purest form of spiritual consciousness, and adopting a more conceivable, understandable form for which man could justify placing his faith in.

Sometime thereafter, there arose shrines to these Gods, and temples as houses in which the spirits of these Gods dwelt in, the need for priests and priestesses soon followed, holy men and women were now required to interpret what the Gods said, meant, or desired. Alas, it was not far to follow before ill designs formed and waxed within the breasts of many a religious holy man, so trusted by the folk they professed to serve, they saw the might of this new power they did wield over their brethren man. Soon, laws, canons, and rules a plenty, were constructed and implemented in the name of the new Christ God, and the organized church became God, and this new way of expressing God became the State of many nations, and in the tumult of it all, God became dead!

Friedrich Wilhelm Nietzsche (1844 - 1900) a German philosopher, often denounced as an anti Christ, wrote; "When the church has become God, then God has died, hence, God is dead".

Though Christianity was now taking root in most of Europe, circa the 2nd century A.D., or thereabout, the Norse/Teutonic people had no use, or inclination toward the new, meek Christ God. For one thing, it contradicted their entire sense of being based upon overcoming life's hardships and struggles with strength and might, and those not inclined by such virtues of strength and courage, were weak by choice; henceforth, they did not deserve to live free lives as independent men and women. Instead, they warranted the lives of thralls, (i.e. slaves) by their design of self accepted pity and weakness! This is indeed a Norse/Teutonic concept of trial and worthiness by overcoming hardship and constant strife! Nietzsche had some profound axioms to offer on this point, one of the most popular and in fluid use to this day is; "What does not destroy me, makes me stronger." To further illustrate this point, he penned; "Independence is a privilege reserved for the strong."

A true and heroic embodiment of this virtue of strength and courage may be found in the historical account of King Odin - whom all the virtues, powers, and adventures of a God were attributed to. (Myths of the Norsemen by H.A. Guerber 1909). King Odin was a Chieftain of the inhabitants of Asia Minor. Threatened with destruction, or slavery at the hands of the Romans, King Odin led his people out of their native land around 70 B.C., were they migrated to Europe. He is said to have conquered Russia, Germany, Denmark, Norway, and Sweden, leaving a son on the throne in each conquered country.

As his end drew near, King Odin assembled his followers, and then in public, he cut himself nine times in the breast with his spear, (a death ceremony called "Geir-odds"). He then told them that he was going home to his native land "Asgard"; he then lay down and died. There is indeed record of this very much loved, King Odin, and of his great feats, in the Black Sea area of what is today, Odessa, Ukraine, (the Rites of Odin by Ed Fitch 1990). The ancient lore suggests that great Odin himself was once a man like any other, but by his own search for wisdom, courage, and much work at understanding the primal state of being of folk consciousness, he became master, holy man, priest, king, and ultimately, he attained Godhood!

Perhaps, through this great man's heroic deeds, our ancestors ascribed his name to that of the Allfather. Or, perhaps, he himself, understanding the scheme of things being what they were, in and of natural order and therefore, the laws of cause and effect, was inspired by the voice of Odin - Allfather (the ultimate primal spirit-consciousness). And perhaps, as Dr. Jung had posited, even had a face to face meeting with him, and thus thereafter, understanding that he possessed the spirit of Odin within all along, adopted/ assumed the name and persona of Odin in human form, (matter as opposed to the purely mind/consciousness) as opposed to the purely spiritual form. This would be no more unbelievable than that of Jesus being the flesh embodiment of Yaweh as God.

We have seen, even offered plausible explanations, (as plausible as any other) as to how things have evolved in the religious hierarchy via organized church/ statehood for profit, power and greed. This contributed greatly, if not solely, to the decline of the true God - self relationship in its truest and purest form. So, what then can we do about this malady, which increases ever more with the vast advances of technology? How can we regain this elite understanding and relationship with God(s)?

The answer is simple, though the practice thereafter is not so simple, nor may those whom self accept weakness benefit from the simple answer, any more than those lacking in courageous demeanor...once again, we "Ourselves" must become Gods! This is not a comfortable notion for most, nor does it afford any instant reprisals from the fears, or horrors of life's realities! Further more, it will not find a popular audience with the meek sheep like people of the gray masses!

Like Nietzsche's ideal of the Übermensch, or super human, we must shun the inanely, mundane and strive for higher idealism, higher consciousness, hence, higher state of being. We must use the Gods as archetypes, models for which we must base our own actions on, they are our dearest friends, and we are their divine descendants... They are our divine consciousness on a pure and collective level, and one day, each of us shall return to that primal source of our being, but only if we are strong enough to find our way back to it. To do so, is to prepare now by listening to, and heeding the ancestral voice within.

When we look upon the images of our God(s), or enter into their Temples of worship, let us worship them by honoring ourselves, and what is divine within each of us. For that is what they are there for, to remind us about and inspire us to return to a time when we were truly divine, and to a place in the future, where we will once again find that which is divine within us (while we are in the here and now, in the form of physical matter). That we might achieve the required strength and courage to be worthy enough to one day return to the primal God source! If you want to know God(s), then you must endeavor to live your life as a God, for therein lies the truth of man, and God, and of a time when we were Gods!

QUEER NOTIONS

Recently we received an email from a Rev. Gothi Ynglsson regarding the HNO's anti-homosexual policy. In his email, he refers to homosexuality as 'very benign' and a 'natural occurrence'. He further asserts that homosexuality is both rampant and a common occurrence within the animal kingdom. He cites "monogamous gay avian couples will take eggs abandoned by their straight counterparts and raise them as their own." Furthermore, "Homosexuality does have its own niche and place in nature." Elsewhere in the Rev. Gothi's email he contends that followers of Frey in Sweden held rites where men dressed as women and danced around a wooden phallus. He then goes on to catalog a number of our myths which he says illustrate gender bending roles such as Loki transforming himself into a mare which gives birth to Sleipnir, Odin learning Seith/seidr from Freya and Thor cross dressing as Freya to obtain Mjollnir.

Initially, I opine that any self respecting heathen would be hard-pressed to refer to oneself as 'Reverend', which according to Merriam-Webster Thes: states; reverend: noun, Christian religious officials. While, in all fairness, the definition does include 'worthy of reverence: Revered. Still, why would any genuine heathen/pagan equate oneself with a title which is most widely recognized in association with Christianity and its clergy? Next, I must assert that I believe that the Rev. Gothi is most probably a homosexual himself, or so it would seem so that his queer notions regarding Vor Siðr (Our Faith) would infer as much.

While we of the HOLY NATION OF ODIN are interested in genuine fundamental Odinism and not popular new age liberalism, we do not concern ourselves with the burden of defending our religious/spiritual policies to outsiders, nor apologize for what we believe to be Odin's law (laws of nature).

That posited, I offer the following for those whom may be confused by the myriad of so-called Odinist or Ásatrú organizations which cater to the Universalist and Homosexual host at large.

The HNO is an Odinist/Wotanist Ministry/Church whose theology/philosophy is fundamentally sound. We don't see an incestuous act of perversion occurring twixt Frey and Freya in the physical sense, but rather a metaphorical paradigm of fertility in mythical proportion.

Nor do we consider homosexuality to be either benign or natural! Furthermore, wherefore 'Natural' animal mating rituals and copulation are in regard, I must contest the Rev. Gothi's assertion that homosexuality is both rampant and a common occurrence. Certainly all species of life on Midgard have within their host those whom are confused about their role within the scope of the laws of natural order. That this may occur to a lesser degree, most assuredly fails to qualify as either rampant or common.
Wherefore the Rev. Gothi cites monogamous gay avian couples assuming the duties of incubating eggs abandoned by their straight counterparts, I say Balderdash! What makes these birds homosexual? Because they incubate eggs?!! I believe what the Rev. Gothi is referring to is a study of penguins some years back, which had erroneously stated that homosexuality among male penguins was a common occurrence. Later more recent studies have since refuted this absurd notion. In the penguin society, females abandon their eggs and the males incubate them. This however is not exclusive to the penguin genus of the avian species. Where male birds of certain species exclusive to colonies, wander across stray and unattended eggs, they will assume the responsibility of incubating the egg to ensure the colony's lineage and strength will survive and continue. This is natural instinct, not homosexuality. It is nature's imperative! Where the Rev. Gothi insists that homosexuality does have its own niche and place in nature, I must concur, albeit not in the same vein as the reverend. I opine that homosexuality assumes the quality of abnormal behavior within the breadth of natural order.

It defies nature's scheme and until the latter part of the twentieth century, when Zionist media outlets waged a campaign of social acceptance in an effort to undermine western civilization via the vehicle of moral decay and deviancy, it was considered abnormal and taboo by the overwhelming populace of western society.

Wherefore the reverend postulates that the followers of Frey in Sweden dressed like women and danced around a wooden phallus, he further fails to illuminate the facts surrounding such strange behavior among our ancestors. The fact of the matter is that in the era of which this example is written, only males were allowed in the Gothard (Priesthood). The rite of dancing around the wooden phallus was one of importance regarding fertility. Since only male priests were allowed on the sacred ritual land at that time, they dawned the garments of females so that it would not appear to be a homosexual act. The phallus of course was/is synonymous with Frey's fertility properties while the priests dressed as mock females, formed a circle or ring around it to symbolize genital penetration twixt male and female. Had the male priests simply danced about the phallus as themselves, the inference would certainly have been one of homosexuality, albeit this was not the case at all.

Where the reverend had sought to sully the Gods character and nature in his own endeavor to justify homosexuality and bolster his defense therefore, he cites that Loki had turned himself into a mare which in turn gave birth to Allfather Odin's steed; Sleipnir, Odin himself practiced Seith/Seidr and that Thor was a cross dresser...

In the myths and old lore, Loki did indeed alter his shape into that of a mare. This he did in an effort to distract the stonemason's mighty stallion once it was discovered that the stonemason building the wall around Asgard was in fact a Jötun, whom had tricked the Æsir when they negotiated the terms of work, time frame and compensation. Loki had not counted on, nor intended to be caught and mounted by the stallion. Nor was the act considered by "ANY" in the myths to be an acceptable practice to engage in. Rather, they viewed it as an unfortunate circumstance which had arisen from Loki's effort to keep the stonemason from completing his task. Next, according to the lore, Freya did teach Odin Seith/Seidr, which was practiced primarily by females. That she taught Allfather this knowledge should not be taken to imply that he dressed as a woman, did perverse things or even practiced the craft. In fact, nowhere in the lore does it say that Odin practiced Seith/Seidr, only that he was taught it by Freya. This was merely in concert with Odin's relentless quest for knowledge and wisdom of all! In all accounts of Odin's employment of magic within the old lore and myths, it is always Rune/Galdr magic. Always!

Regarding Thor dressing as Freya in order to recover his Hammer Mjollnir in order to continue his role as defender of both Asgard and Midgard, he clearly is distraught at the prospect of dawning feminine garb, albeit he sees it as a means to an end. A Trojan Horse tactic, if you will. None of the afore stated examples even come close to a viable argument in favor of homosexuality.

Cornelius Tacitus (b. 56 CE - d. 117 CE), affords us a window into our ancestral past within the pages of his GERMANIA. In chapter eight of this record of history, he illustrates the very power of gender specific roles twixt our male and female ancestors when upon the fields of battle our warriors appeared to be at the very brink of defeat when their women goaded them on to victory! They exposed their breasts and encouraged them to fight on lest their women folk be subjected to captivity and the horrors of being used by their captors. It was understood by all, that this would mean certain death of the tribe's lineage. And this was unacceptable to the Germans of old! In chapters eighteen and nineteen the strict code of marriage (twixt one man and one woman) and the immense value placed upon a woman's role and virtue are outlined, thus indicative of a monogamous and healthy heterosexual society as practiced by our Aryan ancestors.

The Poetic Edda itself offers us a much clearer picture than the homosexual and liberal camps would ever care to concede. In Harbard's Song, stanza 42 has Odin disguised as Harbard saying to Thor:

> 42 I'll compensate you for that with a ring for the hand
> which arbitrators use, those who are willing to make a
> settlement between us.

The ring for the hand to which Harbard alludes is analogues of a man's anus! And as such, Thor takes exception to this slight in the very next stanza.

> 43 Where did you find such despicable words?
> I've never heard words more despicable!

Were homosexuality not a shameful act within the Eddic context of our Gods, Thor would not have been so severely offended.

In Thrym's Poem, stanza 17, Thor clearly states his aversion to the suggestion that he dress as Freya;

> 17 Then said Thor, the vigorous god:
> The Æsir will call me a pervert,
> if I let you put a bride's veil on me.

Once again, this Eddic paradigm evidences the Norse-Teutonic aversion to anything the Gods had perceived to be an 'Unnatural' act (e.g. Homosexuality).

In the Havamal, we are shown several accounts of matters of love and lust, all of which occur twixt man/God and woman/Goddess/ Jötun. Stanza

> 79 The foolish man, if he manages to get
> money or the love of a woman,...
> 81 At evening should the day be praised, the woman when
> she is cremated.... the girl when she is married,...
> 82 ...in darkness chat with a girl: many are the eyes of the
> day; use a ship to glide along, a shield for defense,
> a sword for blows, and a girl for kisses.
> 90 Such is the love of women...

Stanzas 96 through 102 describe Odin's own desire for Billing's daughter. In the following stanza, Odin advises his neophyte, Loddfafnir, to heed his advice:

> 130 ...if you want a good woman for yourself to talk to as
> a close confidante,
> and to get pleasure from,
> make fair promises and keep them well,...

And finally from the Hávamál, in Odin's Rune Tally, stanza 161, we get the crux of Aryan man's sexuality as well as his racial desire and responsibility...

> 161 I know a sixteenth if I want to have all
> a cleaver woman's heart and love-play:
> I can turn the thoughts of the white-armed woman
> and change her mind entirely.

> 162 I know a seventeenth, so that scarcely any
> <u>maiden</u> will want to shun me...
> and
> 163 ...except the <u>one woman</u> whom my arms embrace.

And finally, from the Old Norse language we get the word(s) "Ergi / Regi", which means unmanly behavior, homosexuality. It was the worst of all insults among our Norse-Teutonic male ancestors. Given such considerations, why/how could anyone draw the conclusion that homosexuality was either condoned or tolerated among our ancestors? Any such arguments fail to either support or validate such queer notions!

To be certain, such arguments in favor of homosexuality, <u>**will not**</u> find any support from the Administration or membership of the HOLY NATION OF ODIN ! ! !

THE SKEPPSLÁG CONTRA KINDRED

Skeppslag (ON/Old Norse): Ship's Crew
Félag (ON/Old Norse): Fellowship (Pronounced: Fay-lag)

The mission of this composition is to educate, if not enlighten, our Folk to the negative aspects of forming Kindreds, prior to all involved affording due deference and full consideration to the long term consequences, which potentially lurk beyond the scope of what may initially seem to be fully positive in the nature of such Kinships.

While the primary target of this service is the incarcerated Folk, it is equally applicable to Free world Folk as well, wherefore establishing a new Kindred is in regard.
Kindreds, be they Odinist/Wotanist, Ásatrúar, etc., call for Oath Bonds. This is to say, the members of any such Kindred must enter into oaths of Kinship and Troth (fealty/loyalty). These oaths are life long!

"That I advise you secondly,
that you do not swear an oath unless it is truly kept;
terrible fate-bonds attach the oath tearer;
wretched is the pledge-criminal."
- Sigrdrifumál 23
and
"A hall she saw standing far from the sun,
on Nástrond; its doors look north;
drops of poison fall in through the roof vents,
the hall is woven of serpent's spines.
There she saw wading in turbid streams
men who swore false oaths..."
- Voluspa 38 and 39

The negative aspects, in addition to potential dangers, associated with forming Kindreds, or accepting new members into already existing Kindreds prior to a very thorough vetting process can have far reaching consequences. I have personally been a party to such consequences in addition to witnessing thus with several others over the past two decades alone.

Where the incarcerated Folk are concerned, one must always consider to the fullest degree, the very environment of prison and the myriad of circumstances in concert with said prison life.

When you forge an oath bond with just one other man, let alone several others, considering the afore written, you are accepting the fallout and consequences associated with that man's/those men's (or women where our incarcerated sisters are in regard), actions as well, as they pertain to said's vices, politics, already existing Kinships he/she may have, or any future Kin Oaths said may enter into (see Hávamál 43 regarding this). And this barely scratches the surface. Many are the hazards which may arise from such oath bonds which are attached to membership in a Kindred.

The afore posited thus far should not be assumed as any inference upon my part that I am against the fraternal bonds and benefits of sworn oaths and/or oath bonds and Kindreds, for I am very much in favor of such! I am merely seeking to impart some hard gained wisdom for your own consideration regarding the subject.

Conversely, a Skeppslág (ON Ship's Crew) is an ideal alternative wherefore men/women are interested in gathering for spiritual/religious fellowship is at issue. Derived from the Viking Era, the purpose of the Skeppslág was to wax in adventure and wealth. A Chieftain or Jarl whom owned one or several Lángskipps (ON Long Ships/Longboats) would put out the word in the mead and ale halls during the winter, that he was assembling Skeppslágs for the coming raiding season. Men would then pledge to join his ship's crew for that intended purpose. If he was a man of success and renown in previous seasons, he could count upon the most able warriors to seek to secure a place on his crew(s). When the snows thawed and gave way to favorable sailing conditions, the Skeppslágs would set sail and a viking they would go!

The oaths they made to the Chieftains/Jarls and one another, extended only across the breadth of the Viking season. Once they had returned home, all the oaths, having been fully honored by this time, were now expired.

When it comes to gathering together for spiritual/religious fellowship, the Skeppslág paradigm is ideal by design. It calls for no oaths save for each man (or woman) assembled to honor the virtues of our sacred way. It matters not if two brothers (or sisters) belong to one Kindred and four others belong to a Félag and all others are independent of any outside oaths, etc. for example. In and before the Skeppslág, all are equal. Every man (or woman) has a voice and vote beneath the overturned Long boat.

That is the manner in which a Skeppslág, out a Viking, would meet in council. They would make shore and overturn the long boat and gather beneath it, to hold council and call upon the every man vote. This in fact engendered the modern parliament of today's western world and in Denmark, Norway and Sweden some assembly halls and at least one government hall have ceilings which purposely look like over turned Long ships, that council may to this day be held in like fashion with the original ancestral concept.

In this, the Skeppslágs fashion, if ever the rapport of any among the assembled is damaged beyond reconciliation, Folks involved may go there own way without the stigma and dishonor of being an oath breaker, which of course is among the North Folk's greatest sins!

The longevity, integrity and power of an oath sworn, should always remain in the forefront of all, not to mention the wording of such oaths when and where they do occur. Be mindful of your words when entering into an accord or oath. Choose your words wisely so as to commit to whatever it may be, with honor and integrity on your end.

And that you will adhere to it no matter what, until the oath/accord is completed/fulfilled or the other(s) involved break or dishonor the oath betwixt you. Leave yourself an out in your word choice so that you do not end up an oath breaker. This does not mean start making oaths lightly, cheaply or with the forethought of getting out of it when it doesn't go your way! It merely means, exercise sound reason, logic and discretion prior to swearing any oath. Think long term...years into the future, whenever you are considering binding yourself to any oath. Remember also, that willfully witnessing oaths sworn, renders you a party to that oath as well.

Regarding the group dynamic wherefore spiritual/religious fellowship is concerned, be it in prison or the free world, the Skeppslág will serve you well.

If after a considerable amount of time elapses with sound fellowship, you are seeking more than just the Skeppslág, perhaps consider progressing to a Félag (ON Formal Fellowship). Long term success enjoyed at this level may pave the way to a formal Kindred. Though if you are incarcerated, I strongly urge against this, as transfers are ever looming realities and turnover rates in concert with said transfers do not negate or void oaths sworn when becoming a member of a Kindred. Wherever you land you may find other men (women) with whom your bonds are limited with due to previous oaths. Something to seriously consider.

By adhering to the Rede (counsel) herein this service, you have nothing to lose or suffer and everything to gain wherefore spiritual advancement is in regard.

HALLOWED HAMMERS VS HOLLOW HAMMERS:
A Reality Check

It seems that more often these days one may bear witness to any number of falsehoods in evidence in our daily lives; from empty promises by government officials, entities and politicians, to merchant and consumer advertisements. It is all akin to the false neighborhood on a Hollywood movie lot. For all visual purposes - an entire neighborhood of large beautiful homes line both sides of the street. But once you open the doors and step through them, there is nothing substantial. The houses are merely false fronts made of particle clapboard and plywood.

Sadly so, this unpleasant reality reaches into the spheres of religion and those whom move about such circles. Of course, all religions suffer from such a reality and none are exempt. Within the reaches of Vor Forn Siðr (Our Ancient Religion), the most readily recognizable symbol is Thor's Hammer. As the Christian dons the crucifix around his/her neck, we too don our most visible sacred symbol about our necks. While we have several holy symbols, many which are worn within the corpus of Northern heathen religion, be it Odinism/Wotanism, Ásatrú, Irminism, Vanatrú, Greater Theodism, etc., etc., the Thor's Hammer has and continues today to endure as the embodiment of the might and strength to overcome that which is a threat! As Big brother Thor had employed his mighty Hammer Mjöllnir to protect both Asgard and Midgard (Gods and Man) from the forces of chaos which had threatened harm (the Jötuns/Etins), we too are reminded daily by the Hammers which we wear, that we too wield the awesome might to defend both Asgard and Midgard, just as brother Thor does. Our will, desire and resolve constitute the very fortitude and rectitude which is our Hammer!

We ourselves are and become the very Hammer of Thor when we live our lives in concert with the Æsirian Code of Nine, the 14 Codes of Aryan Ethic, the Nine Noble Virtues, the Rede of Honor, the Code of the Northern Warrior and 1519/Living Einherjar, and any other applicable Aryan Code of Honorable Conduct. It is we, the noble men and women of the Aryan Tribes which give substance and energy to the great Hammer of Thor, within our living religion of Fundamental Odinism/Wotanism. Thor's Hammer is employed to hallow and consecrate all that it blesses. But it is us, we noble Folk which hallow and consecrate the holy hammer itself with our noble deeds! When we honor our oaths, the sacred hammer waxes in might. When we live our lives by our honorable thews and virtues, the hammer grows in strength. When we honor our Gods and Ancestors and the gift which they passed onto us (our blood/DNA), the hammer hardens! The hammer is made great for both us and Thor to wield in defense of our Folk and Forn Siðr, by the substance which we lend to it with our honorable and virtuous deeds. Alas, when the oath breakers squirm about like the worm kin of the Midgard Serpent, the hammer weakens. When the Trú and noble Folk, split and fracture and disunity replaces fraternal solidarity, the hammer weakens. When worm tongues speak out of both sides of their mouths and their ill actions contradict their noble words (talk North while walking South), the mighty hammer weakens and suffers.

You see, "WE ARE" the Hammer... We, the holy Folk, are the very might of Thor's Hammer. Both individually and collectively.

When others look at us, be they our own Folk and race; whether Heathen or not, or other races look at us, they either spy a mighty Hammer in service and defense of our Gods and Folk, made so by our might, will and noble behavior and example, or they will spy a hollow hammer, made so by the oath breakers and other Níthlings who justify their reasons for pernicious and derelict behavior and associations.

But while there might be ten Níthlings whom dishonor our mighty Hammer which others may see, just one truly hallowed hammer is still enough to let those looking on know, our hammer yet lives! Just one or two One Harriers (Einherjar / Living Einherjar), in a crowd of a hundred Níthlings or foes, harrying their odious attempts to shame our holy an noble way, lets all know that our hammer is mighty yet!

"Ek hinn Hammar!" (I am the Hammer!), let this be your mantra... Let it be your creed of iron... "Ek Einherjar, ok Ek hinn Hammar!!!" (I am of the One-Harriers, and I am the Hammer!!!), let this be your will, that you may live your life as a Hallowed Hammer, in service and defense of Vór Forn Siðr and our Folk. Let us "be" the very might of Thor's Sacred Hammer that we may yet fulfill our own destiny as a Folk. Let us "be" the very might he wields when he goes to battle against, and smashes those who would seek to destroy our ancient and sacred way and our noble Folk.

Let us be unyielding and unapologetic in our willed determination to live our lives as hallowed hammers. And let those who refuse to assemble beneath this noble standard, fall by the wayside as yesterday's forgotten kin and hollow hammers. Waste naught your time or energy with such níthlings, for they are merely distractions with designs to deter you from your noble deeds. They are fueled and driven by their own selfish desires and self-justified weaknesses, you cannot help them, they won't even help themselves. You may think that you are doing something good and noble and that you are getting through to them...but you are not. And more so, you are only hurting our Folk and our sacred way by wasting your efforts on such lost souls. From these hollow hammers, seek no accord, alliance or kinship. Those in their host, whom are capable of self-transformation in a positive fashion, may one day achieve thus, albeit it must be of their own volition. As for the overwhelming rest of their wretched lot, they shall wander through this life with their heads and souls filled with the blinding and perpetual fog of Níflhel... slighted not by the fate of the Norns, but by their own hands.

Individually, our character is a quality which we alone assume command over, for better or worse. Collectively, we, as a religion and to a greater extent, as a Folk, shall either thrive or suffer based upon our collective character. The quality of said character shall be determined, not by a multitude of equations, but rather, a single one... Those who shall break the precarious balance and tip the scales in their favor; Those Hallowed Hammers in service to the mission of the sacred way and the 14 WORDS, or those hollow hammers, who go to great lengths to look and sound as though they are of our Folk, when in reality they are Surtr's kin; the sons of Muspell (the agents of destruction). Just how it will all end is something which only the myths may allude to, and the Norns and Allmother Frigga may know. This much is a certainty; while our collective destiny awaits concealed in the shadows of Skuld's dark veil (the future), "WE" own and control today and what we are willing to do in service to our Gods, Folk and destiny.

Choose to "be" the Hallowed Hammer and then strike trú and hard, all the days of your life, that all the wights (beings) of the Nine Worlds (the Multiverse) will hear the great thunder and witness the blinding flash which announces to all; "We shall not be denied our destiny in the halls of honor and posterity!" By our noble deeds, our descendants shall have their day.

Heil Allfather Odin and his holy Folk... the Hallowed Hammers!Ek Einherjar, ok Ek hinn Hammar. I remain yours in Fraternal Solidarity.

CONFUSION IN GERMANIC MYTHOLOGY
(A Religious Perspective)

Earlier this day, Harvald Odinson and myself were discussing the complexities surrounding the realities of the Germanic (Norse-Teutonic) myths, as it were. Harvald had posited that the myths point out that the Valkyries were/are led by Freya, yet Odin is their father. So, he queried of me, 'who is their rightful and correct leader?'

This of course led us to converse upon several differences within many of the myths; i.e. if Freya gets to choose half of the battle slain, how then does one know who makes it to Valhalla contra who makes it to Freya's hall at Folkvangr? Such complexities require anywhere from many years of exhaustive study of the myths, to a lifetime of cumulative said field of lore and myth. I've long since come to realize that anyone whom believes themselves to possess all the answers has long since suffered an arrested state of progress regarding such. That asserted, what follows is the sum, thus far, of my own nearly forty years of research and meditations regarding the subject at hand.

Initially, we would all do well to consider that what constitutes the corpus of our ancestral mythology of the Gods and Folk of the Aryan Tribes, most certainly did not occur all at once. Nor were they committed to text by a single writer or in any single period. Ergo, just because our myths arrive from our illustrious past, packaged or bound in a single volume, or in the case of one, Jacob Grimm, several volumes, should not infer that they came down to us from a single era, or geographical locale. For any such inference would indeed be erroneous.

What constitutes the body of the Norse-Teutonic myths within the full scope of their entirety, most certainly had come about over the span of millennia. To be even more precise, those which we identify, albeit erroneously so, as the "Viking Age" myths, are in fact a product of several different clans, tribes and Folk which comprised the Aryan phylum, and over the breadth of myriad generations as well as geographical value within the vicinity of both Northern and

Western Europe. To wit, in Southern Germany, the two distinct Goddesses; Frigga/Fricka and Freya/Freyja, were considered to be one and the same in days of yore. While in most probably, all other areas, they each assumed their own unique identities. Yet, a further example, albeit this one as a matter of time and generation span, as opposed to geographical in character, is that of the God and patriarch of the Vanir (Earth, water and fertility deities), 'Njörd. The farther back we trace the origins of this God, he had, by some scholarly accounts, evolved from first, Goddess (Nerthus=Mother Earth) only to achieve transformation as a gender neutral (Hermaphrodite) God/Goddess. This may be due in large part to the quality of the gender role which both male and female must play in a concerted effort to produce new life within the grand scheme of natural order. Hence, we may easily arrive at our ancestor's perspective of the dual (God/Goddess) persona of Njord/Nerthus as fertility deity. Eventually, the two deities assume gender specific roles as the God and Goddess of fertility and ultimately, Njörd goes on to assume the station of primacy and thereafter sires the twins Frey and Freya, both deities of fertility and the sexual desire required to procreate.

Now when we factor into the equation, geography as well as generation span, we may descry not only a distinct separation betwixt Njörd and Nerthus, but we may additionally bear witness to the plethora of names ascribed to the Goddess of the very one and the same role as Earth mother/Goddess, to wit; Ertha, Erda, Erde, Ercce, Fjörgyn, Hlódyn, Jörd, etc., etc., etc., all of which are synonymous with Nerthus.

In this vein of example, the same may be posited in regards to variations in name, albeit, in the main they are more oft than not, linguistic only in nature. To wit, Odin, Oðinn, Odhin, Othin, Woden, Wodan, Wotan, Wutan, Wuotan, Wednes, etc., etc., etc.. And Thor, Tor,þórr, Donnar, Donar, Donner, Donnor, Thunaer,Thunor, Thunar, Thurs, etc.. And Tyr, Tiw, Tiwaz, Ziu, Tiuz, Tues, etc.. Such a study in semantics regarding names, nature and character in conjunction with geographical differences and time span, is and always will be an exhaustive one.

Next, we must consider that as a history addressing our myths, we are still in our infancy in as much as the history of research of Germanic mythology commences with the onset of the 19th century (see Dictionary of Northern Mythology by Rudolf Simek). The Codex Regius which is the very manuscript whence came the Poetic, or Elder Edda, is the very heart of our myths, both religiously and recorded. It is the oldest known compilation of the myths and its exact age is unknown and may not be dated with any certainty since the many vellum pages were composed over the breadth of time spanning the multitude of ages. These stories of ancestral lore were verbally passed from one generation to the next for incalculable ages whereby the time of their actual recording in print is most assuredly lost to the recess of history. As a matter of historical chronology, the myriad of velihm sheets which comprise the Poetic (Elder) Edda, which themselves were composed over an unknown yet certainly wide range of time, were compiled as an actual manuscript circa 1150 Common Era. However, it was not until 1275 CE that it was produced as the Codex Regius of Eddic Poems. Conversely, Snorri Sturluson composed his Edda (the Prose or Younger Edda) circa 1220 CE. He also authored the famous Heimskringla and is believed to have been the author of Egil's Saga, as well.

Since the 18th century, numerous volumes by equally as many authors, have been composed on/about the Germanic (Norse-Teutonic) myths, and each author has in turn, interjected his/her own influence and interpretation in the rendering of each's own account of the epic and heroic myths.

Upon such considerations, we must add yet another to the equation. That being that <u>all</u> of these volumes have been composed as an effort or study in mythological history, as a form of entertainment or as a primer to understand the ancestral pagan-heathen religious state of mind. But <u>never</u> have any of these works been composed with the deliberate intent, or from the vantage point of a surviving and 'Living' religion, or spiritual philosophy. Which is exactly what our ancestors did and it <u>must</u> be kept in mind when considering the ages in which these stories were told and retold by word of mouth, as they had been passed down until they were eventually chronicled by the hands of Christian monks upon the very vellum pagesfrom which ancestral, albeit Christian scholars would eventually compile the volume(s) that would be named/called the Eddas which are the source of what we today know as the Germanic Myths.

Given the myriad of clans and tribes, eras/time span and migration, locale and geographical variations, it can be no wonder that so many differences have appeared from what once may have been the same story in certain instances. Be that as it may, there is always the common denominator, if you will. The kernel of similarity (and truth?) which reoccurs within the variations of the myths. That is the common denominator and one of the primary points of authority which we have available to guide us in our own quest.

Next, we must take into account that unlike the chroniclers and scholars of our myths, we actually live the religiosity of these tales of virtue, character traits, morality, honor, loyalty, Folkways, etc., as they have come down to us and yet survive!

In actually ''living' this spirituality, we enjoy a relationship with our Gods and Ancestors. We are connected with and to them, where others are disconnected. And as thus, they speak to us through our blood/DNA and ancestral memories.

There are many confusables within the corpus of our myths, upon initial consideration. But further, advanced and extensive study of our myths, lore and Sagas will guide you well like a true compass always leading you north toward the home of our Gods and Ancestors. It will enable one to unravel the mysteries (Rúna) and the tangle of any confusion. And, in the end, isn't that what any spiritual quest, journey or pilgrimage is all about?

So then, what of my reply to Harvald''s query? Who is the leader of the Valkyries? Why, Allfather Odin, of course. Yes, it is so that beautiful Freya is the leader of the Valkyrie host, which both she and Allmother Frigga are counted among as well. However, she, as well as all of the Æsir and Vanir, submit to Odin as do children to their father (Prose Edda; Gylfaginning 19 - 20).

And if Freya gets to choose half of all battle slain, how does one know that one will go to Odin's hall; Valhalla, or to Freya's hall; Sessrumnir at Fólkvangr? Well, once again, upon exhaustive study of our myths and lore, one may descry that such an allusion must be associated with those who may have been followers of the Gods in general, or perhaps even Thor, Tyr, Frigga, Frey, etc.. For Odin shall claim the souls dedicated to him! No matter how they die. Any who are initiated unto his ways, Gothar (priests & priestesses), or his warriors, those whom rightly wear the Valknut, the Valkyries even those slain to him in sacrifice, shall he alone claim! In the Heimskringla, chapter eight of the Saga of Ynglings, Odin says that all who are cremated (a funeral rite of those dedicated to Odin), shall arrive in Valhalla, and with whatever riches or possessions that are burnt with thee.

In sum, these analogies are mythological in association with the Eddas, our lore and Sagas. However one elects to view them in reality based upon metaphysics, metaphors, Theology, Theosophy, Philosophy, or even quite literally, is up to each man/woman whom adheres to Fundamental Odinism as a religion/spiritual path.

For my own part, I employ extensive research and endless study of our myths, lore, Sagas, history as a Folk/People and race in concert with lengthy (sometimes very prolonged; days, weeks even a month) silent meditation. Additionally, I fully exercise traditional ritual practice (observe Holy Rites), Runic application and of course, my own personal relationship with our Gods and ancestors. But above all, our father, Allfather Odin/Wotan.

May he bless you well in your own journey North and may our Folk of the Aryan Tribes always know his venerable name and his victory. Heil Allfather Odin! And heil the Gods and our noble Folk, in his name!!!!

TWILIGHT OF THE GODS

If there is any one malady which plagues both our sacred way and Folk more so than any other, it is surely the willful lack of fraternal solidarity and unity. This malady of which I write is a construct of the human condition, to be certain. For in the realm of divinity stands a hall called Valhalla. And in this most sacred of places, exists the Einherjar and Valkyrjar. Here upon Midgard, we humans, we of small minds, no matter how intellectually gifted we may be, we fancy ourselves as those men and women who are in command of our psychological and emotional faculties, more so than the common and complacent man. Thus, we comprise the ranks of the, somewhat, initiated. From this phylum, come those of us whom comprise the ranks of the Living Einherjar and Valkyrjar, albeit we fall severely short of their grace. Not for such mundane reasoning that we yet live on in the physical realm. But because we fail to grasp the necessary lesson which is most paramount to the very survival, let alone, advancement, of our sacred way and Folk. This epic Nauthiz (ᚾ) (need) is perpetuated without end in Valhalla, though sadly so, not among the corpus of our living champions, those whom have pledged to defend and serve our Gods, Folk and Vor Forn Siðr.

Everyday, the Einherjar, in Valhalla's court yard, go off to battle. To hack apart and slay one another until all are dead. Upon the culmination of the day's battle, Allfather Odin raises all to yet live on and enjoy the pleasures of the night in Odin's Hall… feasting upon the sacred boar's flesh, consuming horns of mead which never run dry and delivered unto them by the beautiful daughters of Odin, the Valkyries.

The essential component is fraternal solidarity. No animosity is harbored. No grudges to bear .The very task of the Holy Army of Odin, requires said component in order to succeed. Many of these souls, at the least, half of them, were mortal enemies in life. That must all be set aside now would the sacred mission at Ragnarok succeed.

And yet we, their mortal kin ... Those of us avowed to serve and defend the very same mission while here upon Midgard, just cannot seem to forge and maintain the very bonds of fraternal solidarity required to fulfill our sacred mission.

What if we arrived in Valhalla and Allfather Odin said to us; "You do not belong here. For your valor is stable, alas, you do not know how to fit in where the bonds of solidarity reign supreme!" For myself, this would be the most devastating cut, which my soul could incur! To be certain.

If we fail to bring about and thereafter, secure this state of Aryan unity of which I write...Then surely our kind shall perish from the very phylum of humanity. And with the extinction of our Folk (blood), the very twilight of our Gods shall be complete. Our Gods, which live in our blood, and the race which they engendered, shall cease to be.

Extinction is forever!!!

Are we so small minded and selfish as to fail to support our noble oaths of service to our Gods, Folk and the mission of the 14 WORDS, with actions just as noble? Are our egos so self important that we fail to heed Odin's own paradigm of self transformation? "Myself to myself did I sacrifice." Or valiant Tyr's own self sacrifice for the greater good of the Gods and Folk, beyond his own self interest. Per the world census of 2013, the White Race comprises less than 12% of the entire world's population.

The numbers don't lie. The facts are inexorable. We will perish, as will our beloved Gods, as well as our posterity's future if we fail to grasp and apply this simple albeit epic principle.

If you are perusing these words, I implore you to consider their weight, lest it be our own hands which let slip the very bonds of fraternity and thereby, set free the wolf and usher in the twilight of the Gods.

Ragnarok beckons. The Gjallarhorn sounds its deafening blast! Where do you stand ...friend or foe?

Let us all assume the mantle of the genuine Living Einherjar and Valkyrjar and seek to strengthen the very bonds of fraternal solidarity. May the Gods we love smile upon our noble efforts... May the Norns smile upon the fate of our Gods, Folk and future!

FUNDAMENTALS OF ODINISM/WOTANISM
True Blótar Dates and Funerary Rites

As Heathenism/Paganism had sought to re-establish itself throughout the latter three or four decades of the twentieth century, many well-meaning Folks set about laying the foundations for more than the re-institution of authentic heathen/pagan religious/spiritual rites and customs. Indeed, our own Ancient Way/Religion), and then they went and labeled it all one faith - Ásatrú.

That none among our religious leadership had ever sought to correct such maladies, but rather continued to perpetuate them, says a great deal to the serious seeker, of our legitimacy as a religion. Especially if such a seeker, has amassed a deep knowledge of our lore, myths and sagas.

We must, however, never forget the contributions that those forerunners did in fact contribute to our beloved religion. We certainly owe them a great debt of gratitude, to say the least.

That posited, we at the Holy Nation of Odin have sought to correct the afore mentioned maladies over the past ten years. While we have made some important strides toward achieving thus, we have a long haul ahead of us yet. To be certain, it is a continuing labor of love and an honor and privilege to serve our Gods and Folk; One which we don't take lightly.

One look at most Ásatrú or Odinist/Wotanist calendars of religious Rites will illustrate the legitimacy of what I have previously asserted. One will note that both solstices and both equinoxes assume the dates of primacy. Thereafter, the four cross quarter dates assume their place in many calendars. Then follows several localized observances in addition to days of remembrance. In addition, I point out that none of this is a bad thing. It is just not traditional nor fundamental, wherein accuracy is in regard.

The Solstices are representative rites and observations of agrarian significance as are the equinoxes. And to be sure, these were important seasonal tides of the year for our, and every other, farming folk in the world! They remain equally as important today among farmers. However, they are not the traditional dates of our Ancestors of Northern Europe. Therefore, they do not constitute nor represent the genuine fundamentals of Odinist/Wotanist Blótar dates. They are in fact, the dates of primacy among Wiccans and New Agers. There is nothing wrong with holding Blót on these dates. I do. It is after all a matter of respect for the sowing and reaping of the fields, and Harvest celebrations definitely have their place among our Folk traditions. However, with the exception of the Winter Solstice (Midvinterblót) during the Yule Tide, the Summer Solstice and two equinoxes should not assume the predominate stations in our Fundamental Holy calendar.

In chapter eight of the Saga of the Ynglings (Ynglinga Saga), found in the Heimskringla, (The History of the Kings of Norway), Odin institutes the law regarding Blótar (Sacrifices.) A sacrifice (Blót) is to be made for a good season at the beginning of winter. This is the Winter Nights (Veturnaetur) which occurs on both Saturday and Sunday (Laugardagr and Sunnasdagr) which begins on the first Saturday between the 11th and the 17th of October (Hunting.) A second Blót is to be made in midwinter for good crops. This is the Mid-winter Blót (Midvinterblót), the actual Yule (Jól) which occurs on the Winter Solstice. And the third Blót is to take place in the summer (Summarsdag) for victory. This occurred in the month of Ostara (April) which is the date of summer's beginning in the old calendar. So for us today, whom are Fundamental Odinist/Wotanists, these three Blótar dates are fundamental dates:

- Veturnaetur/Winter Nights – which begins on the first Saturday between the 11th and the 17th of Hunting/October – Dísa Blót
- Midvinterblót/Jól/Yule – which occurs on the Winter Solstice, on or about the 21st of Yule/December
- Summarsdag/Sigrblót/Victory Blót – which occurs on the 14th of Ostara/April

These dates and they alone, are the only recorded dates of mandated Blótar which occur anywhere in print within our Sagas, Lore, or Myths. Period!

Nowhere else in any of our texts will one find any sacrifices/blótar mandated by Odin. Nowhere! This is not to infer that all other rites and Blótar are insignificant or somehow relegated to the office of the non-important. For this would be a grave error indeed! It does however illustrate what is fundamental, as by Odin's mandate. And what is not, but rather predicated upon regional, tribal and geographical differences.

Just as Odinism/Wotanism and Ásatrú are not the same religion, Fundamental Odinism/Wotanism is not the same as mainstream Odinism, for lack of a sounder terminology. We seek to draw our theology, philosophy and liturgy from the annals of history rather than the flights of fancy and whimsy, nor wishful sentiment. We are not politically correct, we don't not apologize for this, nor do we espouse any Universalist, egalitarian, or airy-fairy warrior type agendas.

We are the Living Einherjar! We are men and women of stalwart and genuine warrior ethic, ever ready we stand to defend our Gods, Folk and future!

Fundamental implies just that; that which is rooted in origin and history. Let us consider for the moment, funerary rites from the Fundamental Odinist perspective... While anyone may elect to mark the end of their time upon Midgard/Earth as they wish, once the Gods have gathered them up, why would any Odinist, let alone, fundamental Odinist choose anything but cremation? For Allfather Odin tells us that fire speeds the soul upon its way. There is a reason why we say as a part of our religious liturgy, during the lighting of the Scared Flame, portion of the Blót, "It is the first mystery and the final mercy." The final mercy is the all-consuming fire, the pyre/cremation.

Once again from chapter eight of the Yglinga Saga; "Odin ordains the burial rites: All the dead are to be burned on the pyre (our ancestor's cremation) together with their possessions, and that everyone would arrive in Valhalla with such wealth as he/she had with them on the pyre, and that the ashes were to be scattered at sea or buried in the ground. Cremation is a fundamental rite in Odinism/Wotanism, which marks one's journey home to the Gods and ancestors. It is ordained by Allfather Odin!

The fundamentals scribed herein warrant our devout consideration as genuine Odinists/Wotanist, for those of us whom adhere to Vor Forn Siðr, it is absolute for us to respect and observe first, what has been passed down to us by our ancestors as far back as we may discern. Certainly millennia further back than the Viking Age (8th century to 11th century.) And it's good thing too, because if we based the origin of our religion in the seat of the Viking Age, we'd all have to die with a sword in our hands to get to Valhalla! By going back as far as we can to the cradle of our Folk's origin, we merely have to live true to our Gods and Folk and live lives predominated more by virtue than by vice. Heil Odin!!!

FUNDAMENTALS OF ODINISM/WOTANISM
Remaining True to the Elder lore

We've all heard tell of that old adage; Old habits die hard. More so, we all know it to be true.

The overwhelming population of Northern Heathens were not born thus. Rather, most of us were in fact born into a society of Abrahamic faith to some extent, greater or lessor. Here in Vinland (North America, U.S. & Canada), no matter our family or household, we were, from our earliest memories, exposed to, and indoctrinated with such subtle and subliminal messages regarding Christianity, for the most part, in what amounts to state sponsored religion if one is to be honest enough about it all, via the vehicle of such simple everyday occurrences within our lives such as money (In God we trust), sworn testimony (I swear to tell the truth, so help me God), likewise does that same statement occur in all forms of public, military and civil service swearing ins (...so help me God). The Pledge of Allegiance (One nation under God), God bless America, God save the Queen, God shed his light on thee, etc. etc. etc. The assumption is a fairly sound one that this God whom is always referred to is indeed the God of Abraham; Yahweh, of Biblical repute. Certainly it is 'He', whom is referred to rather than she, or they/them. Were the postulation put to a poll, most, if not all would arrive at the same conclusion as posited above.

Thus asserted, we may assume with some degree of confidence that those whose eyes peruse this very content were in fact exposed from the cradle up to the point at which they sought to reconnect with and return to the Gods and ways of their ancestors. Whether that is fifteen years or fifty, it is great deal of brainwashing to undo, akin to a giant tangle of twine which must be untangled!

So then, no matter what Abrahamic faith you were exposed to at home, or even, lack thereof, you were deprived of religious freedom, via the Federal government, regarding who your notion of God was/is. You were told who God was/is every day of your lives, in one way or another. So then, deciding to pursue the old Gods and ways of your ancestors is laden with the awful burden of guilt! It certainly took a great many years to brainwash you. It will now require a very self-aware and conscious effort to eradicate that guilt. Acknowledging this is the first step forward. Now one must wade through the endless seas of available information out there, both erroneous and correct. That asserted, I'd like to point out at this point, that what works for anyone regarding their own relationship to that which is divine, is and should always remain a personal choice if such is to remain a sacred experience.

What available information one elects to educate oneself with in an effort to arrive at such paramount and lifestyle altering decisions, is another matter entirely.

For example, those who began their quest back to the elder way in the 1990's of the Common Era, had a great deal of the way back mapped out for them while those of us who began our journeys back in the 1970's CE had to figure it all out ourselves and in fact became many of the map makers in the 1980's CE, for what would constitute the way back to the old Gods and way.

To be certain, what would amount to my own first Blót in 1979 CE was really more in line with what we know from the lore today to be a Sumbel rather than a Blót.

Then there's the entire 'reconstruction religion' affair, which seemed a harmless enough enterprise in its infancy, albeit the decades which would follow would demand more. Reconstruction implied cult like status as did it borrow a great deal from other pagan paths, etc. In essence, Ásatrú as it became known, as we knew it back then, was really just a form of New Ageism with the trappings of Norse (Viking Age) culture. Norse Wicca is more an accurate mantle with which to identify what was being called Ásatrú in the early 1980's CE. And as such, it was a reconstruction religion, to be sure.

The 1990's CE saw some positive changes within Ásatrú, albeit, the old way remained grounded in the Viking Age (8th to 11th century CE), as did much of the New Ageism remain in lieu of genuine tradition culled from the lore or added to some traditions. By this time, the more separatist minded movement of Odinism, having its roots in the mid 1980's CE, began to seek further back than just the Viking Age Ásatrúar and into the Teutonic camp at that, rooted at the least, in the Bronze Age (4,000 to 500 BCE).

A comprehension of the entire Norse-Teutonic macrocosm demanded a respect for the entire composition of that which comprises the cultures and heritage of the Aryan Tribes on the whole, not merely the roughly three hundred years which constitute the Viking Age, nor merely the Scandinavian peoples within that three centuries. This became the Odinist pursuit. And the inclination of many Odinists to separate further from the Ásatrúar was the latter's penchant toward come one, come all Universalist attitude regarding that which inherently belongs to the people of the Aryan Tribes exclusively... The Gods of our blood!

By the dawn of the twenty-first century, so many different groups and people were calling themselves Odinists, that it became necessary to widen the chasm betwixt those who call themselves Odinists but fail to live as thus, and those who ARE Odinists and do live as thus on a daily basis.

For those of us whom gather beneath the Banner of Fundamental Odinism, no New Age dribble will do for us. For all which we do is rooted in the Lore (religion, myths, sagas, philosophy, histories, architecture, psychology, wisdom and traditions) of our ancient Aryan Ancestors. Not merely one age or another. And it is this lore which has become and remains our sacred foundation from whence we may wend forth from.

At the Holy Nation of Odin, we are indeed Fundamental Odinists. All of our Blótar, traditions and rituals are derived directly from the historical accounts of our Ancestral Lore. Not what we 'Think' may have been the instance, but were in fact the instance! There is no mixing and matching of traditions here, unless it is in fact Norse-Teutonic (Germanic), across generational lines.

Following this model, the seeker will be exposed to the fundamentals of Odinism as they exist in the Lore. In this discipline, the reader will be able to disconnect from the lifelong brainwashing which he or she suffered, while benefitting from a regeneration of spiritual/religious/traditional knowledge as it is derived from the genuine ancestral sources, as opposed to the modern new age - reconstruction perspective.

For us, there is no break in the link with our genuine ancestral past for us to reconstruct. We merely need to read it, apply it and live it.

PART II

"Val Freya" painting by Gð Dr. Casper Odinson Cröwell, 1519-CCG An adapation of an original Luis Royo, title unknown.

Faith

HOF SERVICE for Júlmoon (Yule, Winter Solstice)

TOWARD HIGHER IDEALISM
(For Family, Faith, Folk and the Future)

When considering where to begin, my mind traces the very silhouettes of the old stand bys; Blótar, Runes, Sumbels, etc., etc.. While these components are indeed essential to the traditional practices of our ancient faith of Odinism/Wotanism, as we have come to know it through the spiritual Re-awakening of our Gods and faith, so much has already been committed to print by so many accomplished writers. And so, I shall not rehash any of it. Well, at least, not at this time. I will venture to presume that those whom peruse the contents herein will be familiar, to one degree, or another, with the basic essentials of our faith. So then, where shall I begin? How about with Family! For this Júl/Yule tide season certainly holds great importance wherefore the scheme of family is in regard.

It should be painfully obvious to even the simplest mind, just how significant the family unit is to the survival, growth and advancement of our faith and our folk. For most, the Júl tide is the opportunity to gather with family. The season has remained virtually unchanged in that respect, over the span of the past millennia, albeit, what families do with the time they spend in each other's company has changed in a multitude of ways. So many families will get together this Júl and argue over trivial and unimportant issues. Just as they have the previous years in which they have gathered. This is opposed to capitalizing upon the gift and opportunity which they have been afforded. Not only is this selfish, it is disrespectful to both the living family as well as the family's ancestors!

We so oft take it for granted that we will be afforded

another opportunity later in time to right the wrongs which occur with our loved ones. All too oft failing to realize that life does not occur on our schedule, or by the rules and dictates of our personal desires. Death arrives as an uninvited guest and he claims the lives of our loved ones without consent, or consideration to the circumstances surrounding our lives, or the many things we have yet to resolve in our lives wherefore our personal family relationships are concerned. What if the Gods gathered you up to them right this instance? Have you the peace of mind in knowing that you have done all that you can to have your Wyrd and Ørlog in order and all worked out? Don't answer that right away.

Our ancestors have left us many gifts, not least among them, the ability to learn from their errors and to apply that knowledge in an effort to avoid repeating the same errors in judgment. Our Sagas are ripe with examples of what occurs when the family unit breaks down. The Clan/Kindred unit suffers the same tragedy. Although, the greatest tragedy is that in the past, this has led to complete dissolution of the Tribe(s) and that has nearly cost us today the sacred faith of our fathers! By the grace of the Gods themselves, a few folk were blessed with the fortitude and persistence to keep our holy ways alive when the great family breakdown occurred, a millennium ago. And it could happen again!

Today, so many families suffer the effects of the dysfunctional family unit to a greater or lesser degree. Sad but true. And so many would seek to avoid this uncomfortable truth as opposed to embracing the reality and working together to resolve that which plagues them.

People say hurtful things to one another, then allow it to fester until they no longer speak to one another for many years, if ever again at all. The ancestors would not smile on such base behavior! For in the days of yore, when the family unit existed in a state of disharmony it meant the fields did not get worked the way they should and the harvest thereafter suffered and failed to yield its full potential. But this was by no means the sum effect of a family's disharmony, nor is refusing to speak to one another today the sum of ill behavior towards one another.

So then, here we are - another Júl/Yule tide season. It's another opportunity to set things right with the family unit in an effort to restore harmony, strength and unity to the family and the Clan/Kindred and Tribe, thereafter. Ultimately, the folk and our beloved faith can only prosper as a direct result.

If you are out there in the free world, take this season as the opportunity for which it is. Get together with family and enjoy each other's company as opposed to arguing over trivial matters when the liqueur starts to flow. Seek to edify one another rather than belittling each other.

And no matter where you are when your eyes rest their gaze upon these words, if there exists unrest and discord in your own family's harmony, take this opportunity to right a rift between yourself and your loved one(s). Reach out to them in an honest effort to secure a peaceful resolve to gap the chasm between you. And do not get angry if they fail to capitalize on the opportunity, or your own effort to move forward. You cannot control another's animosity or their lack of desire to restore frith (harmony & peace) between you. But you can take solace in the knowledge that you did your part to restore the balance.

There are so many among our folk whom will suffer the absence of a cherished family member this Júl/Yule, due to prison, war, perhaps the recent passing of a loved one. Whatever the case may be, don't let anger and harsh words be the reason why you don't see, or speak to your loved one(s) this Júl/Yule, for it is unnatural! No other animal in nature acts in such a base manner! The very cornerstone of our faith is family.

I direct your attention to the AEsirian Code of Nine: 1) The Code is Honor: Honor your family and friends with reverence and respect. Honor is the mark of strength and nobility. 2) The Code is to Protect: Protect with savagery your blood and Kin. Protection is the mark of a warrior spirit. And from the Noble Nine, Kinship is better than alienation. From the Nine charges: 5) To suffer no evil to go un-remedied and to fight against the enemies of Faith, Folk and Family. And from the Nine Noble Virtues of the Temple of Wotan: Without loyalty to family, faith and folk we are nothing and can achieve nothing. Be courageous in defense of your family, faith and folk! Be generous with tolerance, assistance and sharing of knowledge and wisdom within your family, faith and folk. Let's take a closer look at these virtues:

Honor your family with reverence and respect! This means parents, BE parents to your children. Siring, or giving birth to a child does not render you a parent, per se. Sure, it makes you a biological parent albeit there is much more to good parenting than any biological title may confer. It requires a commitment to rear that child and provide without fail for that child. It means being accountable for the children you bring into this world and remaining responsible for their welfare and healthy growth. Not passing them off on someone else to rear, or passing the buck when things get tough! Children, honor and respect your parents. Respect your elder kin and the sacrifices which your ancestors made so that you could receive the gift of life that you now enjoy. They are not just faceless family members that you never knew. They did their part to protect the family line so that you could one day do the same. Next time you think that your life is your own to do as you please, consider this; "You" would not be here today with out them first being and fighting to secure your right to be here today!

Husbands, honor your wives. Show her the respect she deserves. Worship her like the goddess that she is! Do not cheat on her! As the Mother Goddess, "Frigga" resides within all of our women, if you abuse and disrespect them, you are abusing and disrespecting our Allmother Frigga!

Wives, honor your husbands. Do not belittle, or demean his manhood when he's down. Do not spit on him when he's low. Do not cheat on him with another. Lift him up with your love. Assure him that he has something worth fighting for in his wife (and children). The both of you must strive to honor and protect the very gift of love which Freya gave you and the gift of marriage and family which Frigga blessed you with. Strive to not tear it asunder. Kinfolk, be Trú Kin to our Kin! Seek always to edify them and be slow to belittle them. Seek not to break, or destroy the bonds which hold you fast as Kin, but rather, seek with vigor to always strengthen the Kinship between you.

These are but only the obvious and immediately apparent measures of virtue we may exercise, not only this Júl/Yule tide season, but everyday that we awake to journey forth upon Midgard. Let this be our will and our purpose towards the end of creating, securing and maintaining the healthy family unit. For when we achieve this we not only may achieve a return to a healthy folk community, complete with healthy Tribes once more. But, we too shall then achieve the will of Wotan/Odin and the will of both our Gods and ancestors. And that will only serve our descendants yet unborn by reinforcing prominence in the future.

May all of your Hammers strike Trú, and may our holy Gods bless your noble endeavors! (Perform traditional Blót to Patroness of family, Frigga)
Fara með Goðanum, ok Góðan Júl!
I remain in service to the Gods and folk of the Holy Nation of Odin… Heil Allfather Odin!

*remember always my stalwart and noble Kin and Kith;

"A Community of honor will always attract the honorable. But a circus, well, a circus only attracts clowns and children."
-- Casper Odinson Cröwell, Ph.DD

HOF SERVICE for Yule (Yuletide, Winter Solstice)

AND THE WHEEL GOES 'ROUND

Yule is upon us and this can only mean one thing... "NO!" Not Santa. Settle down, settle down. It means that the holy wheel of the year (Jera) goes 'round yet once more.

To begin with, the Yuletide delivers the holy year unto the alter of death. It is a culmination in the grander scheme of nature's cycle as made evident in the winter landscape. But this reality is by no means restricted to the bosom and valleys of Mother Jord, or Frigga if you prefer. Wherefore metaphor is in regard, we too have an opportunity to burn, or bury non-conducive and pernicious habits. You know, those less than admirable qualities which have long since overstayed their visas as they had existed in our past lives, prior to our walking the Northern Road. Yes, kinsmen and kinswomen, this is an eventful time in which we may slay those ignoble character flaws which have been detrimental to our past on both a personal level as well as the damning effects which they have had on our families, our faith and our folk community. This is a chance to shed the fetters of self accepted weakness and thralldom from our lives and leave them as burnt offerings upon the alter of death! Vices, selfishness, lack of accountability and responsibility for faith and folk. Lack of genuine self respect and respect for the path we claim to tread and all that it encompasses. Yes my noble kin, true freedom begins in the pyre's flames where old destructive habits are turned to ash and self liberation is born anew from the flames of a new beginning! Beneath Sunna's radiant smile and victory giving light, we may discard the shackles of vice and self accepted weakness. What joys and pleasures we would seek in this life must be balanced and tempered by moderation if we would be counted among Master and Commander of our own lives. The very possibility for self transformation resides within the shadows of the season's death. And the Mother Night brings forth the new year and a fresh start to all.

It is debatable among the Northfolk as to what day the New Year actually begins. Some believe that it begins on the 20th of

Yule (Mother Night), while others believe it begins on the actual Yule (the Winter Solstice). And still others place the Northern New Year in the middle of Snowmoon (Jan). For us, within the HOLY NATION OF ODIN, so as to establish uniformity within our own liturgy and traditions, we shall fix the Nordic New Year of our calendar as occurring on the Mother Night, the 20th of Yule. It is the night which the Julleuchter is lit, symbolizing the need-fire and the glory of Sunna's light and power. The Mother Night also presages the longest night of the year which occurs on the Winter/Yule Solstice, which will also be the shortest day of the year. The 9th of Yule is a Day of Remembrance for Egil SkallaGrimsson. We may all take a cue from Egil's stalwart and unyielding disposition, in our own pursuits of fortitude, courage, self command and mastery over our actions and lives.

So then, where the Mother Night begins the Twelve days of Yule and the New Year for us, the Solstice itself heralds the rebirth of Sunna as she now begins to grow in strength. The majesty of her smile will produce a bounty of magnificent floral and fauna spectacular to behold at the Summer Finding as the Goddess Ostara spreads the joyous gift of renewal and rebirth all about Mother Jord! Ah, but that is yet another season to come. With our new year comes the fresh prospect to infuse our own lives, and the life of our faith and folk community with new strengths and joys. New freedoms and liberations from old and pernicious habits. Step out of the shades and shadows and into the glory of Sunna's victory giving light! For the wheel doth indeed, go 'round.

Perform a Yule Blót, enjoy good Kin's company and eat some pork. Meditate upon and Galdr these Runes: Thurisaz (ᚦ), Dagaz (ᛞ) and Sowilo (ᛋ). Begin your meditation of the past year on Mother night. Consider and swear oaths on Yule. Don't forget to set a place for the Ancestors.

I remain in service to the Gods and Folk of the HOLY NATION OF ODIN. Prosperous new Jera to you all. In Frith with thee...

Heil Odin!

"Life does not render unto any man, greatness. A man's own noble character does."

-- Dr. Casper Odinson Cröwell, Ph.D.

HOF SERVICE for Snowmoon

FRATERNAL SOLIDARITY

Brother! Sister! Kinfolk! What do they all share in the way of commonality? Sadly so, it is a rather debased distinction. One which entails, more oft than not these days, a hollow or empty sentiment attached to the very definition which encompasses such nouns.

It is often cited that one may not choose one's family. Such is the decree of the Norns (Fates). And still, we would fight for and defend those less than desirable, or worthy family members wherefore the need arises. Though were they no Kin relation, we'd neither mingle, nor converse with their ilk! Albeit, born of a sense of duty to Kin, for reasons some may neither fathom, nor discern with ease, if indeed at all, we are compelled to do what we must.

Yet, in this Wolf Age in which we live, so many elect to enter into the bonds of Blood Siblinghood and Kinship, of their own free will, though it seems these days, seldom will so many honor those sacred bonds of oathed allegiance! Why is that? More so, one has elected to enter into a family relationship of one's free will (family by choice), though one may very well abandon said relation in difficult, or unfashionable times. Why and how does this occur? Why it occurs is no mystery at all. In fact, the reason "WHY", is the same reason why that is consistent wherefore other social maladies of the day occur. Lack of sacredness assigned to the achievements we strive for and attain. To place this in its proper context we must revisit the nobler and honorable eras of our ancestors whom placed the greatest degree of pride, duty and honor upon Kinships oathed freely and the loyalty attached thereto. For to fall short of the freely oathed Kinship arrangement was not only a matter of shame and dishonor to the one whom desecrated such sacred bonds sworn before our Gods, but it also brought to bear the stigma of shame and dishonor to the oath breaker's entire blood family as well. Seeing how the two most common reasons for forging oathed Kinships in days of auld, were to either create a stronger Clan/Family to Clan/Family alliance to stave off war/aggression, end a feud, or prepare stronger defenses for war, or to enter into the sacred bonds of brotherhood among war bands for those about to go a Viking. One may easily descry, and thereafter argue that it was not merely prudent to enter into such compacts of Kinship, it was more oft than not, an outright matter of sheer survival!

While I certainly would not debate thus, I must assert and submit for your consideration the following query: Is the survival of both our faith and folk not of paramount importance today? Does not our future hang upon such acts of honoring the bonds of oathed and freely entered Kinship in an effort to re-establish a sacred order of fraternal solidarity?

As to the "HOW", it occurred, well that is easily illustrated as well. We live in an environment which purposely creates dissension among ourselves so as to enable those whom promote thus to drive the many wedges between us necessary to achieve the divide and conquer tactics which they employ towards the end of succeeding at their mission goal - Destroy any fraternal solidarity wherever it exists in order to more readily maintain control of the overall population via the vehicle of disunity.

Today's society seeks the very same and employs the same techniques of divide and conquer in a concerted effort at so many levels in order to create and promote an overwhelming state of consumerism. Faith/Folk identities and the solidarity attached to them, resplendent with honor integrity and self respect are all antithesis to both, the prison systems which further promote decadence, moral abandonment and lack of self respect, lack of respect for faith, folk and fraternity as well as bonds of honor, integrity and solidarity which will ultimately contribute to our Faith/Folk community, and the World Trade Organization -"New World Order", which seeks to rob all peoples of their indigenous folk identities and the sense of sacred respect, responsibility and loyalty to them in a collective effort to hawk their wares and get richer at the expense of any legitimate honor, spirituality and morality in concert with virtue.

I realize that for some of our readers this may be a bit much. But I can assure you that it's all too real. Not because I say so, but because the facts say so! Research it all for yourselves and ye shall see.

Fraternal solidarity (True Brotherhood & Sisterhood) will prevent further moral and social breakdown which we as a folk have

thus far suffered. Especially wherefore lack of folk unity is in regards. As individuals, no matter how equipped and prepared we are, we are weak before our collective adversaries/foes. But where genuine solidarity is established and fiercely promoted and defended... We may wend further down the Northern Road toward victory. It is not guaranteed, this victory we seek on behalf of our faith and folk. But it is an honest effort at achieving it. This much I am certain of; without the effort and fraternal solidarity we are destined to perish, both faith and folk!
I implore you all to establish the sacred bonds of Kinship amongst ourselves in an effort to create a Tribe of fraternal solidarity and defend it thereafter with the viciousness of the Wolf Pack and without remorse.

Seek communion with Allfather Odin, Allmother Frigga, Tyr and Heimdall as the very progenitor and protectors of sacred Kin and Kith and loyalty thereto.

Compose and/or perform a Blót to our Ancestors and Descendants yet to be, and oath to them that you shall protect, defend and advance our beloved Faith and Folk!

Meditate upon and Galdr these Runes:
Othala (ᛟ), Laguz (ᛚ) and Elhaz (ᛉ).

In Frith with and in service to thee...

"Call no man happy until he is dead."
- Herodotus, from the Histories

HOF SERVICE for Snowmoon

MODERN HEATHENRY AND THE NORTHERN TRADITION

Merriam-Webster defines a heathen as: 1. an unconverted member of a people or nation that does not acknowledge the God of the Bible. Thes: Pre-monotheistic. Syn: Pagan, pantheistic. Ant: monotheistic.

Today, Heathenism/Paganism is well on its way to re-asserting itself in the mainstream communities of post modern society. Gone are the days of yore in the late 1960's and early 1970's when the only places we thrived were in the wishful hearts and minds of the cultnics and the new age, / head shops which they frequented. Indeed, today, true to evolution, our religion has ascended beyond the "One-size fits all" box our holy faith once fit so neatly into!

When fine folks like the late Else Christiansen, (my own mentor and many others as well) and Steve McNallen of the Ásatrú Folk Assembly began to sound the Gjallarhorn and alert our folk to the great Re-awakening (as it has since come to be called) in those early days of the 1970's, those whom adhered to what we call today; "Odinism", merely set about referring to our faith as the "Northern Tradition", as it hails from the North of Europe and the folk which inhabited the regions of North and Western Europe. But, the Northern Tradition, as it were, is not the same generic spiritual philosophy á la Viking influence today that it was some forty plus years ago. In fact, quite the contrary!

While some in our Faith and Folk community would disagree, albeit without merit, nor validity, there are several denominations of our faith within the Northern Tradition. Though, since we are a faith absent a centralized system, most adopt the local flavor and customs of the Temple, Hof, Church, Kindred, Garth, Individual, etc., from which they were introduced to our faith and as the years progress and they with our faith over those years, folk will come to stubbornly believe that the names, words, teachings, pronunciations, etc., are the only correct one associated with our faith. In fact, outside of the obvious common denominators, e.g. our Gods and Goddesses, Sagas, Myths and shared heritage, folk whom have followed our ancient ways with one Kindred would most likely find many foreign elements to what another Kindred calls the same faith. And there is a simple answer for why that is - Different denominations. That's right Folks. So many folk believe that Odinism/Wotanism and Asatrú are one in the same, though Kinsman 'One' may not easily descry what Kinsman 'Two' is calling the same spiritual path. I've been an Odinist/Wotanist for thirty-nine years now, and folks, I've got to tell you that Odinison/Wotanism and Asatrú are Not the same path! Not at all! Odinism/Wotanism is a path akin to the path of Asatrú. While the latter literally means to be "True to the Ǽsir, or Old Gods" (Which also includes the Vanir today), its adherents seek to embrace and honor equally, all of the Gods of the Ǽsir and Vanir. While adherents of the former seek to honor and embrace the All-Father Odin first and foremost and then the Gods of the Ǽsir and Vanir thereafter. While all are honored, Odin rules the roost where the Odinist/Wotanist is concerned. Odinist/Wotanists will subject themselves to strict regimens of physical and psychological ordeals, rites and self disciplinary practices. They tend to be very structured and some would even say, fanatical at times. They forfeit their voices with vows of silence which have lasted over a month at a time and fasted up to nine days at a time. There are Vanatrúar whom are devoted to the Vanir (Earth Gods). Theods, which subscribe to an Anglo-Saxton variation, Irminists, whom subscribe to a German variation. There are Thorists, Tyrists, and Freyans all devoted to their respective deities, and there are lesser known denominations. And while it is of course, an excellent opportunity to reach out and serve a wider range of our folk in concert with the evolutionary nature of our Norse-Teutonic Heathen religious community, it should not be a source of consternation and division within our Faith/Folk community! But the reality is, that is what occurs. Certain denominations assume an elitist attitude and thereafter disregard the significance and import of all others as if they matter little, if at all. Have we learned nothing at all form the monotheistic religions with their bitter divisions and "un" – Holy wars?

We must strive for "Pan-Folkism and Pan Heathenism" unity and solidarity within our faith/folk community. We must seek to edify each other, not belittle, lest we fall prey to the new wave of Christian fundamentalists and their unjust attacks on Heathenism/Paganism. A folk and its faith will thrive and advance only as long as their actions remain conducive and beneficial to all members of said community whom endeavor to affect a healthy and positive attitude towards those ends of a united faith/folk community.

Let the posers and pretenders dissent into the ranks of Loki until they sever the bonds which tie them to us. It is, after all, the teaching of Heimdall that the unworthy always exclude themselves. Let the rest of us bestow honor upon our sacred Gods, ancestors and descendants yet unborn… Let us bring honor to ourselves by edifying one another and uniting our faith/folk community. Choose to say "Yes" to pan-folkism within our faith/folk community.

The Sons of Odin, 1519 – Vinland Kindred will neither condone, nor contribute to any of the chaos, or bigotry towards other good folk, or denominations within our own community. We must hold ourselves to a higher standard than those whom have gone before us. We must hold ourselves accountable to our Noble virtues and edicts of honor. For without that we truly have naught!

Individual dignity begins with an individual's accountability for his/her actions, or lack thereof. When we espouse such an attitude as individuals our faith/folk community advances collectively and therein lies not only the dignity of folk and faith, albeit the very majesty some of our later ancestors either once forfeited, or outright had taken away form them by the Church in Rome! Point Blank!!!

Let us "All" cease playing the 'Pass the Blame' games with our folk, especially due to the differences in the way we each approach practicing our sacred Northern Tradition. Let us edify each other and celebrate the different denominations within our faith/folk community. Let us protect and advance what we hold sacred today, as our fathers' fathers did before us and we too shall afford our descendants the same opportunity to do so. Just like our folk wrote about over forty years ago, when they spoke so lovingly about our future generations and their right to inherit our faith and our duty to protect and defend them.

Seldom does any living entity retain its core simplicity as it evolves, and our faith is no exception to that rule. Our faith/folk community assumes the same, erroneous and self serving burdens which the monotheistic religious communities have suffered from over the past two millennia. It's quite the contrary. We have it at our collective disposal to employ the lessons of the past and apply them to our own concerns today as the circumstances present themselves.

And, we must take heed to and apply the lessons and examples of Asa-Tyr if we are to achieve a comfortable success in the future. We've all seen success claim many casualties. This needn't' be the instance at all. Evolution is all about transformations and forward progress, as is it undisputedly the truest way of All-Father Odin. Asa-Tyr inserted his hand in the gaping jaws of the vicious Fenris wolf so that he could be bound. Knowing all too well the price he'd have to pay. He had accepted the voluntary loss of his hand in a noble effort to protect and advance both the Gods in Asgard and our folk on Midgard. Now then, who among our leaders will act in a valiant way, like a God! And, do the right and honorable thing for the good of us all? I will and I implore all others to do the same, lest we suffer the wolf's voracious appetite on the morrow's tide. For tomorrow is too late. We must act now, today with haste to heal our community and we must achieve this victory in spirit of protecting and advancing Family, Faith and Folk.

Hail the holy Ǽsir and Vanir… Hail All-Father Odin!!! (Perform Tyr Blót and reflect upon duty and service to faith and folk.)

Runes for meditation are: ᛏ ᚨ ᛋ.

I remain in service to the the Gods and folk of the Holy Nation of Odin.

"Be naught a today without a tomorrow on the horizon, lest you perish as yesterday's forgotten Kin.."

-- Casper Odinson Cröwell, Ph.D., DD

HOF SERVICE for Snowmoon

HONOR: THE AGELESS VIRTUE

While the Odinist New Year began on the Mother Night (Dec. 20th), we still find ourselves, for all practical purposes, moving in the time flow of the Current/Common Era wherefore mainstream calendars and schedules are in regard. As such, the first day of Snowmoon / January began with what may at first observation, seem to be some odd little ritual. Of course I'm alluding to the New Year's Resolution. Actually, this ritual begins prior to the new year and in many instances, is already being broken by New Year's Day. Furthermore, upon closer inspection, one may descry that the very origin of this ritual is neither odd nor little!

For you see, this ritual has its roots entrenched in the customs of the culture of the Aryan Tribes. More pointedly, the Odinist Faith as it were! Oh sure, some tribes in different geographical locations about the European continent may have varied as to which day this had occurred, for instance; on the Mother Night, or on the Solstice, or on the Twelfth Night, but it most certainly occurred never the less among our ancestors. At some point during the Yule Tide (the Twelve Days of Yule Dec. 20th to the 31st), sacred oaths were sworn in grand fashion. Before the assembled Kin and Kith, Norse-Teutonic warriors would boast, sometimes arrogantly so, about what they intended to do in the coming year. These oaths were sworn upon the sacred boar/hog/pig at this particular time of the year, albeit I'm sure the usual Oath Rings, Thor's Hammers and Spear tips were employed just the same.

What is of key significance thereafter is that oaths were not broken!!! It did not matter that Svein was three sheets to the wind when he swore to go a-viking in Angle Land (England) in the spring tide, or Rolf swore to personally construct two thirds of the newly needed rampart with his own two hands. These boasts were fulfilled or the oath maker himself had perished in his honorable and noble efforts to fulfill them, lest his Kinfolk bear the burden of being related to an oath breaker! Our Lore and Sagas are filled with such accounts as mentioned above.

So then, how did we arrive at such a place in time where the descendants the Aryan Tribes could swear such honorable oaths and later justify why they are reneging on them? What shame do such folk bestow upon the memory of our majestic Gods and ancestors??? Surely I could lay it all out for you if I had both time and space to facilitate such. Alas, thus would exceed my allotted space. What's more is that it is not nearly as important as to how we have arrived at such a place, but rather what we may do about it. The beautiful thing about Honor is that it does not matter what you did yesterday, so-to-speak. But what you elect to do today and tomorrow! This does not mean to infer that one may exist within the parameters of odious and lecherous behavior and get right tomorrow only to repeat the cycle. Not at all! What it does mean is that we are all prone to committing errors as part of the human condition. If some of those errors mean that no matter what, you will not find favor again among old comrades, then so be it. But you still may elect to act in an honorable fashion for yourself and those to whom you have ties and liaisons with.

It is never too late to live honorably or to begin to honor old oaths that you once swore and then perhaps, later swore off. Your Ørlög and that of your Kin and Kith will always be tied to your oaths and actions, for better or worse.

Of course, a great deal of our Folk, do honor their oaths and suffer great consequences for it sometimes. But the rewards associated with the integrity of genuine honor will always serve as salve for the wounds.

Remember this; there is no shame in admitting to erroneous ways. The true shame arrives only when we have acknowledged such pernicious ways and yet we elect to abide by such ways rather than correct them.

Let this be the year that we all make a full return to the ways of our ancestors...The way of HONOR. Let today be that day when others admire or despise us for living Trú!

The power is ours alone to succeed or fail. The honor or shame is our descendants to inherit.

Runes to meditate upon & Galdr are:

Fehu (ᚠ) Uruz (ᚢ) Thurisaz (ᚦ)

Heil Allfather Odin and Heil the truly Noble Folk in his venerable name!!! I remain yours in Frith, Service and Fraternal Solidarity.

"What for, this honor, if for only a fleeting moment?" queried the young squire.
"Then for naught else but a brief moment, was I a God!" replied the Knight."

- Dr. Casper Odinson Cröwell, 1519-CCG

"ANY RELIGION OR TEACHING WHICH DENIES THE NATURAL LAWS OF THE UNIVERSE IS FALSE."

-- the 1st Precept, David Lane

HOF SERVICE for Horning

CONCERNING TOLERANCE

If I were to posit the word "Tolerance", to say, twelve individuals, I'd evoke twelve independent conceptions of the quality of the very nature, if not the definition of tolerance. Each individual would most likely assume a line of association to the word in concert with what is deeply seeded within the very recess of their subconscious reflections. The conclusions which they would arrive at would therefore be an equation or sum of repressed feelings of guilt wherefore a past experience which found that individual lacking in tolerance once occurred and now lives on in some far forgotten corridor of their subconscious, only now surfacing once more at the behest of the word tolerance which has triggered the memory attached thereto.

It is human nature, this quality of intolerance and it must be overcome by a willingness, or desire to arrive at a personal compromise if it is to occur at all. We of the Northern Heathen Traditions, whom find ourselves incarcerated, are generally an intolerant lot to say the least. And while the morally bankrupt and socially ill environments in which we are housed do indeed contribute largely to intolerant attitudes, it most certainly is neither the predominant, nor underlying factor which is responsible for lacking the quality in character of tolerance. That very culprit would be our own lack of desire to effect a positive alteration in our individual program.

Too often have I been privy to a rather sad display of some Kinsman being discounted, shunned, or even outright ostracized as opposed to being embraced by the folk of our noble faith, merely due to said individual not fitting into our ideal mold! I myself must confess that I too have been guilty of this very crime, albeit, not in many years, thankfully so.

If we espouse this negative attitude of intolerance while we are incarcerated, several negative factors will most certainly occur as a direct result thereof including but not limited to; We cut off potentially good folk from our/their indigenous Gods/Faith, we carry this negative attitude back to the free world where it continues to influence one's perspective on a myriad of accounts and, well, I could catalog a plethora of fallout which of course, far exceeds the scope and space of allotment in concert with this service. Suffice it to say, the chief agent of detriment is that our faith/folk community, both within and without the collective prison system, suffers the ramifications and the consequences attached thereto, not to mention the stigmatism our faith is branded with! As it were, we find ourselves constantly on the defensive and having to explain our faith to the multitude of prison administrators whom we must endeavor to convince they should afford us the deference of tolerance toward our faith which is more oft than not labeled racist! In addition, it leaves our free world folk in an uncomfortable time and energy consuming position of having to explain to their friends, family and employers why they subscribe to a prison religion which exhibits racist concepts? This of course is a stigmatism which we must work to shed and ascend above. Such will always require the tolerance and open minds of the skeptics. And yet, we would deny tolerance to our own folk and others whom are deserving of it? This train of thought is rather ironic and perverse, wouldn't you say?

Both Tyr and Forseti would have quite a bit to say about this I believe… For, in justice one may always find tolerance in residence. But injustice will always find tolerance tardy if not altogether absent!

As we prepare to celebrate the feast of Vali, let us not forget that Vali's very mission was to avenge the death of his gracious and bright brother, Baldur. Let us then consider the goodness and benevolence of Baldur whenever we revisit the word, tolerance. And let us honor both Baldur and Vali, let us be worthy of their divine union with us. Intolerance resides in the camp of Hodur (the blind, dark and negative), let us elect to edify and emulate the righteousness and goodness of both Baldur and Vali (light, positive nature and progress). And let us prosper as a Faith/Folk community on a continuum and as a whole.

(Perform a Baldur Blót and meditate upon good will and tolerance towards Trú folk in the spirit of maintaining Frith.)[3]

Runes for meditation are: ᚹ, ᚾ, ᛋ, ᛊ and ᛏ.

3 Author's Footnote: This essay should not be employeed erroneously to embrace Nithlings in an effort to justify incorrect actions/deeds as an act of tolerance.

Let us seek advancement and transformation in our own noble efforts.

"Fear naught the coming darkness, nor the voice within, let the righteous light of noble deed and the order of self discipline keep the dark agents of chaos at bay."-- Casper Odinson Cröwell, Ph.DD.

"Tolerant men are never stupid... And stupid men are never tolerant."

– An ancient proverb

HOF SERVICE for Horning

ODINISM AND PRAYER

Any folk among us who may lay claim to a history, say, a decade, or longer within the Odinist, or Ásatrú community may be wondering about the title of this Hof Service to some end. I am of course referring to the "prayer" part, that is. For nearly all of our community produced literature has sought to deter the strong willed Northman/woman from all things in concert with the monotheistic faiths in an honest effort to re-establish the faith of our fathers' fathers, hence, eradication of prayer has been a component included within the scope of that noble effort. However noble the intention was, it was erroneous in my opinion and additionally so, one which continues to rob our faith today of a measure of its sacredness and majesty.

First let me assert that in the nearly three decades which I've been an Odinist, I have always prayed! In fact, no less than three times a day for over the past fifteen years now. Upon waking, midday and just prior to bed each evening. Now before folks get all sideways in their thoughts regarding prayer, please allow me the latitude to allay any preconceived misconceptions which you may harbor. Please consider the following facts as they both exist and apply. A great deal of the Christian faith's rituals was in fact usurped from our ancestral faith in an effort to convert folk by incorporating the very rituals and traditions which they were accustomed to. Eventually they morphed into the more recognizable rites of the Christian faiths which we are familiar with today, albeit, they have their rudimentary foundation in the faiths of our forefathers.

Next, and equally as important, I'm not referring to prayer on bent knee, or in the form of begging for favors from Allfather Odin, or any of our beloved Gods/Goddesses... Not even close! What I am suggesting is that we restore sacredness to our beloved faith by openly re-embracing prayer just as our ancestors surly did. Yes, you read correctly! I said our ancestors did. Just think about it for a moment. Do you really think that Herman (Arminius) did not go into the sacred forest of the Teutons (Teutoburgerwald) and talk openly, or silently to Odin prior to launching his assault against Varus' Three legions? Or what about Ragnar Hairy Breeks, do you suppose that he never went to a natural spring, or sacred grove to speak with his God, Odin? Lore accounts have him calling out to Odin during his death song. Is that not prayer? What about Egil and Eirik the Red? Do you suppose that they never called out to Odin and Thor? Of course they did! What about today? Do you suppose Kinfolk in say, Wyoming, have not spoken aloud to our Gods while on, or around the Grand Teton Mountains, or any of its numerous meadows, valleys, or forests?

I've gone up on Mt. San Jacinto, over looking Palm Springs, California, on so many occasions just to openly commune/pray to our beloved Gods, especially Allfather Odin. I've done several rites upon that mountain. I did a Land Taking Rite whereby I named the site -"Wotan's Platz" (Odin's Place). I held this place to be so truly sacred, that I had only ever taken two others up there with me. I've done three day Utisétas up there twice, with positive results. I've had others request that I take them with me, but I ignored their protests as I felt that they were not worthy enough yet to set foot upon such holy ground. Two even went hiking all over the suspected area in search of the sacred site, but to no avail, (smile).

I am not the first to write about the place and validity of prayer within the Northern Faith. In 1994 CE Maddy Hutter and Stephen A. McNallen, wrote about it in the booklet which they composed entitled; "A Book of Uncommon Prayers". I am not certain as to whether or not the booklet is still available. You may elect to contact the Ásatrú Folk Assembly, regarding thus if you are interested.

Prayer is merely a form of communing with that which is divine, our Gods, Ancestors, the natural and unsullied environment in its many manifestations which reflect and echo the very faces and voices of our beloved Gods! Why, Blót itself is a form of prayer where we speak openly to our Gods... Must we restrict this sacred affair to only official Blótar? I think not.

I don't suggest that anyone do anything which they may be uncomfortable with. Though, it certainly escapes my comprehension as to how anyone could be uncomfortable speaking to their Gods. Just as their ancestors most assuredly did in locales ranging from mountain tops to valley floors. From meadows and sacred groves, to shorelines by the fjords.

I had previously asserted in this Hof Service, I pray no less than three times per day to our Gods, though mostly to Odin. Why three times? Three is a sacred number to all heathens/pagans and it is of course very Odinic in nature. I face the North, the direction of the Odal/Othal lands from which our Ancestors come and where our Gods and Faith first took root and spread forth throughout Midgard, wherever our folk may be found. Next - I Hammersign myself. Though, I must concede that my own Hammersign varies a degree from the traditional one. I go Odin, Baldur Freya and Thor. Why do I replace Frey with Freya? Because I find it erroneous that our faith speaks of such respect for our Goddesses and women folk with equality, and yet not one Goddess is named in our Hammersign blessing, the most recognized rite of reestablished Northern Religion. Hence, I have done something about it for the past twenty years or better now... I replace Frey with Freya and I don't think he minds at all. I certainly afford him his due!

Next, I assume the Irminsul Statha/Stada: (ᛘ / ᛘ) turning myself into the mighty world pillar and I speak my mind for a few moments. Once I've finished, I Hammersign myself and go on about my business. Like I said, I do this upon waking, some point during the course of the day and just prior to retiring for the evening. The benefits are that it keeps me connected to my Gods throughout the breadth of the day and I usually have insightful dreams about our Gods in some context, or another, at night. In addition, it is my way of restoring a sacred respect for the Mannaz (ᛗ) union between myself and Odin in an effort to exhibit that I never take him, or the Gods and their gifts, for granted. I also meditate while facing North.

Follow your hearts, remain Trú to yourselves and to our Gods. This is the secret to a fulfilled and spiritually prosperous life. Live an enriched life with our Gods as your compass, and just as a compass only works when you employ its Rede, so it is true of our Gods.

Perform a Blót to your preferred God(s), or Goddess(es). Pray as oft to them as you desire. Meditate upon and Galdr these Runes; Mannaz (ᛗ), Ansuz (ᚨ) and Gebo (ᚷ). I remain in Frith with and in service to thee.

"Man is what he honors."
- An Odinist proverb

HOF SERVICE for Lenting (Ostara, Spring Equinox)

ADDICTIVE PERSONALITY

When one hears the phrase; 'addictive behavior', one's mind most likely conjures the notion of an individual who suffers from an addiction to some form of narcotics, chiefly speaking, and then perhaps one whom suffers a penchant for gambling, overeating, consuming alcohol, etc., thereafter. And while I surmise that this would probably be the overwhelming consensus of society, and it would be by far and large, correct, it most certainly would not encompass the breadth of addictive personality in its entirety, or those whom suffer the effects thereof.

Addictive personalities and behavior are a component of human nature which the vast majority of us succumb to, to one degree or another, and most would vehemently deny this. But any honest self examination would reveal the reality of the matter.

Most addictions exist in such a minute form and state of socially acceptable normal behavior so that few laymen readily recognize them as such. But upon closer scrutiny, one may begin to descry several identifiable characteristics which fit easily into the criteria of addictive behavior and personalities. To illustrate my study of the human condition and bring my point to bear regarding this service, I direct your attention to three certain types of addictive personalities. The first type (Type A) of people demonstrates a propensity for seeking out and forging detrimental relationships and friendships. Others of Type A are attracted to and gravitate towards high drama and controversial social circles. Type A is therefore addicted to crisis, whether it is in the capacity of the participant or the spectator. The second type (Type B) of people exhibit an authority or elitist attitude and usually suffers from superiority complex in concert with said attitude. Type B therefore may suffer an addiction to ego while the split side of Type B is those whom suffer from inferiority and low self esteem complex, it's the same addiction. Finally, wherefore this illustration is in regard, there is Type C. Type C people exhibit impulsive behavior and thrive on the presence of danger and threatening circumstances and the adrenalin rush which such behavior produces.

Type C people are addicted to uncertainty. The myriad of addictions are too numerous to catalog here, obviously, in addition to the obvious ones: drugs, food, alcohol, pornography and gambling. What is of importance here is that we endeavor to recognize what constitutes defective, demeaning and destructive behavior associated with addictive personality disorders. Once we have identified these characteristics, we embark upon a journey contrary to the negative behavior which we have espoused for so long; both to the detriment of ourselves and our loved ones and to a wider scope, our faith/folk community at large.

Lenting (March) is the season tide of the Spring Equinox and the Goddess of the season of renewal, rebirth and regeneration, "Ostara." Fresh starts abound during this bountiful time of rejuvenation which expresses itself most visibly in nature as the fertile fields of Mother Jord (Earth) explode in a riot of magnificent and brilliant colors! Such reminders of new life are Ostara's way of gently reminding us of her glorious gift to and within each of us... The ability to discard and shed the dead, negative, tired, obsolete and detrimental factors in our own nature, and replace them with the new, fresh, healthy and conducive positives which exclaim; "I say yes to life!"

By adopting such a healthy attitude, we demonstrate our appreciation and gratitude to the Goddess of renewal, her joyous season and most significantly, we alter poor judgment and behavior and replace it with psychological, emotional and spiritual perspectives which are ad rem to our state of sound mental health and well being. This will not only enrich our own personal lives, but also the lives of those entwined with us, in the immediate sense in addition to the entire faith/folk community in the grander scheme of prosperity and spiritual advancement.

May the holy Goddesses, Ostara, Eir, Frigga and Freya bless you all!

(Perform a Blót to Ostara, or Frigga and the Summer Finding, and meditate) (upon positive alterations, renewals and rebirths in the self.)

[Runes to meditate upon are: (ᛒ), (ᛗ), (ᚷ), (ᚹ) and (ᛋ).

I remain in service to the Gods and Folk of the Holy Nation of Odin. In Frith with thee always.

"Mastery of the healthy self requires compatibility between one's virtues and one's actions.
Whereby it is the natural inclination of strength to despise weakness, one must learn to evict that which is incompatible with the mastery of the self."
-- Dr. Casper Odinson Cröwell, Ph.D., D.D.

HOF SERVICE for Lenting (Ostara – Spring Equinox)

ZEAL vs. COMPLACENCY

Merriam-Webster defines 'Zeal' as - a noun: Eager and ardent interest in the pursuit of something; Fervor. Synonym: "Fire in the belly". Antonym: Complacency.

As a religion we are posed with many facets which, initially may have served a greater purpose in the grander scheme of reawakening our folk to the Northern Faiths, since the late 1960's CE.

However, today as we seek to assert our innate right to pursue our indigenous Northern Faith along side of the mainstream and monotheistic faiths, some of these facets have morphed into maladies which pose a genuine threat to the secure existence and advancement of Odinism in much the same manner as a boat at anchor in the bay, which will, without a doubt, incur the storm's fury, while the other boats, free of such a malady, may put out to sea in an effort to escape the storm, save themselves and survive. Well folks, the storms are coming and we must pull up anchor and put to sea if we would see Sunna's smile on the new 'morrow!

For one thing, at the risk of sounding harsh, Viking period dress and re-enactment sectors of our faith community undoubtedly contributed greatly to the current Northern Renaissance we all enjoy, albeit, such folk in our collective faith community barely constitute a cult. So many more of our searching folk would not pass us by as a faith, if we only offered them an alternative to the monotheistic faiths in the same contemporary context.

Next, we require a united front of Northern solidarity, albeit, one which acknowledges and accepts the fact that there are several different denominations of the Northern Faith, not merely one with several names!

We need to be proud, and openly so, about who we are as a faith and folk, as opposed to constantly offering up apologies and politically correct explanations to outsiders! I most certainly can grasp the need for valid public relations, regarding our faith within the greater mainstream community at large. But that must never entail apologizing for our proud heritage and natural desire to survive as both a folk and a race. Nor must we embrace any ideology which is politically correct in order to achieve some sort of uneasy compliance with a morally ill society.

Here then is the reality at point blank range:

As a Faith and Folk, Zealousness equals endurance and progress. Complacency equals stagnation and inevitable demise.

It is truly that simple. Holy wars have been waged by zealots for as long as man has inhabited Midgard. Those strong enough and serious enough to do what must be done, they live on to continue the fight until they either attain victory, or perish in their noble efforts to do so. But those unwilling to do so are just enslaved until they simply cease to be! I am not inciting some fanatical Holy war, nor am I insinuating such is necessary at this juncture. I am saying that if Odinism is not holy enough for you to do, without remorse, what the circumstances of history may one day warrant must be done, then this religion, along with its holy Gods, does not belong to you! You have no right to anything which you are not willing to fight to the end for. If this seems extreme and militant, so be it. Only the child like mind believes that the world may continue on in its present social course when so much immorality and wanton disregard for our natural environment is rampant. The child like minds and arrogant rulers of today, that is.

As the laws of natural order once set the cadence and reigned supreme, so too shall they once again. And at such time in the epochs of humanity, no paper decree of constitution will wield any weight, or credibility. Those strong enough, whom maintain a zealous posture in their indigenous faith and defend the sacredness of that which they hold to be divine, those whom live in concert with the laws of natural order will not only survive, they will thrive as once before, long ago before our ancestors forfeited what we should have inherited, but must now fight for on a continuum, wherefore parity with others is in regards.

Is zeal tantamount to militancy? Perhaps. But any way one may descry it, zeal equals survival and we as a faith need to concern ourselves with that in an immediate sense. And once we secure this, then and only then may we surmount progress and advance. We must rid ourselves of ill character traits and bad habits which we have accepted as normal for far too long now! We must invoke the courage of Tyr in order to alter the way that we selfishly think in terms of ourselves as 'individuals', as opposed to as a community of faith minded folk!

We must eradicate weakness wherever we find it within our character make up and replace it with strength and zealousness if ever we are to regain victory over the state of complacency which once robbed our ancestors of our beloved faith and Gods, and still continues to do so with the overwhelming majority of our people, today!

The answer lies in assuming a zealous attitude wherein redefining ourselves in the noble and honorable attributes of our holy Gods are in regards. May Allfather, Victory bringer, smile on us all in our noble endeavor toward thus.

Perform a Blót to Odin and Tyr. Meditate upon and Galdr these Runes: Tiwaz (ᛏ), Eihwaz (ᛇ) and Sowilo (ᛊ).

Don't forget to perform an Ostara Blót during the summer finding to celebrate the Spring tide, the season of renewal and rebirth. Runes to meditate and Galdr upon: Berkano (ᛒ), Ingwaz (ᛜ), and Fehu (ᚠ).

Ves Heil, ok Fara meth Odin! I remain in Frith with and in service to thee.

"Only your Kith, or Kin may betray you. From your foes you expect it!"

- Dr. Casper Odinson Cröwell, Ph.D., DD

HOF SERVICE for Ostara

TAMING THE EGO

Oft I am echoed by my Apprentices and other well seated Gothar whom once were my Apprentices, much in the same fashion a musician may experience feedback from his amplifiers, thereby informing him to adjust his output. Hearing those I counsel, echo my teachings affords me the opportunity to adjust my own output, if you will.

For some years now, I have emphasized the need and desirability to slay one's ego in concert with achieving any meaningful progress. I lived by this very rule myself. However, as I listened with great interest one day not too long ago, to another Gothi and Kinsman of mine (who was once my Apprentice) echo my hero's journey metaphor regarding slaying the ego in order to advance and ascend to the next level of initiation. I was both proud of his teaching mannerism and his point hitting home with the neophyte. More so, this other Gothi had taught me something when he echoed my own teaching, albeit unbeknownst to him.

It seems that the very reverberations of my lesson to him had penetrated deeply within my subconscious, which would, more than a week later, surface in my own meditations and thereafter inform me of the inadequacy of my earlier teaching; thus warranting some adjusting. Feedback indeed.

Though I had always stressed the difference between the positive and negative ego, I had never the less advised, and staunchly so, the suppression of the ego in order to advance upon our Northern path. This would be an oxymoron wherefore I teach these same men in esoteric studies-the need to embrace the dark as well the light if they would come to know and understand the balance in all things. For does not the ego exist in both, the shades and the realm of light? Indeed it does.

In light of the afore stated, I am now compelled to adjust my earlier teaching to encompass the positive ego and the negative ego as two separate egos in relationship to the self in its entirety as the id. In asserting thus, I must now advise that while I continue to advocate the identification and suppression of the negative ego as a means of procuring progress and advancement, I would be remiss if I omitted to equally assert the validity of the positive ego and the role it assumes as the id in aiding in our subjective, evolutionary transformation on a continuum. Be it not for me to leave the matter at bay in the shallows of assumption that it was to be an automatic understanding.

The inroads to the Northern path are manifold and oft fraught with uncertainty. It is neither my desire, nor inclination to contribute to the myriad of uncertainties at large within our path, wherefore your growth and endeavor toward ascension and self transformation are in regard. Quite the contrary. For it is my sincere desire to guide those worthy souls over the Isa Bridge and into the very clutches of mystery and the esoteric in an effort to assist the seeker in descrying that wisdom via the vehicle of experience.

I realize that this month's Hof service is more academic, or exoteric than my usual fare, albeit, I believe it will go a great distance towards taming the ego and thereafter afford one the means to achieve a greater degree of advancement in the deeper and esoteric studies of our noble path.

Certainly more than the usual food for thought, albeit well worth the contemplative journey during the tide of new beginnings and growth.

Perform an Odin's Blót and meditate upon the following runes: Ansuz(ᚨ), Dagaz (ᛞ), Eiwaz (ᛇ), Kenaz (ᚲ), Hagalaz (ᚺ), Nauthiz (ᚾ) and Mannaz (ᛗ).

I remain in service to the Gods and folk of the Holy Nation of Odin. In Frith with thee always.

"If struggle, controversy and hardship are absent from your life... Surely you must be dead inside and therefore, incapable of growth."
-- Dr. Casper Odinson Cröwell, Ph.D., DD

HOF SERVICE for Merrymoon

ALONG THE LINES OF HONOR

I'd like to bring to light the topic of Northern virtue. More pointedly so, honor and that of freedom as it applies to free will. We all have the right to this conceptual quality of free will, though it is not absent of one's duty, or responsibility to bear the joys of the rewards, or the burden of the consequences attached thereto!

Let us consider the following example. From the "Vinland Sagas: the Saga of the Greenlanders", we may glean an example of primacy wherefore Freydís Eiriksdottir is regarded. In short, Freydís embarked for Vinland with a pre-arranged compact in place with the brothers, Helgi and Finnbogi. Each party would have a host of thirty fighting men aboard their ships and each would have a half share in any/all profits from their journey. But from the out start, Freydís had violated the terms of their agreement by concealing five additional warriors, so that the brothers would not know of her oath breaking and deceit. Nor would this prove to be the extent of her treachery or its far reaching severity!

In short, Freydís would go on to orchestrate the malicious and unprovoked murder of both brothers and their entire host! Furthermore, when none of Freydís' men would kill the women in their host, Freydís herself grabbed hold of a battle ax belonging to one of her men, whereupon she commenced to killing all of their women folk herself. According to the Saga of the Greenlanders, the conclusion of this historical matter would infer that neither Freydís, nor her men were dealt any sanctioned penalties once back in Greenland for their unconscionable acts of depravity and greed. Though the mere ostracism she incurred socially, circa 1000 CE, would be total and complete and in fact, tantamount to life in prison today. For without social ties to the folk community, one would certainly have been as bad off as a leper. Especially considering both the harsh environment of Greenland and the high degree of value placed upon honor within their society. There are indeed accounts of both Father, Eirik the Red and brother, Leif disowning her and encouraging the whole of society to do the same!

This much is certain, Freydís was branded an oath breaker and wicked soul by all in her society for her odious deeds. The consequences of Freydís' actions far exceeded the scope of exercising one's free will.

Obviously, any among us now may be able to descry the aforementioned abuse of free will. Although, what may not so easily be descried by all whom peruse this, is that free will today must be accompanied by consequences as well. Though this seems a no brainier, I assure you that it is not! Just look around your self within our faith/folk community today and you may easily bear witness to any of several accounts of oath breaking being justified by the oath breakers among us. An oath breaker is just that! No exemptions, or excuses would be in the offing by our noble ancestors, and so none should be extended today by us, their descendants.

Where one has violated the compacts of an oath, let he or she assume the full weight of accountability for thus, and endeavor to consider future oaths at greater length prior to swearing any other oaths (so as to afford them the respect and power for which they were intended). To merely refuse to acknowledge one's short comings and failures will not erase them or make them disappear as though they had never occurred. No, it will only widen the chasm between those whom choose honor and those whom freely forfeit it. Redemption may only be had by one's own deeds and one's character adjustments and improvements.

Free will is a great Northern virtue, indeed. But it does not trump the Northern virtue of honor! Nor does it excuse any among us from accepting responsibility and accountability for the consequences which accompany the choices we make in the name of free will. And an oath broken is an oath cursed; "The curse upon himself made by the oath taker, should he break it, also belonged to the oath as such." (see Old Norse texts. Heidarviga Saga 33, Grettis Saga 72, and Gragas 114... Cited as, "Oath" pg. 238, Dictionary of Northern Mythology by R. Simek).

The power of an oath sworn should be every bit as irrevocable as the consequences attached thereto those whom freely embrace the known oath breaker! Never should any among us encourage, or embrace the caviler attitudes of those whom would seek to water down or dismiss the very integrity of noble character which our ancestors hath passed onto us! Honor is timeless and I for one would rather stand alone with my honor, in tact, against the raging tempest, than to forfeit my honor in exchange for the company of dishonorable or half honorable men whom will always fail to stand up to the fiercest storms! Let no man convince you that honor may be purchased with broken oaths!!!

Consider the gravity of free will and honor.

Perform a Blót to Var and Heimdall, the Patron Goddess and God of oaths and honor. For, it is they who punish the oath breakers and odious characters.

Meditate upon these runes:
Ansuz (ᚨ), Gebo (ᚷ), Tiwaz (ᛏ), Jera (ᛃ), Othala (ᛟ).

I remain in service to the Gods and folk of the Holy Nation of Odin. In Frith with thee always.

"Beware of them who favor only the sunshine's warmth.
For they hath grown complacent and their honor suffers wantonly for it."
-- Dr. Casper Odinson Cröwell, Ph.D., DD

HOF SERVICE for Merrymoon

TRÚ NORTH
A Case Against Universalism

Many are the spiritual paths/religions of today which are devoid of any legitimate history in which they may anchor their theology/philosophy. Indeed, the history of many non-Abrahamic faiths of today are little more than New Ageism albeit with a myriad of names attached thereto. Many of the so called traditions attached to such philosophies are merely borrowed or outright usurpations from a host of other spiritual paths/traditions. One instance in particular (out of many), are the Norse-Teutonic Runes in their many Futharks. Just how do Wiccans come to claim them as a traditional component of their path, when all, lore and mythology has the very discovery of the Runes inexorably seated in the Norse-Teutonic heathen way. It is Allfather Odin whom discovered the Runes while hanging upon the World Tree; "Yggdrasil". He thereafter gave the knowledge of them to the Gods and Aryan man.

Comprehension of their value was very basic and exoteric (academic) wherefore the uninitiated were / are in regard. Those who elect to abide by a lifetime of initiations in an effort to achieve self transformation on a continuum (Being and Becoming) are privy to the Runes' greater and esoteric (hidden) qualities and use.

Now, this is not an attack against Wiccans or any spiritual path, as it were. And certainly anyone can do as they wish wherefore religious/spiritual affairs are in concert with their own belief system so long as it is not imposed upon others with neither the desire nor penchant for such beliefs. I am merely seeking to set the stage, so-to-speak.

You see, new Ageism accounts for a great many maladies within otherwise, genuine ancient religious traditions. The concept of Universalism, among adherents of the Norse-Teutonic/Germanic Tradition is just such a malady of new Ageism. It is the Universalist camps among Vór Forn Siðr (our ancient religion) which like to claim that our ancestors were not so Folkish as we claim them to have been. I will be the first to concede that at some point in our lineage, a breakdown in the unsullied awareness of the blood did in fact occur. Only an uneducated idiot would debate what must be stipulated as fact. Be that as it may, there are equally in fact, hosts of

contributing factors for such a negative turn of events. Chief among them is the advent of Christianity with its questionable theology. But that is not the direction in which we are going with this work. What is, is whether our ancestors espoused a Folkish or Universalist attitude, wherefore community, mating, breeding and free association are all in regard.
You see, the Universalists are fond of pointing out what they posit as the mythological argument for universalism via the vehicle of miscegenation and more pointedly so, the mixed race parentage of Odin himself, and Thor and Thor's Kinder.

Mythologically speaking, I concur with the fact that Odin is born of a God (Father-Bor) and a giantess (Mother -Bestla), or that Thor is born of mixed elements (sky and earth), Odin (a God, his sire) and Jörd (a Giantess, his mother), and so on and so forth. However, what must equally be asserted as a matter of fact, albeit is always omitted by the Universalists, is that all of the racial elements in question in regards to this argument, are ALL of the same Norse-Teutonic (Aryan) racial phylum! That is to say, they are not mixtures of the blood in terms of other racial phyla (i.e. Asian, African, Latino, etc.), but rather, such an example in literal context of humanity and race, would be tantamount to a Celtic woman marrying a Teutonic man. It still occurs within the Aryan race. And since mythologies are by-products of cultures and heritages attached to specific racial groups, it would require a grand departure from any one race's mythology and entrance into another race's in order to achieve any cross phylum miscegenation. I know of no such conditions existing in any race's ancient mythology. It most certainly does not occur within the scope of Norse-Teutonic mythology!

Further more, I posit the argument against universalism in terms of Eddic lore as well, whereby Aryan man and woman, from Askr and Embla on down, are indeed descended from our Nordic Gods and rather specifically, Allfather Odin, at that. Therefore, our religion and our Gods are an ancestral inheritance of the blood, to wit the runic properties of Othala (ᛟ). Conversely, universalism seeks to incorporate a myriad of miscegenation.

Additionally, once again citing Eddic lore as a point of authority, we must consider the very words of Allfather Odin, himself...From the Hávamál, stanza 161;

I know a sixteenth if I want to have all
a cleaver woman's heart and love-play;

I can turn the thoughts of the **white-armed woman**
and change her thoughts entirely.

Of course, I could go on and on, but I believe that I have articulated my point. This is neither an attack on any other race or religion nor is it an endorsement therefore. What it is is unabashed pride in our Gods, ancestors and the fundamentals of our beloved religion of Fundamental Odinism!

Herein I have clearly, if only concisely, presented facts as they are based in our Eddic Lore and Myths, to discredit the alien notion of universalism within Odinism (or any other Folk's heathen tradition for that matter), by demonstrating that our's is a religion of the blood, and as such, it therefore begins with the very beginning of Aryan lineage as we exist upon Midgard (Earth).

One Thanksgiving, I spent the day with my wife and her parents. My Mother-in-law is from Norway. She told me that growing up in the Raumariki District of Norway; she had no notion of what it meant to be prejudice because she (nearly all of the folk there) had never seen a non-white person! In fact, she said the first time she had ever seen a person of color was when she married my Father-in-law and departed Norway. Both of my in-laws were quick to point out from one of their more recent trips to Norway, that while prejudice was once a foreign concept in Norway, due to the influx of non-white immigrants and the strain placed upon the available social services, that nation now fully comprehends racial prejudice as it now exists there too.

While I am a servant of my/our Gods and Folk, I strongly encourage other Folks to seek out and embrace the indigenous traditions of their own ancestors. For nothing so rich shall ever await us in the traditions of others not of our own blood, as those voices of our own ancestors seek to impart to us.

Great riches await the Aryan man/woman who seeks out the indigenous ways of our ancestors. Sincere reverence for that from whence we hail shall yield great wealth in what today amounts to uncommon wisdom, for it travels through the blood, from Odin to us! May your compass always lead you Trú North. Perform a Blot to Odin, perhaps a Sumbel in honor of our lineage. And meditate upon and Galdr the following Runes; Ansuz (ᚨ), Perthro (ᛈ) and Othala (ᛟ).

"Truth requires little explanation. Therefore, beware of verbose doctrines. The great principals are revealed in brevity." *David Lane, the 11th Precept*

HOF SERVICE for Fallow/Midyear (Midsummer, Summer Solstice)

BALDUR RETURNS

Fallow-Midyear / June 21st, or thereabout, is Midsummer, the Summer solstice as it were. Depending upon where one resides, the legitimacy of this event will occur at several different times. It is, of course the longest day and shortest night of the year. Sunna (the Sun) has reached her zenith. In terms of the wheel of the year, this year has reached its maturity and after today, it will progress towards its natural culmination at the Yule Tide.

Today we celebrate the return of Baldur; brightest, most revered, cherished and beloved of all our Gods! He is the unblemished son of All-Father Odin and All-Mother Frigga. He is blameless in all things and he is symbolic of the sun and its light whose radiant beams are said to be Baldur's flowing blonde hair, or his dazzling and benevolent smile. We are told by the old lore, myths and Eddas that Baldur will return to reign supreme after the Ragnarok and he will rule the new golden era with peace (Frith ok Wunjo). He is therefore the epitome of the promise for a better tomorrow, albeit, only if we create a better today for our kin and kinder (folk and children). We must hold ourselves to a higher standard of personal accountability than do those who wander aimlessly without a sound sense of higher purpose.

In today's western civilization, we are experiencing great upheavals in the most fundamental sense of personal responsibility and accountability for the choices we elect to make and the consequences attached thereto. Our society in which we live has become morally bankrupt and those who would deny this most basic of truths, or are simply not able to descry such a reality, are those whom suffer the greatest infliction of the rampant corruption which spreads like a virus and permeates throughout the whole of western society today!

It is not too late to alter the current course of dissension which we are on. That which those who so cavalierly charted for us without regard for our natural inheritance of the strength and fortitude which comprises the Germanic Folk soul! We must shake free from the fetters of self accepted weakness, the bonds of thralldom. We must once more learn to live like the very Gods we honor and look to as examples which can afford us the very majesty and state of grace which we so oft seek. We will not, "cannot" begin to ascend to such maximums if we refuse to accept accountability for the myriad of maladies which contemporary western society affronts us with. The very destiny of our Faith, Folk, Heritage and culture is incumbent upon the actions of us today, both collectively and individually.

Does the whisper of Baldur's rebirth echo within the depths of your soul? Does it course through your veins like an ancient and mighty river whose head waters sprung forth from a holy glacier some forty millennia ago?

Is your resolve and constitution as everlasting as Sunna herself? Is your resistance and defiance against alien creeds, the hammer, or the anvil? Is your desire to see Baldur return, as true as the day is long on Midsummer? These are without a doubt, queries worthy of your consideration. In fact, they warrant an honest examination at some considerable length!

As the days begin to grow shorter now, we are provided with an excellent archetype and thereafter, opportunity to take measures of our own to decrease the power of any negative factors in our lives. The opportunity to increase our strengths as our weaknesses begins to wane. If we would usher in the return of Baldur, not only annually, but perpetually, then we must seek to emulate him to some degree. Sure we cannot hope to be completely blameless in our journeys north. But we can strive to live our lives beyond the reproach so many in today's western society suffer from. Let us each seek to restore the splendor and majesty of Baldur and the old Gods by seeking our own transformations on a continuum. Let us edify our faith and folk with honorable and noble endeavors and let us endeavor to honor our ancestors, living folk and descendants yet to come with actions which reflect the very brightness of this holy tide of the year!

Perform a Blót to Baldur and the Midsummer and meditate upon and Galdr the following runes:

Sowilo (ᛋ), Wunjo (ᚹ), Berkano (ᛒ) and Kenaz (ᚲ).

I remain in service to the Gods and folk of the Holy Nation of Odin...Heil All-Father Odin! Heil the Holy Ǽsir and Vanir in his name. In Frith with thee.

"If we seek beyond the mundane and the modern trappings of artificial and temporal gratifications of the day we may easily descry the fact that Baldur truly lives!" -- Dr. Casper Odinson Cröwell, Ph.D., DD

HOF SERVICE for Fallow/Midyear (Midsummer, Summer Solstice)

RECLAIMING OUR ODHROERIR

This thing, this living, breathing and ever evolving organism we call Odinism today: Faith, religion, spirituality. It is all of these and yet, any and all of the afore fail to encapsulate the very essence of the thing itself. For Odinism is more! It is a way of life and how we elect to approach the myriad of life's joys and heart aches. What's more, it is "our" way of life. A Hammer and a Sword passed on to us by divine and ancestral hands which have journeyed long and far, having traversed the breadth of some forty millennia. And we have both willfully and eagerly accepted the very gift which they have handed us... This noble way of life which when wielded correctly and without shame, or guilt, will always surpass and ascend the mundane parameters and self imposed confines of man's inferior laws.

Prisons are a device of man's construct and socially ill design. And yet, they keep within them only those whom capitulate to such a detrimental state of mind. Those fettered by the perverted nature of a beast called "Corrections" and it's socially ill sibling "Institution-alization". And not all whom suffer this affliction are incarcerated. Digest that for a moment or two.

A brief description of the chief components surrounding "Odhróerir" and its corresponding metaphysical qualities become essential in order to further illustrate such a reclamation, hence follow hereafter. It should be stated initially, that the following descriptions in no manner what so ever exhaust the comprehensive knowledge to that which they are associated. Indeed, quite the contrary is the instance. For such descriptions serve only as a vehicle to further comprehend the exercise herein and the actual metaphysical qualities attached to the mythological concepts are indeed severely complex and quite exhaustive in their respective natures, whereas here they appear vague at best!

KVASIR: An ancient God of both heavenly (Æsir) and earthly (Vanir) lineage.

ODHRÖRIR: (the drink of divine inspiration), the blood of Kvasir. The innate property of those whom possess consciousness (Gods and Man). The Divine Mead. Initiation and knowledge synthesized equals numinous wisdom. The progression of this discovery on a constant path of transcendence towards the ends of achieving legitimate spiritual enlightenment will ultimately lead the neophyte to the dais of ascension. This ultimate awareness of divinity within is realized within the very primal waters of Mimir's Well. That is to say, one's ancestral memory which resides within the blood/soul/DNA!

SUTTUNG: An Etin/Jötun (chaos devoid of the property of consciousness). The external and unfocused circumstances and forces of life as they exist and become manifest on a continuum.

THE TRISKELION: (Triple entwined horns). The three vats/horns which hold/contain the divine mead; Odhróerir: 1) Odhröerir - the Wód stirrer, or exciter of inspiration. 2) Són- repayment, or re-investment. And 3) Bodn - the container.

GUNLOD: An Etin/Jötun (Suttung's Daughter). She guards the divine mead which her father hoards in an endeavor to withhold it from the Gods and men. She is symbolic of life that is randomly lived, devoid of any focused will.

TRIPARTITE ODIN/ALLFATHER: 1) Odin - consciousness. 2) Vili - the will. 3) Ve - the sacred enclosure/container. Thus constitutes the original Odinic gift we receive at birth, albeit we ultimately forfeit via a life of constant exposure to the artificial components of technology which we are all inundated with as we progress in age. The conceptual winning of Odhróerir may be viewed as a re-connecting with these original divine gifts and a re-investment in thus thereafter (i.e. disregard all dependency upon the unnatural and cultivate and nurture that which is natural such as intuition, etc.).

We are all born with and begin our life's journey with this Odinic gift in tact, this sort of innocence and complete connection to our natural environment, and awareness of the divine multiverse and its host corpus in its entirety. Just as any other animal! And just as any other animal, we never lose the ability to exercise theses natural qualities. Alas, as we age and are exposed to the continuum of external, mundane and unnatural entities/circumstances of life, we grow keener in the artificial laws of man and technology, albeit we grow apart from natural and divine law/order. Hence, our most innate natural senses suffer a retardation on a constant basis until we either suffer a complete arrest in our natural senses and the prospect of their development all together! Or, we awaken to such an unnatural reality in which we exist and we resolve to take charge and do something about it by seeking to stimulate our desire to ascend once more to our natural majesty of being a part of that which is divine as opposed to being apart from it. We achieve this by reclaiming the very Odhróerir with which we were born. For just as Kvasir was born of both the Æsir and Vanir, so too are we North Folk.

The agents of chaos amassed against us are not merely external. Our collective emotional states, pride and temporal, albeit mundane desires are more so the culprit as they more oft than not go about unchecked. It thereafter must follow that the inter actions of our own internal weaknesses and the chaos of life's non-willed and undirected events/circumstances within the scope of our lives, inevitably results in a lack of command of one's self which thereby stunts the awareness in a natural and divine presence and prohibits ascension toward one's own divinity!

If we would seek to consume the Odhróerir, then first we must learn to utilize the original gifts of Allfather Odin which we were born with; our consciousness/conscious thought (Odin), our will to act upon such thoughts (Vili) and the ability to substantiate that focused and directed will (Ve). With these faculties properly and willfully employed toward the ends of self mastery, one may eradicate all self accepted weaknesses and eventually all external/ objective baggage which so frequently inundates the subjective reality with its deluges and thereby confining one to the very prison of self accepted limitation.

This quest, this desire for authentic spiritual enlightenment, it will not be cheaply purchased, nor are any such short cuts in the offing.

The Rúna (secret) is this; the first vat/horn of the precious and coveted mead is "Odhróerir" it is our Odin employed - our focused conscious thought. The second vat/horn "Són", it is our Vili - our directed and focused will, a re-investment in that which Odin gave us originally. And finally, the third vat/horn "Bodn" - it is our Vé, our container/our ability to effect that which is both numinous and natural within ourselves. There is the Rúna Odhróerir, seek not without, but within, if you would raise the most sacred horn and taste the draught contained within it!

Midyear is the time of Midsummer, the solstice and tide which Baldur the beautiful is patron of. His shining mane is Sunna's own life sustaining rays. Baldur is the God of the very promise of hope for both the Gods and man. Beyond the obvious being that this is the longest day and shortest night of the year, it too is a time for divine illumination and hope thus so reflected in the very archetypal essence of Baldur in addition to the afore presented contemporary paradigm of the Rúna of Odhróerir. The gifts and blessings written about herein are divine, to be certain! However, the ability to effectuate thus lies solely within our own personal desire to connect with and utilize the very spark of divinity within ourselves. Therein lies the very soul of the Galdr/mantra; "Reyn til Rúna!" (Seek the mysteries).

Perform a Baldur and Midsummer Blót to celebrate the observance of the Summer Solstice. And Galdr and meditate upon these Runes:
(ᛋ) Sowilo, (ᛗ) Mannaz, (ᚲ) Kenaz and (ᛚ) Laguz.

I remain in service to the Gods and Folk of the HOLY NATION OF ODIN, with Frith and fraternal solidarity. Megi Odin Blessi thig allr... Heil Allfather Odin!

"If we fail to escape the bonds of complacency,
how then shall we ever hope to bask in the radiance of divinity?"
-- Dr. Casper Odinson Cröwell, Ph.D., DD

HOF SERVICE for Haymoon

OUR GODS, ARE THEY REAL?

I am inquired of on a continuum by folk and non-folk alike as to whether our Gods are in fact real, or not? Well, to cut through the chase, the answer is; "Of course they are real!" In fact, they are every bit as real as you or I. However, simple as it is to assert thus, it is never so cut and dry in explaining it. For each individual who I have conversed with in an effort to explain what seems to be tantamount to an enigma to their way of thinking requires an approach to rendering such an answer which makes sense in correlation to their particular query. For example, one gentleman whom places his stock in with the sciences poses the age old science vs. nature (i.e. Gods) angle regarding whether or not our Gods are in fact real. He set about debating divinity by what I asserted with equations of science and thereafter asserting that science does not lie! I calmly explained to him that that was/is not the fact at all. Quite the contrary! The truths and facts which we have arrived at through science, in many instances, are being reconsidered and amended these days on a rather frequent table. I further posit that if we are merely to attribute the wondrous grandeur of life's spectacle, within the realm of nature, with mere reductions and deductions in the name of science, then no such mysteries remain! There is no purpose to life, no synchronicity; everything is just one random act after another! What of the inadequacies in the theory of evolution, I queried? What of the metaphysical? He admitted that I levied some decent arguments, but how do I know that the Gods are real? You obviously comprehend the quality of synchronicity within the realm of science, I proffered. Well, yes, of course, he said. Well, the Gods occur within the realm of nature just as much as we ourselves do...all of us, Gods and man alike are an integral component of nature and the laws of nature. The realm of the cosmos which you so simply wish to explain away with science, is the very conduit which trans-personal energies are conducted through from God to man, man to

God, man to man wherefore the commonality of a shared folk soul and conscious are in regard, it all occurs within the web of warp and woof at play about us at all times, within the realm of natural order. And therein lies the foundation for the occurrence of synchronicity within the realm of nature. Example: Several members of a shared folk located in several different parts of the world and totally unaware of one another, are all thinking the same thing at the same time - that is synchronicity. And the shared folk conscious is what is responsible for affecting such a thought in so many at the same time. That collective conscious is a God and it has existed long before man existed. It has simply always been! Now then, explain that away with science. It cannot be done!

When you feel an instinctive gut feeling that tells you to do this, or that and you later learn that it saved you from some unpleasant event, the science of psychology calls this quality – intuition, though they cannot afford us any explanation of plausibility. That is because that voice inside is (in my opinion) the voice of our Gods and/or ancestors.

And so then, be this the case of validity, would not all Gods be the component personalities of the 'one' divine spirit, as it were? Absolutely not! There is nothing so simple wherefore such entities of vast complexity are to be considered. In today's Universalistic oriented society, such one size/one god fits all mentality is certainly more oft than not, pandered by those with the Universalistic/Egalitarian agenda which are designed to elicit the very destruction of any and all genuine diversity wherefore culture, heritage and religion are all concerned. Do not be misled by such pie in the sky, fantastical thinking. There will never be any total peace on earth and any Theological doctrine, or philosophy which promises thus, is promoting an egregious lie!

Just as the myths, culture and heritage of a people are unique unto that people, so too are their Gods as made manifest via a myriad of vehicles including, but not limited to, the very voice of our Gods, the primordial Folk consciousness which permeates the primordial Folk soul which resides in the very blood of our ancestors, which flows through our veins. In fact, to reiterate, they are timeless qualities which have always been, aeons prior to the dawn of humanity. And so then, it goes without saying along such lines of reasoning as posited above that for each race of people exists indigenous Gods as genuine and unique as each race's culture, heritage and myths.

The evidence of the reality of our Gods is all about us and easily witnessed. And they will not abandon us simply because we elect to disavow them, for that is a human error, not a divine one. Alas, those who continue to insist that the Gods, any Gods, are merely a construct of man, or those whom seek to reduce them and the laws of natural order, to simple scientific formula, will not only deprive themselves of a working relationship with that which is truly divine, they will miss out entirely on the very majesty of life's experiences with the wonderment and magical qualities that only the Gods may provide.

Our Gods are real. They are not some mere archetypes of natural forces. Natural forces are the very result of the Gods fulfilling their role within the realm of natural order! As we approach the month of Haymoon, let us each endeavor to pay our respects to our modern era founders. Not just those who live on in our hearts and praises, but those whom we can easily enjoy the company and wealth of wisdom from, the living. And for Gods' sake, and yours too, seek to commune with our Gods in some special place and in some special way.

Ves Heill! Conduct a Sumble to honor our Founders, living and past, and hail our beloved and stalwart Gods.

Meditate on and Galdr theses Runes; (ᛟ) Othala, (ᚢ) Uruz and (ᛗ) Mannaz.

I remain in service to the Gods and Folk of the Holy Nation of Odin... Heil All-Father Odin! Heil the Holy Æsir and Vanir in his venerable name. In Frith with thee.

"I have experienced normalcy and I have rejected the entire experience!
For it is the normalcy of contemporary man that has sought to eradicate the very Gods which have taught me how to love life and myself!"

- Dr Casper Odinson Cröwell, Ph.D., DD

HOF SERVICE for Haymoon

FOR THE LOVE OF FRIGGA

It would seem as of late, what was once well concealed, for fear of ridicule, or worse, is now not only out in the open, as it were, for all to see, but widely hailed and celebrated and outright encouraged. Yesterday's taboos are quickly becoming the norm, and not merely accepted as thus, but vigorously promoted, in many instances by programs which are federally funded. Where battles for sovereignty and Nation once engendered nobility in character, they were supplanted by wars for equality of social and racial classes which soon led to a state of arrested development in moral standards which has paved the way for the decline of the western world wherefore social issues hang in the balance. Today's government sponsored battles are for promoting the once taboo and morally deplorable conditions and lifestyles of yesterday in an effort to alter the social and political campaigning climate of our society in an effort generate more income and support for what is termed the liberal choice. But IF homosexuality (a lifestyle choice and sexual preference) is to be accepted in our society today as a normalcy then what's next? How about bestiality or pedophilia? I mean, after all, they too are sexual preferences and lifestyle choices. Seems a bit far fetched does it? So was homosexuality only thirty years ago.

In today's society of moral bankruptcy, far too many men have succumbed to emasculation at the hands of government programs which promote morally questionable programs under the guise of public services and the liberal choice. Yes folks, the same liberal choice government which wants to disarm its citizens by taking away their right to bear arms, ostracize and ridicule white folks who openly display pride for their heritage, culture and ancestry all the while hailing all other peoples for doing the same, and in fact even encourages, promotes and sponsors it with tax payers dollars!

Hmm, sounds a lot like a targeted effort to eradicate an entire race of people along with their heritages and cultures... "Our" people! Our men are taught to embrace effeminate demeanors while our women are encouraged to pursue careers as opposed to marriage and raising a family. This does not bode well for the survival of our folk and if our folk perish so too shall our Gods forever!

Our liberal choice government is so concerned with censoring white racial pride, free speech, raping us of our constitutional rights and disarm citizens of their right to bear firearms in order to create a defenseless sheep like class of people which shall pose no threat to a corrupt and tyrannical government, yet they do nothing about the graphic and gratuitous vulgarity, violence or the demeaning fashion in which our women are portrayed in the media, theatres and video games. Two entire generations in western society have been taught to disregard any semblance of ethical behavior let alone genuine morality. Males are taught that our women are mere sex tools and cum receptacles, there for their entertainment. Free to abuse at will, and more and more of our teenage girls and young women begin to assume an attitude that it is acceptable. I assure you, it is not!

I see it occurring with frequent acceptance these days, this open disrespect of our women in depictions of women as mere pleasure providers to any and all takers, in the verbal and physical abuse women incur on a daily basis and in the demeaning language employed towards them and even by them. Teen girls and young women address one another too often in terms of Ho, insinuating whore, or Bitch. Though these titles serve as terms of affectionate greetings among them whom employ such terminology, it is detrimental never the less. Is it any wonder why so many women today suffer from low self esteem issues, or depression disorders?

Chivalry once dictated that man defended woman's honor, no matter who she may have been. The womanly virtue of the fairer sex was filled with the promise of hope for a people's future and the gift she had to give to a worthy suitor, was something to be prized and held completely sacred as was the union entered into by man and woman! What happened to the attitude of chivalry towards our women? What happened to the promise of our folk and Gods thereafter? I'll tell you what... Disrespecting our women and imbuing them with a low self worth, that's what! Men addressing our women as ho's, hookers, sluts and bitches. And our women and teen girls accepting it.

Our women are the very images of our Goddesses incarnate. Everything beautiful and desirable about our women is the very embodiment of sweet Freyja. Every hope for new life and continuity of racial and family lineages is the embodiment of Ostara. Every time we rest our gaze upon our folk's young girls, we are beholding the youthfulness of Idunna. And every time a man looks into the eyes of his new bride, or holds his newborn infant he is experiencing the very presence of Allmother Frigga! Who among us would call any of our beloved Goddesses a ho, or bitch? Who among us would call Allmother Frigga a ho? And what man among us would stand by and do nothing about it? Well, I'll tell you, it is the same thing when we address, or allow for our women to be addressed in such an ill manner. We wouldn't address our own mothers as "HO". Yet, in the grander scheme of the spirit of our Goddesses residing in our women folk, that is exactly what we would be doing. So then, for the love of Frigga, let us endeavor to correct this pernicious behavior that all who encounter us look upon us and our faith with the respect thus warrants. Let us heal our selves from what a morally bankrupt government seeks to promote in an blatant effort to profit from it.

As we celebrate the moontide (month} of Haymoon, let us be mindful of the manner in which we engage our women folk and girls who will one day too become our women folk. If we would desire that they conduct themselves with the refinement of a lady, then we men must honor and address them in such a fashion.

Haymoon 4th is 'Founders Day', a day of remembrance for those modern day founders of our noble faith. It is due in large part to such founders as A. Rudd Mills, Sveinbjorn Beinteinsson, Thorstein Guthjonson, and the beloved Folk Mother, Else Christensen, and their noble efforts, that we now practice the Northern faiths which we do. And these noble efforts are by no means limited to those which the Gods have gathered up to them. So then, this Haymoon 4th, perform a Sumble to those gone to the Gods halls that brought our beloved ancestral faith back to us. And Heil to those stalwart keepers of the Northern Faith!

Meditate on and Galdr these Runes: (ᛟ) Othala, (ᚢ) Uruz and (ᛗ) Mannaz.

"What then shall they say of us one day as they stand b'fore the memory stones, our posterity? That we stood fast in our ways and defense of their right to 'be", with honor! Or shall they cast their glance downward in shame and with quiet voices, as they recount how 'WE', their ancestors, nearly cost them their right to 'be', with our lack of unity and refusal to band together with iron bonds of fraternal solidarity! Only the Norns know the final outcome. But each one of us knows within the measure of our hearts, just what we are or aren't willing to do for our descendants yet unborn."

-- Casper Odinson Cröwell, Ph.D, DD

HOF SERVICE for Harvest 2256 RE (August 2006 CE)

GOOD HARVEST

Heilsan Folk! The month of Harvest brings to us the celebration of 'Freyfaxi', toward the month's end. Freyfaxi was local to Scandinavia and Iceland as a Harvest festival honoring the horse. Since the sagas hold many accounts which relate the sacredness of the horse and Frey as deity of the horse, such as Hrafnkel's Saga, we may ascertain that priests were known to regard their horses as; 'Freyfaxi' (Frey's Mane). These horses were not ridden, or worked in the fields for they were deemed sacred to the God Frey. Many events associated with both Frey and horses occurred on this day of harvest celebration such as horse fights and horse races.

When we celebrate Freyfaxi around the twenty-eighth of the month, let us each be mindful as we partake in the Blót to Frey, that while he is indeed the God of joy, plenty, fertility and the harvest, seldom does anything worthwhile come from nothing! The age old axiom comes to mind here; "We reap what we sow". The more focus, attention and care we invest our energies in wherefore the positive endeavors of our lives are in regard, the greater will the harvested reward be too. Just as the fields of auld would not yield a harvest, save for the horse's partnership which afforded our ancestors the means to plow and sow, said fields. So too it remains so today. We may see the quality of the Ehwaz (ᛖ) Rune in terms of that which aids us in our worthy endeavors as did the horse aid the farmer. Here, our horse is called "Ethic". For it is the quality of sound ethics regarding work, industriousness, perseverance and self discipline which will guarantee the good harvest. We will always get back an equal return to what we are willing to invest. Food for thought folks.

Harvest too is also the holy time of 'Odin's Ordeal', whereby All-Father hung upon the world tree; 'Yggdrasil', for nine days and nights in order to win the sacred Runes which he passed on to us, his Kin...

"I know that I hung on that windswept tree
nine nights long,
wounded with a spear, dedicated to Odin,
myself to myself,
on that tree which no man knows
from where its roots run.
No bread did they give me, nor drink from
the horn
downwards I peered;
I took up the runes, screaming I took them,
then I fell back from there.

Hávamál 138 - 139

Once more, following the train of thought, you receive from something only what you are willing to invest in it. Do you suppose that All-Father may have descried the the very secrets of life's mysteries, had he not been willing to invest all he had and thereafter, travel to the very threshold of death? I think not. This time of 'Odin's Ordeal' which is, Harvest 17th through the 25th, are nine days and nights which are sacred to many. For the Gothar, Brothers and Apprentices of the SONS OF ODIN, 1519 - Vinland Kindred, they are the holiest nine days and nights of our lives! Each member will 'Hang on the Tree', as we call it, for the entirety of the nine nights. We forfeit our voices during this time and sacrifice them to All-Father Odin. Our Apprentices will not speak the entire course of nine days and nights and they will fast as well during this sacred time. In addition to this, they will perform the true blood ritual of "The Valknut Rite". If an Apprentice allows so much as a single peep to escape his lips, the journey is over for him until next Harvest!

Many members elect to repeat much of the entire rite annually, while others wish to simply fulfill the nine night requirement of silent meditation. I have personally completed the entire rite nine times in the past eleven years. We have had several fail. If you think this a mere simple task, attempt to remain silent for only two, or three hours, with people trying to speak with you. And then reconsider those whom do it for nine days and nights straight. One needn't be an Apprentice or member of any holy order to venture forth on such a noble endeavor and thereafter reap the harvest of thus. Each of us, whether we are seeking admittance into any order, kindred, etc., or are just seeking spiritual growth and wisdom, may find these nine days and nights most appropriate as each one's own personal rite in concert with 'Odin's Ordeal'. For in doing so, one may grow closer to Odin and to one's self! May you seek and discover... May you possess the courage to approach the gallows and the well, and may you not hesitate to drink deeply of its sacred water! Heil All-Father Odin!

Perform a Blót to Frey as part of your Freyfaxi celebration and meditate upon and Galdr these Runes: Ingwaz (ᛜ), Jera (ᛃ), and Ehwaz (ᛖ).

For the Nine Nights of Odin's Ordeal, make a self sacrifice; seek to understand a new mystery.
Perform a Blót to All-Father Odin and meditate upon and Galdr these Runes: Ansuz (ᚨ), Eihwaz (ᛇ), Elhaz (ᛉ) and Dagaz (ᛞ).

I remain in Frith with thee.

"Drink deep of the well's holy waters. Drink until you are sodden with that sacred mead. Drink until you have drowned the agents of that Bedouin's faith, those whom have denied you your birthright! Drink until you spy the eye of Odin, and let no wight bar your way north!"

- Casper Odinson Cröwell, Ph.D., DD

HOF SERVICE for Harvest

TOWARDS CREATING THE ÜBERMENSCH

Honky, Cracker, Peckerwood, Wigger. All words/names with demeaning connotations. Honky = Loud mouth, Cracker = the color of soda cracker and which crumbles easily, Peckerwood = Female genitalia/vagina/ slang: Pussy; Wigger = white nigger. All names/words coined by non-whites with the intended purpose to demean and degrade the recipient of the insult. And yet, so many white men proudly embrace them. Why, many white men in Vinland's Black hole, otherwise called the Corrections System, proudly exhibit these words as badges of honor in ink upon their person. Like many, I once was such a man. So, what's the big deal, right? Wrong! In fact, it is a very big deal in terms of influencing younger generations wherefore the declining nature of Aryan character becomes acceptable as opposed to the natural character of the Aryan to be driven toward ascension in a quest towards creating Nietzsche's Übermensch. We have gone from noble and majestic people whom employed the King's English, to Modern English which is a bastardization of what was once a beautiful and melodic cadence of the spoken language. Why, we have gone from embracing the meter of Sir William Shakespeare to emulating the erroneous Ebonics of the likes of Vanilla Ice and Kid Rock! This is NOT ascension... It is decline at a rapid advance.

This pernicious behavior is more than just about some crude and derogative decline in speech. It too sows the seeds of credibility among our youth wherefore espousing cultures which are counter conducive to the upward rise and advance of our people, faith, heritage and cultures are in regard. Consider for a moment, if you will, that in Japan, China and Korea (North and South), the youth, in the main, enthusiastically embrace a love for classical music, the Arts, fine literature and the sciences.

Now contemplate this; In Vinland today an overwhelming sector of white youth are failing miserably in the forum of rudimentary academics. They are emulating African-American youths from the projects and ghettos. Talking, dressing in apparel, getting involved in the substance abuse culture, dropping out of school, whiling the hours away with violent video games and mimicking the content of those games by committing acts of crime, violence and domestic violence as not only acceptable, but glorified behavior! Clearly the antithesis of the normal standard behavior in Asia's youths. Sure, there are always exceptions to the rule. They have troubled youths in Asia. And we certainly have some very bright stars on the rise within our own youth here; albeit, both are the exception to the general rule of the populace climate.

Embracing these ill standards of a monoculture will breed a desire to breed down in society. Someone with little or no education is likely to breed with, and/or marry and breed with someone of the same background. If both of these people in the example are white, then we are breeding dumb whites. If one of them is white and the other is not, which is the most likely scenario, then we are no longer breeding white folks at all... We are breeding the inevitable demise of our race, our faith and our Gods!

So then, what do we do about this state of retardation and decline? Do we take away these video games and anti-Aryan culture music from our youth? No. We set the example for them to follow by living, acting, and speaking in concert with the higher states of mind of Aryan culture. We strive towards creating a higher standard to live by in a concerted effort to bring about the Übermensch. We expose our youth, on a continuum, to the superlative cultures of their Aryan Ancestors. It is never an acceptable practice to identify ill standards and thereafter accept them as normal, nor must it ever become thus, lest we desire to witness the promise, and hope for the future of our faith and folk succumb to a corrosion of the will to survive!

So then, what do you say, Peckerwood? It's only a word, right? Yes. Yes it is. But words lead to actions and actions more oft than not will ultimately substantiate the rise, or fall of a living thing... Say, a folk and its faith. Say, our folk and our faith!

Harvest is the time of "Odin's Ordeal". It is a time for the Sons of Odin, 1519, to search out the depths of their own souls during the nine days and of nights. It is a time of severe introspection regarding just what one is willing to sacrifice in service for the good of our faith and folk, and deep consideration of what Allfather Odin had pledged and continues to deliver on to this very day in the lives of those who seek to know his burden and Rúna (mysteries), and even more, those who are bold enough to approach the well and pay the required Fehu (fee) to consume its sacred contents.

The 1st of Harvest is a day sacred to Odin and Frigga, the 9th is a day of remembrance for King Radbod of Frisia, the 17th-25th constitutes the nine days and nights of Odin's Ordeal, and the 28th we celebrate FreyFaxi.

Perform an Odin's Blót and meditate upon these Runes:

Ansuz (ᚨ), Eihwaz (ᛇ), Elhaz (ᛉ) and Dagaz (ᛞ).

Perform a Blót for FrayFaxi and Galdr and meditate upon these Runes:

Ingwaz (ᛜ), Jera (ᛃ) and Ehwaz (ᛖ).

"Where one seeks to understand the nature of Rúna, one must first understand the nature of oneself."
- Dr. Casper Odinson Cröwell, Ph.D., DD

HOF SERVICE for Shedding (Autumn Equinox)

A CALL TO ARMS

Shedding, a gentle month of transformation. Shedding is the month which begins the holy year's quiet segue from waning light to that of the shades. For it is seated deeply in the month of Shedding that darkness begins to assert itself over the fading light. On the equinox we celebrate the 'Winter Finding'. This is the time of the year when the days and nights rest in the cradle of equality, but the morrow's eve, will see the nights now grow longer than the days. Stephen A. McNallen once wrote, "The sun continues to decline to its nadir at Yule. It is a time of inward turning, of conserving the personal and group resources as we seek the things that will help us struggle through the approaching death of the sun. - Ragnarok in miniature."

The Winter Finding further reflects All-Father's journey to wax in knowledge and wisdom concerning the fate of the Gods and men at Ragnarok and how to better prepare all for this cataclysmic event! Just as Odin sought the mead of inspiration, "Oedreher", the winning of the sacred Runes by hanging on the windswept tree; "yggdrasil" and pledging one of his eyes to extract and consume a draught from; "Mimir's Well", all in a concerted effort to better protect and prepare the Gods and men from the inevitable doom. So too may each of us seek the sacred knowledge and wisdom required to defend and protect our noble Gods and Folk and our holy Faith which was nearly lost to us a millennium ago. Let us all endeavor to ensure that such will never be the sad case again. If we are to protect and defend our holy faith, Gods and folk, let alone restore it to its former majesty and thereafter advance it, then we cannot, must not simply pass the buck to others, simply and naively assuming that there will always be someone else to do what must be done! That is a losing attitude! We must all be accountable, each one of us today. We must seek the knowledge and apply it to our lives by experiencing said knowledge and thereby converting knowledge to wisdom by living what we learn. We must learn to articulate what we say and write about our faith. We must represent our faith and its virtues with any and all whom we find ourselves either seeking to educate, or may become engaged in discourse with - be it a Christian Pastor, a Rabbi, an Imam, a Scientist, or a Philosopher. We must endeavor to do so in an intelligent and disarming manner. Let us, each man and woman, resolve to become who we were born to be and fulfill our destinies, both individually and collectively as a folk. Else wise, we are naught but loosely connected souls, bandying about tired old clichés left to us by ancestors of stalwart spirit whom perished millennia ago.

I do not want to be loosely connected with those whom are not certain of their place and destiny. I desire naught less than the true and genuine bonds of kinship with folk of like, whom seem determined to pursue a restoration of our beloved ways of auld and to establish a solid connection to one another and to our Gods as did our hearty and noble ancestors so long ago when faced with overwhelming adversities!

Are you willing to stave off the slavering wolf? Won't you join me, ye of true and valiant dispositions? Let naught the doughtiest of storms dissuade ye, nor turn your hearts...
For somewhere between the strength of the mighty oak and the resilience of the willow tree, burns the soul of the Germanic Tribes, and his name is ODIN!

Perform the Blót of Winter Finding and meditate upon and Galdr the following Runes:

Uruz (ᚢ), Thurisaz (ᚦ), Raido (ᚱ) and Othala (ᛟ).

I remain in Frith with thee.

"Let naught the wolf overtake the sun, nor moon. Let naught Fenris break free of his fetters.
Let naught despair settle into your minds this night.
And when the wolf doth break free, let courage be found residing in your hearts!"
-- Dr. Casper Odinson Crowell, Ph.D., DD

HOF SERVICE Shedding (Autumn Equinox)

SHADOWS AT THE EDGE OF DARKNESS

There is a place I know, and I wend their often. It is a place of both magic and mysticism. More so, it is a place that exists to me only in the reality of Ancestral Memory as it lives on in my blood and reveals itself clearly to my Húgauga (mind's eye). This place, this magical and sometimes even frightening place which I am often drawn to in my dreams and meditations, it surely must exist in reality somewhere in the old world of my European Ancestors, though in my visions, it always assumes a surreal quality.

It is a heavily wooded forest with copious trees so large and with trunks which seem to be smooth, yet knotted and polished to a dull shine. The forest floor is littered with spent autumn leaves in hues of orange and red. So thick is the blanket of leaves which covers the vast entirety of this great and magnificent forest which seems to be my private wonderland. Small animals scurry about and I see my own Fýlgja (fetch) there often. In fact, at certain times he seems to be his own entity, while other times I am he and he is I and I travel about in his form, with a fleetness of foot! It is always Autumn in this place. And 'He' is always there, whether he reveals himself to me, or not. I always feel his presence and hear his voice in my head and...inside my soul. A whisper of rushing wind; "Ooooddddiiinnn!"

I have noticed that in times of great upheaval in my life, something pursues me and sends me back to a childhood memory from about age five. It is a truly frightening memory. In this memory, I am in my bedroom which I shared with my elder Schwester (sister), late at night, when the whole household was fast asleep. Meine schwester was in her own bed about twelve, or fifteen feet across the room from me and she was soundly asleep. Something had awaken me from my own peaceful slumber and had terrified me to the point that I had gotten out of my bed and hid beneath it. I can still recall to this day, the strong and sweet fragrance of the pine wood planks which held the box spring in the bed frame, in addition to my own urine, and chocolate candy which was on my night stand. It was the Yuletide season so there were candy dishes full of various types of candy distributed all about the house. I had wet myself from fright at whatever was in my bedroom, and I recall so clearly those three smells mingling with each other!

Whatever it was that had frightened me so, was only made known to me, as my schwester slept, undisturbed and undaunted, right through it. Though it had occurred only feet from her. And no one else in the house was disturbed by it either. The next morning no one had said anything, including me! Whatever it was, it frightened me so badly that other than the memory of what I have recounted herein, whatever had occurred that Yuletide late night had continued to elude me for over decades! Though, the memory has haunted me with frequency. I have always known that someday I would have to find a way to reconcile with what had transpired in that bedroom all these years ago. This seemed an improbable, if not altogether impossible feat. Until yesterday that is. I spoke of this yesterday with a kinsman. While I was recounting the details of my grim memory, it hit me like an epiphany after decades. I excused myself and immediately went to meditate and consider what had revealed itself to me, as if divinely so!

In 1967 CE, during the Yuletide (Wild Hunt), Allfather had come to me and awaken me from my sleep. The Wild Huntsman himself, in the form of the Terrible one; "Ygg". He reached into my mind with his hand and he activated the Wode Fury within me... Odin had claimed me as his son on that fateful night. Frightened, I clambered under my bed to hide! I was hiding from a divine blessing of which my young mind could not possibly have comprehended.

Shedding is the time of the "Winter Finding" which of course is the beginning of Fall, the beginning of the season of the shades where shadows appear at the edge of darkness!

We all have our places that only we know, where the Gods, wights and ancestors appear to us, and speak to us. It is imperative, if ever we are to enter such esoteric realms, to learn to embrace the shades and shadows and all that awaits us there. For one may not know that some frightful experience decades ago was indeed a blessing, if one is not willing to re-evaluate one's own experiences and memories which occurred under less than pleasant circumstances. The natural law of balance in all things requires that we not only accept the dark with the light, but that we experience it as well. Otherwise, we are out of sync with natural order, and as such, much like an automobile which is out of alignment, as it moves down the road it is always compelled to veer. As the auto's driver seeks to keep the vehicle from veering off course, it creates an undue hardship upon the auto's tires and other parts. If the auto is not fixed to correct this state of unbalance, then it will ultimately be good for nothing but scrap as the condition worsens.

Our own personal lives are much like that automobile. As we travel the Road North, we are moving towards the purpose of our lives. Yet, if we become unbalanced and thereafter elect to remain in such a state, we too shall veer off the paths which we desire to travel. Instead, we will fall victim to any number of pitfalls and detours which will have unnecessary and unpleasant conditions attached to them.

We have been taught throughout life, that the darkness is bad. That it somehow conceals a certain evil element within. This of course is Balderdash! There is nothing to fear within the realms of shadows. For therein awaits the reclamation of balance with the light in your life!

Shedding the 9th is a day of remembrance for Herman, for it was in the month of Shedding in the year 9 Common Era, in which Herman (Arminius to the Romans) laid waste to Varus' three legions (20,000 men) in the Battle of Teutobergerwald, at Kalkriese near Detmold, Germany. Heil this brave German Chieftain for his deeds of daring in the face of what must have seemed to be insurmountable odds, and heil the noble and stalwart Kinsmen who fought by his side to rid the Fatherland of the Romans and their imminent debauchery and whoredom which accompanied them everywhere! Raise your horns to Herman the Cherusker on this the day of his remembrance.

And of course, don't forget the Fall Equinox (the Winter Finding), perform the proper Blót for the season.

Megi Odin blessi thig, ok fara meth Gothanum! I remain in Frith and fraternal solidarity with thee...

"What terror awaits just beyond the shadow's edge? What horrors, that repel so many, yet attract so few...those bold enough to cross from the light into the dark and seize what nature has promised? It is there, lurking just beyond the shadows, the balance of those who abide by the laws of natural order." -- *Dr. Casper Odinson Cröwell, Ph.D., DD*

HOF SERVICE for Hunting

IN OUR ANCESTORS FOOTSTEPS
(Initiative & Perseverance)

I would have loved to have belonged to the Jomsvikings!"; "It would have been so awesome to have been counted among the ranks of the Heruli! "; "I count myself among the ranks of the living Einherjar!" - Admit it. We've all heard one kinsman, or another posit such a remark in our presence at one time, or another. Perhaps we ourselves have even professed such an exclamation. I most certainly have. And sure, why not? It is such an honorable notion in addition to being somewhat romantic as well. I've even spent a considerable amount of time affording such notions both lengthy and weighty contemplation. Daydreaming, if you will.

Considering the current state of contemporary man, resplendent with his myriad of ill social habits, vices and lack of skills required by one seeking to ascend beyond the masses! I am certain that many of you now perusing this have indulged in such wishful and melancholy meditation at one time or another yourselves. I find myself given to sporadic fits of sincere disgust and contempt for contemporary man, nearly on a daily schedule! For contemporary man has brought about the execution of Renaissance man and replaced him with a ghost of men long dead now. In their stead, where majesty once reigned supreme, illuminated by the very flame of desire for godly Ascension, stands some form of contemporary human waste insistent that all are equal simply because the powers that be have drafted a document affirming the death of the valid laws of nature! Contemporary man tells us that the weakest man is just as equal as the strongest. That the man whom would allow any trespasser to violate his family, is every bit as equal as the man who would bring about a reckoning to any such trespasser. I say to you my brothers and sisters, that the laws of natural order are alive and well, and that no arrogance of man can, or will alter this timeless and inexorable fact, with their laws of the land! There is no supremacy for any, save by the sheer might and desire to break free of the fetters of mortality, the absolute aspiration to ascend toward godhood and the exertion and application of one's will in concert with the very laws of nature. No egalitarian, or universalistic fantasies will alter this reality, nor are my assertions herein, any new revelations, or rapturous notions, to be certain. They are the politically incorrect, albeit unabashed truth. I am certainly not the first to posit such truth, nor will I be the last. More so, I offer no apologies to those whom I may have rendered uncomfortable with my open and honest assertions. The truth is often harsh and uncomfortable to embrace. Never the less, it is such men and women of heroic and stalwart character whom seek to embrace the fullness of their realities, especially in the presence of their adversaries whom are both offended by such truth, and thereafter, motivated by their own repulsiveness towards that truth.

Fully comprehending that there are indeed multiple, valid levels of both, initiation and comprehension of our sacred faith and its traditions, I accept the far reaching reality as it does indeed exist. Not all among us are going to be on the same level of understanding as all others with the same amount of time and experience invested in their journey North. One may consider two individuals whom began their journey North, say, three years ago. However, while one may have excelled at an exceptionally rapid pace, the other's growth may be dwarfed in comparison. This, however, should in no way whatsoever, infer a lack of sincerity and devotion to walking the Northern Road, on that individual's behalf, nor should it be interpreted as such. Some folk just simply excel in certain forums over others and vice versa. This is all perfectly normal and fine. What is not fine, nor acceptable are those whom claim our sacred faith and recite the Nine Noble Virtues, etc., all the while they are caught in a frame of mind which fails to elucidate their self accepted weaknesses in concert with their own lack of accountability. These folk suffer from the 'Pass the buck' syndrome. This very lack of self discipline is not only contradictory in terms of the Noble Virtues of "Strength, Honor and Courage", but it is in addition an egregious disservice to oneself wherefore genuine self respect is in regard. Our life long exposure to the very pernicious neo-customs and traditions of contemporary man will not easily be eradicated from our lives. The signs of this detriment are all around us to witness on a daily basis.

Kinsman "A" informs kinsman "B" that it is his opinion that he is not only failing to live up to the honorable and noble virtues which an Odinist encompasses and should outwardly exude in an open effort to lead by example, but he's not even putting forth an honest effort to do so! Kinsman "B" in turn becomes indignant and defensive as opposed to considering the words of his kinsman. Were kinsman "A's" observations valid, then kinsman "B" is about to enter the lack of accountability and pass the buck stages! Rather than see things for what they are and thereafter resolve to correct the erroneous behavior which indeed will continue to impede any progress he would otherwise achieve, kinsman "B" will point the finger, or pass the buck by alluding to some other, "What are you talking about, brother? Kinsman "D" does that all the time!"

Let's consider kinsman "C" under similar circumstances. Rather than assuming the indignant and defensive posture, kinsman "C" plays the ' I wear my feelings on my sleeve' card. Instead of acting out, he opts for the cold shoulder, avoid the kinsmen angle. When he encounters other Kin during the course of his day, he appears not to notice them, all the while secretly hoping that they will approach him with inquiry as to why he has been avoiding the circle, kindred, hearth, etc., to which he then proffers his rehearsed reply which fall along the lines of something like; " You know, bro really hurt my feelings with that comment." Or some such line in concert with said scenario.

My point is this... Every day self professed Odinist's talk about how they wish that they had been born a thousand years ago, yak, yak, yak. When in reality, they would not have gotten away with acting in a manner that was not conducive to the entire Skeppslag (ship's crew) which they were part of. If Svein would have taken offense to something true that Ragnhild had said, he would not have been afforded the opportunity to take his ball and go play somewhere else, per se. Nor would Thorgard been able to pout and mope whilst he elected to sulk in his hurt feelings. Truth of the matter is both would have been thrown over the side of the long boat and told to swim home! End of story.

So then, why is it that we put up with self accepted weakness taught to us today by the lessons of contemporary man when we speak so fondly of walking in our ancestors footsteps? Matter of fact is that less than 10% of our folk who fancy themselves fit enough and suitable to have been a Jómsvíking, Herúli, or a living Einherjar, would truly make the cut. Most would be sorely disappointed in the reality.

So then, do I consider myself to make the cut? Of course I do! Not in any part due to any great status, or place of honor, nor for any reason of arrogance either. But quite simply because I walk the same way that I talk. Were I in the same situation as kinsmen "B" & "C", I would consider what kinsman "A" had to say. Next, I'd inquire as to the validity of what he alleged, with other kinsmen that I respect and I'd seek their Rede. If it turned out to be an honest assessment of my actions, then I'd do the honorable thing. I'd thank kinsman "A" for thinking enough of me as his kinsman to point out my inadequacy and I'd thereafter seek to correct it in an effort to strengthen my own resolve and character and thereby maximize the collective strength of my kin while minimizing any weakness we may have suffered as a result of my deficit.

I know as I have, indeed, done this in the past on more than one occasion. It is the very lesson of All-Father Odin, that of self transformation on a continuum. And so, I continue to strive for that self transformation.

This month's Hof Service is in no fashion or form, an indictment against anyone which I personally have in mind. It is however, an indictment against all who fit the criteria of talking North while walking south! And if I've offended anyone... well, good. Get off the long boat and swim home!

For only through initiative and perseverance will we restore strength and majesty which our ancestors once enjoyed, which we today can re-initiate and our descendants of the morrow may rightly inherit because of our noble efforts! This month finds us paying homage to both Leif Eriksson (on the 9th and his stalwart father, Eirik the Red on the 8th). Were it not for their initiative and perseverance, Greenland and the Vinland expeditions would not appear in the annals of history next to the other accounts of heroic proportion. These worthy sagas have thrilled our folk for generations in addition to eliciting inspiration and a grand sense of adventure. And yet, if we today fail to afford these accounts the respect they warrant, by not living up to our own potential, then they are naught more than that of say, mere fairy tales!

This is also the time of the "Winter Nights" which occurs on the first Laugardagr (Saturday) and Sunnasdagr (Sunday) on or after the 11th. We honor sweet Freya and the Disir as we mark the end of the harvest and thank her for the bounty it has produced with her favor.

So then, there it is, your Hof Service for Hunting.

To the many of you which I know out there and are in good stead with us, I'd like to extend both my sincerest affection. To all members and associates of both 1519 and the HNO, my genuine gratitude to you all for what you do for our faith and folk. It is an honor to count you among my kin! To all my other kin out there, my love and respect. And to the rest of you, to whom this very work is dedicated to, I warmly thank so many of you for the decent missives which you have sent. It is my honor and privilege to serve you and I have no doubt that one day many of us will in fact be kin. It is a thought which warms my heart and one I look forward to. For from you whom I endeavor to inspire and perhaps enlighten to some extent, the leaders of our beloved faith and folk of the near future will come forth. Believe in thy selves as not only I believe in you, but as ALL-Father Odin believes in you, for were it not so-I'd not waste my time on this effort which keeps me from most others.

Perform a Sig blót for success and victory in your efforts and invoke the father of victory. Meditate upon and Galdr these Runes: Sowilo (ᛋ), Tiwaz (ᛏ) and Perthro (ᛈ).

Also hold a blót and feast to beautiful Freya and the Disir during the Winter Nights, and meditate upon and Galdr these Runes: Berkano (ᛒ), Jera (ᛃ) and Fehu (ᚠ).

Ves Heil. I remain in service to the Gods and Folk of the Holy Nation of Odin. And I remain in Frith with thee... Heil All-Father Odin and Heil the holy Æsir and Vanir in his venerable name!

"Now more than ever, we need to fill the ranks of the 'Living Einherjar', and Valkyrjar, for the wolf is at the rampart! It is not enough to keep him at bay. We must follow him into the next life and all the way to Ragnarok to see that the deed gets done. This will require extraordinary folk, not only in desire, but in deed."

--Dr. Casper Odinson Cröwell, Ph.D., DD

HOF SERVICE for Hunting

DISUNITY OR DIVERSITY?

It occurs among the best of us, no matter where one resides. Separations within the Folk! For many, this seems to be a form of dissension or disunity. But take a closer look through the lenses of reason and reality. What many color dissension and disunity are sometimes mere expressions of diversity and naught more.

I am, of course, referring to the realistic necessity for several different Kindreds, Skeppslags and Groups, for a myriad of reasons. There are Folk whom refuse to assemble with other Folk who participate in substance abuse. There are those whom feel some do not take Vor Trú (Our Faith) serious enough. There are a plethora of personality conflicts and there are always the many differences in how our holy thews (virtues) are interpreted. For these reasons and scores of others which would fill any number of volumes, it is necessary to have several groups in order to accommodate all Tru Folk.

That such different groups and attitudes exist, neither implies nor affords any of us the right to blatantly disregard the Noble Virtue of Hospitality or Frith among Trú Folk. For example, there is no valid reason for me to ignore or be inhospitable to one of another Kindred, Skeppslag or Group because we do not see things the same way (very few truly do!), or because we belong to separate groups. So long as this other Trú Man/Woman was in fact Trú to the Nine Noble Virtues, etc., which is what we should bear in mind wherefore hospitality and Frith among Tru Folk is in regard. That we all are defenders of our Gods and Folk is what is germane here. I am in no way at all suggesting that we give a pass to someone who has truly done another wrong, or is in willful violation of our sacred thews. I'm not saying look the other way. Not even close! What I am saying is this, barring any legitimate violation of Norse Law by one among us, there is no reason to be hostile or rude toward others simply because we don't concur with their views or expressions, or because they belong to another group. Such an attitude is contra to the

Fourteen Words in addition to Fraternal Solidarity. They are weaknesses in our defenses, chinks in our Folk's armor!

Let us look to the examples which our very ancestors have left to us regarding this matter...I'll employ a model of the Viking Age to illustrate my point. During this era there existed many different Clans, Kindreds, Tribes, etc. among the people of the Aryan Tribes. To be certain, many did not get along well at all and even fewer shared the same perspective. Be that as it may, since they shared borders and boundaries, efforts of hospitality were extended in order to keep the Frith betwixt themselves. Indeed, when all arrived at the local Thing (Assembly), no such rudeness was tolerated. More so, at the annual Althing (the Great Assembly) any rudeness would have been met with a swift and almost always unanimous call for justice for anyone who would violate the rule of Hospitality and threaten the Frith.

Granted, the afore stated paradigm is simplex in nature, it never the less affords one a clear, concise and honest picture of what Hospitality meant to our ancestors and what it is supposed to mean to us today, as well. Everyone is not always going to get along with each other. That is just the plain reality. Especially wherefore incarcerated Folk are in regards. Would it be ideal if we could? You bet! It just wouldn't be realistic. Be that as it may, it doesn't mean that we can't honor the Noble Virtues which we profess that we do. On the contrary...If we fail to, then it is we who are not living Trú. There are enough agents of chaos amassed against us and our survival as it is. Let us not enable them with our own lack of loyalty to the mission of the Fourteen Words. For selfless service to something higher than our own desires and emotions, is the teaching of Tyr. Let us all remember this when next we meet another Odinist on the route, that we greet each other with a hearty "Heilsa!" No matter our personal differences. And may the Gods smile upon us as others take note of the fraternal solidarity and unity we share, even though diverse we may be. For there is always something much bigger than you and I, at stake... The future of Faith and Folk!

To be sure, the subject of the content herein, is not unique to the incarcerated Folk. This burden affects our Free Folk as well. For anyone who thought that this was only happening in their locale, I can assure that such is not the case at all. I hear from Folk from all over Midgard and it would seem that this occurs in all corners of the globe, both in and out of prison. It too shall continue until we cease to exist, or until we can learn to quit shooting ourselves in the foot, as it were.

Take the time to reflect upon the lessons of Tyr and perhaps conduct a Tyr Blót. Let us too, deeply consider the value of the following

Runes... Tiwaz (ᛏ), Nauthiz (ᚾ) and Othala (ᛟ)

"Who then shall defend Asgard and Midgard and the Holy Kin? Who shall keep the wolf at bay and Loki bound, if not us? We, who with the words on our lips, the blood of Odin in our veins, did vow to defend such a noble way, all the way to Ragnarok and beyond!"

--Dr. Casper Odinson Cröwell, Ph.D., DD

HOF SERVICE for Fogmoon

LERNE ZU LEIDEN OHNE KLAGEN!!!
(Learn to suffer without complaint)

It seems no matter where one resides upon Midgard (Earth) today, great upheavals have been and continue to disrupt the very social environs which we populate and thereafter, the economic state which is directly associated with such discord and so many dismaying circumstances. Midgard's financial and banking institutions continue to founder in their feeble efforts to reform and resuscitate the depressed and ever yet plummeting economy, over the entire breadth of Midgard. The Zionist controllers of these institutions, themselves, suffer no such financial crisis, to be sure.

Accompanying this state of arrested economy, are a myriad of frustrations and fears. Folks are losing money, jobs and homes. Therewith, such despairing circumstances do in fact create various conditions in the manner in which Folk may deal with such troubling times. Some may slip into depressed emotional states and seek relief with alcohol and/or drug use...

No better burden can a man carry on the road
than a store of common sense;
a worse journey-provisioning he couldn't carry
over the land than to be too drunk on ale.
- Odin, Hávamál 11

It isn't as good as it's said to be,
ale, for the sons of men;
for the more he drinks, the less he knows
about the nature of men.
- Odin, Hávamál 12

The heron of forgetfulness hovers over the ale drinking; he steals men's wits;
with the feathers of this bird I was fettered
in the court of Gunnlod.
- Odin, Havamal 13

Alas, one's problems yet remain when sobriety returns, yet further is one now shorter on money for such squandering...

The foolish man lies awake all night
and worries about things;
he's tired out when the morning comes
and everything is just as bad as it was.
- Odin, Hávamál 23

Others may drop to their knees in desperation and beg a Bedouin/Semite god to intervene on their behalf. Making promises in return for the answered prayer. Promises born of desperate minds that never keep such promises once the crisis of the moment has passed...

Any religion which denies the natural laws
of the universe, is false.
- David Lane, the 1st Precept

Looking heavenward at an empty and non-responsive sky, they petition the nothingness of Abrahamic/Zionist design. But nothing yields only more nothing! In these continued states of despair, such Folks will start asking the nothingness; "Jesus or god, where are you? Don't you care about me? How could you allow me to lose my job, money and/or house, etc.?"...

God(s) and religion are distinct, separate and often conflicting concepts. Nature evidences the divine plan, for the natural world is the work of the force or the intelligence men call God(s). Religion is the creation of mortals, therefor pre-destined to fallibility. Religion may preserve or destroy a people, depending on the structure given by its progenitors, the motives of its agents and the vagaries of historical circumstances.
- David Lane, the 3rd Precept

There are no answers in the empty sky! The answers lie in the self-determination and applied will of an individual. Such are the realities of life on this mortal coil that we call Midagard, and are the lessons of 'our' Gods!

COURAGE
HONOR
STRENGTH
SELF RELIANCE
INDUSTRIOUSNESS
PERSEVERANCE
TROTH
HONESTY
HOSPITALITY
the Nine Noble Virtues of Odinism

He should get up early, the man who has few workers,
and go about his work with thought;
much he neglects, the man who sleeps in the mornings,
wealth is half won by the vigorous.
- Odin, Hávamál 59

The examples of our Gods and ancestors <u>are</u> tangible models with genuine application in our lives today! Allow yourself a moment of pause for consideration. How does one go about accepting a nonsensical and foreign theology? For over a thousand years now, the western world has blindly accepted the myths of Jesus and Christianity with little or no practical/reasonable consideration. Little honest investigation, on the whole question, has been posited. And where such inquiries have been conducted and postulated, the preponderance of truth yielded by such, has vehemently been dismissed by the church, while the scholars and inquirers have been branded as heretics anti-Christ's and plain lunatics, for presenting their valid discoveries! Blind faith is the agent of primacy in an arrested appetite for the truth. It robs men and women of average and above intelligence, of their desire to investigate the matter of spirituality for themselves. Rather, such folks place their spiritual welfare in the clergy of a 'Pie in the sky' faith.

I say; "NO THANKS!" I want my pie on the table in front of me in this lifetime. As a Gothi (Priest), it is my duty to teach;

1) That no priest or minister has an exclusive or better means of communicating with the divine (Gods) than you; yourself do! You do not need any 'Official' Clergy member to speak to the Gods for you and translate their meaning. Why, the mere notion is Balderdash! And it has kept the church in business a millennia now...

"...Choose only a guardian who has no interest in the accumulation of material things."
- David Lane, the 42nd Precept

and

The judgments of the guardians, the leaders, must be true to natural law and tempered by reason.
- David Lane, the 71st Precept

2) It is the Goðorð's (Priesthood's) duty to teach Folks how to investigate the matters of spiritual truths and Thews (ethics & principals) which our ancestors passed down to us, for themselves. I opine that no better system of Thews may be found, than those espoused and endorsed by the Holy Nation of Odin, and the entire Fundamental Odinist community the entire breadth of Midgard! To embrace such a system of conduct is to extol a noble life of Aryan chivalry.

3) To afford Folk the opportunity to reclaim that of which they were robbed by the church a millennium ago; a relationship with their own indigenous Gods! To know our Gods and ancestors via the vehicle of "OUR" Folk's lore, myths, sagas, history and traditions, is an Aryan birthright. Not bigotry! And in knowing this, one may discover a rich, diverse and unique scope of Aryan culture and heritage to which you were born by the very Norn's decree.

Start at the beginning... Our ancestors were either forced or duped into accepting this foreign and Semitic/Bedouin faith/god about a thousand years ago. This is an inexorable fact. Mentally digest that for a moment... Only a thousand years ago, compared to forty to fifty thousand years (or longer,) which our Aryan race/Folk have existed upon Midgard. So then, a millennium ago, the chain of corruption had begun. Passed, from father to son and mother to daughter each generation, thereafter, right up to the present era, just accepting this alien creed, based on blind faith. Ergo, lies had supplanted the truth of nature via the vehicle of custom and use. Why, there is not even a shred of genuine, convertible evidence that shows that the Jew Rabbi, Jesus, ever existed in the flesh. Why is that? Certainly, older and truly existing personae left tangible evidence of "Their being", from which we may verify their existence...

History, both secular and religious, is a fable conceived in self-serving deceit and promulgated by those who perceive benefits.
- David Lane, the 6th Precept

and

Religion in its most beneficial form is the symbology of a people and their culture. A multiracial religion destroys the senses of uniqueness, exclusivity and value necessary to the survival of a race.
- David Lane, the 7th Precept

In fact, the first we ever hear of this alleged son of the Semite god Yahweh, named Jesus, is in the gospels of the New Testament Bible, which in and of itself is nothing more than a compendium of dubious accounts of this Bedouin/ Semite religious figure.

A persuasive argument for the "Jesus as fiction", paradigm is the book by Joseph Atwill; "Caesar's Messiah" (see Chapter. 4, 'Building Jesus'). Both Atwill and his book may be accessed at www.caesarsmessiah.com.

This much is a certain truth, at least 85 to 95% of the church's rituals and customs have been usurped from several Pagan religions which had existed for tens of millennia prior to the advent of Christ and his church. This is a verified and inexorable fact, yet the church insists that it is a lie of sorts. So then; 1) why would anyone elect to follow, with blind faith, a theology based upon lies; and 2) a theology whose trappings and rituals are truly pagan in character, having been seized by Christ's priests? Another certainty is that the vexations which we suffer in concert with the depressed economy, corrupt and overbearing politicians and big government encroaching upon the laws of nature ad nauseam, are not departing any time soon!

But we can elect to "Viking up!" And take control of our emotions and actions rather than allow for our circumstances to dictate what we feel and how we respond to the externally generated stressors which assault us daily. An Odinist proverb states; "We cannot choose the joys or terrors which we must face in this life. But we can choose to face them calmly. That is an Odinist's resolve." In other words: "Lerne zu leiden ohne klagen (Learn to suffer without complaint)!"

Oh, I know that this is much easier said than done. Never the less, we must discard the "Woe is me," mentality of the victim, and forge ahead...

Silent and thoughtful a prince's son should be
and bold in fighting;
cheerful and merry every man should be
until he waits for death.
- Odin, Hávamál 15

We may achieve this very noble and stalwart thew by genuinely living the Æsirian Code of Nine, the Nine Noble Virtues, the Rede of Honor, the 14 Codes of Aryan Ethic, the Code of the Northern Warrior (Living Einherjar/1519) the 88 Precepts, etc... By truly living these thews we reconnect with our Gods and ancestors and we participate in our own self-determination until fate has its say and we are gathered up to our Gods.

Shun the weakness born from the womb of lies and despair!!! Seek the light of truth. When you find yourself down and out, transform yourself into a man or woman whom stands erect in the face of adversity, with pride and confidence in the knowledge of your lineage and its very beginning with our Gods. Heil Allfather Odin! And heil his Folk whom paint the canvas of life with the vivid colors of will and fortitude!

Perform a Blot to Thor or Tyr in honor of strength and self-discipline. And Galdr and meditate upon these Runes; Thurisaz (ᚦ), Tiwaz (ᛏ) and Sowilo (ᛋ).

HOF SERVICE for Fogmoon

OLD METAL RINGS TRUEST

Odinism just as any other religion, suffers its share of fools. Though we do not suffer them gladly, as the old axiom asserts. We are a faith ripe for the targeting by all of the so called civil rights bigots and racists in addition to the many poison pens of a plethora of ill informed or just outright slanderous journalists.

We do not promote, nor advocate any hatred for any, save for the mono-culture oriented New World Order. Yes folks, it truly does exist. Just look under "World Trade Organization", which has an agenda that despises any folk which fights to maintain its own indigenous culture. For such folks are serious impediments in their world wide plan for a mono-culture society of consumers.

We certainly do not exercise an open door, come one, come all, policy, which by the way, I do not apologize for, nor should I. Albeit, neither do we advocate, nor promote pernicious action towards those we seek to bar from our cultural and ethnic faith, or those whom disagree with our philosophy.

So then, why do you suppose so many seek to continue wasting our time and energy, reserved for spiritual endeavors, on defending who and what we are? Well, for one thing, it does just that... "Keeps us from pursuing our innate spirituality". And if this were to remain the case, than we don't stand much of a chance to grow as a community. And then there is the fact that our current Odinist and Ásatrú community is pregnant with so many conformist interlopers, bent on opening "OUR" folk's spiritual doors to any and all who would just saunter right through them to employ the sacred traditions of our noble faith, as their spiritual flavor of the month!

These conformists ill represent who and what we are about, all the while they point at us and exclaim that we are the ones who pollute our spiritually clean waters which run so Trú from Hvergelmér to Mimir's Well. They apologize publicly and openly for "our" genuine zealous and righteous troth as we wend our ways on along the Northern Road. Most of these folks/conformists are so called warriors in spirit. So who the Hel is going to defend them and their villages while they are being raped? The adversaries so bent on our corruption, which they cow before like some ignoble Thralls employing our noble Gods names! I don't think so! Real warriors serve and defend Trú folk whom practice our noble faith both, undiluted and devoid of either shame or apology. We shall not, this day, nor any other; apologize for who we are, or what we believe! **Nor do we advocate harm towards any whom exercise their opinion against us**. But make no mistake about it. We have not forgotten what nearly became of our beloved faith a millennium ago and it will not happen again. We are here to stay for as long as our folk are and we will defend ourselves from any and all violence with violence ourselves, as would any reasonable people.

Fogmoon is a month in which we honor those stalwart souls in Valhalla, "The Einherjar" (One Harriers). The very metal they pass onto us, the Living Einherjar, are ancient and rings truest! Sure, our adversaries have what may seem to be an never ending source of means by which they may wage their smear campaigns against us, as well as a battalion, or two of conformists and provocateurs amidst our spiritual community. Albeit, true to the Einherjar spirits which gave their lives for our Gods, folk, and faith. We too can man the ramparts and defend our faith. We can remain Trú to our Gods and courageous in the face of our foes attacks, no matter the score! We must not be measured and found wanting. We must exude the very noble principles and virtues which we profess to love and we must always remain beyond the scope of reproach. We must stand both, together as a legitimate religious community as well as alone as the 'One Harrier' when need arises.

And above all, we must remain true to our Faith and Folk (Note: one's family is a component of one's folk), and live our lives by setting the example of what noble truly means. Only then will our many adversaries see that our survival and advancement is not the threat which they claim it to be, but rather a benefit to an ailing, spiritually poor and morally bankrupt society.

Today, too many 'Fuzzy Bunny' - New age types have ensconced themselves within the greater Odinist and Ásatrú community in an attempt to usurp our sacred and noble traditions, and throw the doors to our Hofs open for all to seek shelter there. We must wrest from these charlatans, any grip which they have established within our faith and folk community and restore it to its legitimate inheritors, the descendants of our hearty ancestors, those among us willing to fight for and preserve our ancient faith and culture. We have no time, nor room left for self accepted weakness, whiners or politically correct dabblers seeking any outsider's seal of approval! That does not require any genuine conviction at all!!! The morrow does not belong to the meek. But rather to the stalwart and bold souls who would own it, no matter their race, creed, or religion. That is nature's law!

We, the genuine and unabashed Odinists are just such a folk. We are they who say "yes" to life and for that we shall not apologize to anyone!

On the 11th of Fogmoon, perform a Blót to the Einherjar Proper. Toast those brave souls in Valhalla during Sumble. Call upon All-Father, victory bringer, to assist you in your own struggle to remain Trú in the face of adversity. Meditate on and Galdr these Runes:

Tiwaz (ᛏ), Sowilo (ᛋ) and Othala (ᛟ).

I remain in service to the Gods and Folk of the HOLY NATION OF ODIN. In Frith with thee...

"Any self proclaimed warrior can face death while in the host with others...
But the truly extraordinary ones embrace it equally alone. We call them Einherjar!"
--Dr. Casper Odinson Cröwell, Ph.D., DD

Meditations and Musings of Goði Casper Odinson Cröwell

"Let us resolve to adjourn now from the forum of corrupt and senseless politics, and get on with the serious business of securing our right to self-determination."

"If we do not forge our swords in the fires of history, how then can we shape our own destiny?"

"If authenticity is truly desired, then one must begin with the very root of origin; for there, may one, glean the fundamentals of such a thing. It then falls upon one to not only take it up, but apply it as well. That is authenticity."

"If mediocrity is the caliber of your big gun, then surely you shall suffer for it when hunting giants!"

Fear naught the coming darkness, nor the voice within. Let the righteous light of noble deed and the order of self discipline keep the dark agents of chaos at bay.

Let naught the wolf overtake the sun, nor moon. Let naught Fenris break free of his fetters. Let naught despair settle into your minds this night. And when the wolf doth break free, let courage be found residing in your hearts!

Life does not render unto any man, greatness. A man's own noble character does.

Do not capitulate to the minions of honor's theft! For they cannot wrest this gift from the Gods from thy soul. Only thou may forfeit that which your mighty ancestor's hath passed onto thee. With your life's risk, hold fast and dear to your heart this gift of honor. For a life devoid of this gift is merely slavery, perhaps even, existence at best!

Any self proclaimed warrior can face death while in the host with others... But the truly extraordinary ones embrace it equally alone. We call them Einherjar and Valkyrjar.

I have experienced normalcy and I have rejected the entire experience! For it is the normalcy of contemporary man that has sought to eradicate the very Gods which have taught me how to love life and myself.

Only your Kin and Kith may betray you. From your foes you expect it.

If we did not feel so inspired as to seek out the warmth of the sun in those rare and unusual places which afford us such serendipitous joys, we would all but stumble about blindly in the darkness until we finally froze in the cold and lonely shadows of the uninspired.

A man is judged by men of honor, by his own deeds of honor: or lack thereof. Not by the libel and slander of his character assassins, that which they seek to assign to him. As for such ill noble characters of poison pens and toxic mouths, their league of allegiance is limited to the small and simple minded...the easily duped!

Flatulence is the language of assholes the entire world over - it is up to each of us to rise above their stench.

If struggle, controversy and hardship are absent from your life...surely you must be dead inside and therefore, incapable of growth.

Beware of them who favor only the sunshine's warmth. For they hath grown complacent and their honor suffers wantonly for it.

If we fail to escape the bonds of complacency, how then shall we ever hope to bask in the radiance of divinity?

People are only bi-products of their environments if they lack the fortitude and conviction to live like Gods. Rectitude is ever an attractive quality to those in possession genuine character.

What terror awaits just beyond the shadow's edge? What horrors, that repel so many, yet attract so few...those bold enough to cross from the light into the dark and seize what nature has promised? It is there, lurking just beyond the shadows, the balance of those who abide by the laws of natural order.

By what measure might we calibrate the strength of a man's character, if not initially by the iron bond of his word?

If gray is made of black and white, and darkness is devoid of any guiding light...then which is the way that shall lead us back to a world that is bright?

Let no man become overconfident in his bearing that he fails to remain ever vigilant and prepared to battle the forces of chaos amassed against him. For they offer neither truce nor reprieve.

Sympathy, the thing itself, is always coveted by the undeserving. For those souls whom warrant it, seldom desire it.

Life is simple. You make choices and then you live with them, you don't look back and torment your soul with what may have been!

A cause devoid of genuine passion is empty, in fact. And therefore always in peril of being filled with whatever comes along to consume such an emptiness.

Be naught a today without a morrow on the horizon, lest you wish to perish as yesterday's forgotten kin.

Mastery of a healthy self requires compatibility between one's virtues and one's actions. Whereby it is the natural inclination of strength to despise weakness, one must learn to evict that which is incompatible with the mastery of the self.

Is a ripple upon the quiet pond an intrusion on peace, or an assault upon stagnation?

Every hour wounds, but the last one kills and none are exempt... A clear conscience is needed, for the final hour always arrives both unexpected and uninvited!

Without darkness we would not be able to comprehend the light. Order is born first of chaos, and with a delicate balance, a synthesizer, balancing in the chasm, 'we are'. And were it not so, this inexorable law of nature, then there would be nowhere, space nor time. Ergo, "we" too would cease to be.

From foul waste often beauty is born; does the rose not begin its journey encapsulated in manure?

Aspirations not acted upon, are merely failures kindly disguised.

Only through self discipline can one come to know the power of will... And only through the will is triumph born.

In rumination, freedoms are born. The mind and soul achieve liberty, or thralldom.

On the wings of perseverance one may wend far. But with only a single oar in the water, the journey is short and ends in a tiring circle.

Confusion exists only in the absence of knowledge. Ignorance exists only where the desire for wisdom is dead. For experience teaches when we listen. Ah...But wisdom only arrives when we learn.

It is a noble virtue to be kind to your kin and kith. Albeit, more so, to be extremely cruel to your foes, and to offer them no truce.

To peer down is to view naught more than debris and despair. To gaze empyrean is to spy the heavens and the stars. But to look within is to behold the abyss; the whole of potential resides therein.

If we do not seek out the mysteries of life, we shall never know they purpose of our life.

The truly wise are never satisfied. Their thirst for knowledge respects no limit. Their appetite for wisdom is insatiable. Ergo, their lust for adventure is naught more than a means to an end... A vehicle in which they may arrive at their desired destination; the well of wisdom.

Self forgiveness? That is when you abandon hope for a better yesterday. That is the only genuine self forgiveness and naught else!

The inexperienced life is merely an existence.

The difference between the warrior and the victim is that the victim never strikes back.

One whom allows weakness to manifest within one's self without resistance is only inviting failure to be a permanent guest in one's life.

A grievous error..."my" grievous error, placing expectations far too high on others incapable of obtaining such an acceptable standard.

Nobility is not a birthright, such as we are led to believe. It is a character trait, defined by one's actions and conduct.

Once the battle has begun, there can be no surrender. And so there shall be none!

If the grass truly is greener on the other side, one still must mow it! Lest it become naught more than a garden of weeds.

Some lessons may not be taught. They must be experienced in order for one to comprehend them.

A league of honor will always attract honorable souls. But a circus only attracts clowns and children.

The colors of life are never so bright, or vivid for those who merely notice them as they are for those who stop long enough to experience and enjoy them.

There is no wrong way to do the right thing. Where one seeks to comprehend the nature of Rúna, one must first comprehend the nature of oneself.

Evil is the absence of empathy where it is warranted.

MEDITATIONS

NEUN NACHTEN IM ERNTE: Nine nights in Harvest

Hereafter, committed to print, for the sake of both insight today to those concerned, and for posterity tomorrow for those who are brave enough to seek, follows the meditative musings of myself, the Herjan of the Sons of Odin, 1519-Vinland Kindred, for your perusal. These of course occur in the form of journal entries as they did in fact transpire over the course of nine days and nights of silence and fasting in some instances, during the initiatory period known as "Odin's Ordeal", which of course spans the breadth of nine days/nights in the month of August/Harvest. This is a deeply meditative journey which is capable of yielding truly profound results wherefore insight is at issue! And while I have been traveling the road of shadows since 1978 CE, each year's new journey has continued to provide me with great intellectual wealth. This year was no exception, and it was truly anything other than pedestrian... The Odroerir yet once more, have I consumed!

Odinsdagr 17, Harvest 2255 RE Day one
(Wednesday 8/17/05 CE)

And so it begins, another year on that holy and sacred tree, the path less trod. Another initiation reserved for the stalwart and noble character. None but the truly brave dare tread this dark road in search of the light. Only those with honest thoughts, who dare not look away from what reality shows them, may hope to approach the ancient well. Only those stout of heart will peer deep and long into its cold, clear water, and only those truly initiated will descry his eye looking up at thee from the depths of Mim's well!

But not without sacrifice will any see the Drighten's face, nor hear his voice on the wind. The ordeal is at hand...what will I see this year? Has the storm abated, or dost the tempest's fury rage yet with the might of the burning pyre?

I step forth now on this first day of nine, eagerly and without pause, knowing all too well, that in my endeavor to sacrifice myself to myself, do I honor the All-Father, my father! And with this holy act do I anticipate spying his face in the reflections of my mind. I stand ready, ready to embrace this ordeal with passion and an undeniable thirst for yet another draught of Odroerir! I ascend the holy ash of Ygg and eagerly await the coming storm.

Thorsdagr 18, Harvest 2255 RE Day two

I have awakened before the dawn, it will be sometime yet before Sunna smiles this day. And so, I sit in the early hours of the dark and silent morn, resigned to the loudness of my own ruminations. But are they in fact "my" own? Or are they not to be attributed to the old Sage himself? I can hear the distant echoes of a thunder which none save for myself can hear. It vaguely reveals itself to my awareness, calling out to me whence it has come. Its origin rooted in that which is ancient and nourished by the Laguz of Urd's well!

Soon, my senses will be assaulted by the cacophony of Loki's laughter as this place comes to life! Such is the torment of residence in Fetter Grove. Fjolsvidr's echo will however, permeate my mind and drowned out the din of the day and the music of Thor's chariot will keep Laufey's son at bay as I hang upon the tree and send hither and tither my mind, in search of that sacred echo which travels the sanguine highway of millennia past...Hail Odin!

Later same day -

It begins with a desire really. To comprehend the ideas and language of great masters of thought; Nietzsche, Wagner, da Vinci, Edison, Grimm, Machiavelli, Aristotle, Plato, Socrates, Hitler, Herodotus, Franklin, Jefferson, Twain, Whitman, Yeats, Kipling, Patton, and so very many more! The ghosts of these men have been my dearest companions for so many years now. They have goaded me on to higher idealism and aspirations. They have witnessed my struggles, watched me stumble and demanded that I get up and refuse to yield to defeat! I have heard them all in my darkest hours; "Pity naught thyself, ye of noble heart and character, for self pity is a whore, a pining thief and she will rob thou of thine senses!"

I seek to join the social order of these sage men, though I dare not assume the pompous air of arrogance in thinking myself worthy as of yet, though I forge on ahead. The wise are never sated, their thirst for knowledge and wisdom shant ever respect the bounds which confine the mundane and complacent minds of the masses... Not ever!

Hail to those great thinkers, for are they not all, each one, but incarnations of Odin himself? Made manifest in the shapes of these men's minds? And thereby bestowing veracity to the fact that the All-Father is often-wandering among us.

He is here, with me now, this very moment. And I shall wax from our intellectual exchange. The wind begins to rock the tree and I rejoice in the fruits of sacrifice.

Friggasdagr 19, Harvest 2255 RE Day three

It is day three of the Ordeal and the resonations of my last words two days ago have now receded into the silence. Sunna's ascension over the Sierra Nevada Mountains this morn was a magnificent and wondrous sight to behold! It is just after 6:30 a.m. and soon this place will explode with the sound of prison life, and like a great beast, it will tear this sacred silence asunder. Today is also the third day of the Festival of Runes, and it concentrates on battling the ego this day, in an effort to achieve victory by sacrificing self to self. This particular guest far exceeds the parameters of this day for me however. For I seek to slay my ego daily, for it is the only thing which stands in the way of one's own progress. Tiwaz (↑) is the runic key for unlocking the door which would otherwise oppose success...to invoke its power is just not enough, one must become it wholly, and so I do. This day I shall know the victory I seek. Hail All-Father Odin!

Lagaurdagr 20, Harvest 2255 RE Day four

Hmmm..., day four is upon me and the pace quickens. My dreams last night were very vivid, graphic and colorful. In these dreams, I journeyed far and wide. Some of it was very pleasant while other portions of it were not. I had a companion with me everywhere, Odin, of course. Over and over again, he advised me; "Trust naught those whom have yet to earn it. And never trust any man whom fears the shadows of darkness, or what awaits him there." My meditations throughout this day and night will find me considering Hár's words/Rede well. On another note, yesterday, a Skraeling who moved into the cell block a few days ago was impressed that I was not speaking for such a lengthy time and for such a noble reason. He said to me; "I have something that you may enjoy." He gave me Black Sabbath CD entitled "TYR"! Three particular songs which all fade into one another are of special interest - The Battle of Tyr, Odin's Court and Valhalla. I reciprocated the Gebo with a CD to him which he was pleased with. The songs are haunting and moving, and that I received and heard them for the first time yesterday...I have no doubt that they are the voice of Odin! Oh, not the singing, but rather the combination of the Gebo, the CD's title in addition to those of the three songs and the lyrical content all occurring in concert with the timing. I have gazed into the eye so blue yet once more...Hail Odin!

This is Thurisaz's day to champion over chaos in the sacred Festival of Runes, Hail to you James Leisinger!

I will tame the Thurses this day and command myself fully.

Sunnasdagr 21, Harvest 2255 RE Day five

My night was without event, save for the dream. Ah yes, it is always the dream...isn't it?

I was at a mini mart of sorts, when a man walked in and shoots dead the woman merchant! He then mutters the words; "I told you bitch!" He glanced at my sister and I, walked out to his waiting car and sped away. I took my sister by the hand and led her away from the place with great haste! Then I informed her that I must return to the mini mart. "No!" she cried, it's not safe. I must go, I affirmed, and I departed for the little store. When I arrived there this time, it was twilight time, early evening. Nothing seemed to be amiss in the store. Then he walked in, firearm in hand and said; "You should not have returned here." He leveled the weapon at my chest and fired three times in rapid succession! I was down, but got back up unharmed. The would be assailant stammered; "But, but I shot you!" I felt a presence in the shadows as I tried to make sense of it all. And then, just as I began to wrap my mind, somewhat, around what had just occurred, the store had transformed into an old European village and I was surrounded by Roman soldiers while the Tribe folk looked on. The Roman was incredulous as his words began to make sense to me; "I ran you through, why are you not dead?" The presence in the shadows had stepped forward now. It was All-Father Odin, and his voice boomed; "You cannot kill the Einherjar, fool! None but the fire of Surtr will put them down in the final battle of Ragnarok!"

Now obviously, in terms of analytical psychology, fleeing the mini mart with my sister in tow was an action born of an overwhelming sense of duty to "Family", to safeguard & protect my sister. My imminent return to the mini mart must be attributed to a sense of living the Nine Noble Virtues, more directly to the point of the warrior's duty to protect and not merely stand by. And then there is my execution in rapport with defending the Folk. Odin restores my life for honoring my oath to serve the Gods and Folk, or so it is which I equate with the former.

The voices and lessons of our Gods and ancestors can and do speak to us on many levels, not just via the medium of our myths, lore and sagas, but via our dreams as well which speak directly to our souls! One need only learn to become aware and listen. I will consider the lesson and gift of their voices, the voice of Odin, from this dream, all day in my meditations. Hail All-Father Odin, hail the seeker...hail to those who not only seek, but find as well!!!

Manisdagr 22, Harvest 2255 RE Day six

I awake yet another day to bear witness to Sunna's majestic ascension beyond the apex of the Sierra Nevadas. It all occurs with such grace, accompanied by a loud silence heard only through the eyes. The nocturnal world recedes with the first tell of dawn's stirring. One must truly be aware to grasp the Dagaz at work here, if only for a few brief moments. The truths of both night and day enjoy a brief harmony with one another, just as they do at the end of the day. This is a time when one may look upon the face of Odin, when the light and dark hang in that precarious balance just long enough for one to consider whether or not they had just looked upon the face of God! Only the initiated will meet him in that succinct yet sovereign place. Doubt not what the mind would seek, would thou know and you shall know truths unparalleled which powerful Runes shall reveal.

Sunna shatters twilight, day has begun and with it arrives so much raw potential...so many possibilities awaiting the initiated, those bold enough to reach out and seize them!

Tyrsdagr 23, Harvest 2255 RE Day seven

It has occurred to me, and not for the first time, that so many who claim to know Odin, know him naught! Especially some so-called authorities of renown whom have authored a number of books. In fact, they have merely interpreted what they have read somewhere and then furthered it with some rehash in eloquent, albeit often verbose fashion. I have perused books on numerous occasions, whereby the author asserts how Odin has betrayed his own! I have no inclination to be disrespectful to any among our folk whom have authored such books reflecting thus. Though I would strongly suggest a deviation from the same old fare regarding Odin's betrayal of his sons and daughters for it is altogether devoid of any merit whatsoever and is valid only in the same vein as mere rubbish is!

Odin does not betray his own, not those who remain true at least. Folk betray themselves by failing to identify and thereafter, accept reality. Odin grants wisdom and wit, he grants victory to those of us brave enough to embrace reality beyond the minute and unrealistic scope of political correctness! Any trú son or daughter of Odin knows all too well that the day **will** come when he will come to collect his portion of the avowed Gebo exchanged between you and he. He will come to gather you up to him, or send his Valkyries to do so. That was the deal which any trú son or daughter has made with Odin via the oath of the Valknut; that it is understood and accepted that Odin may gather you up to him any time he sees fit to, that's the deal and shame on those who failed to read the fine print of the very contract they signed in their own blood! For you have betrayed yourself, Odin certainly has not betrayed you, or any other loyal son or daughter!

Such folk whom entertain such an absurd notion and even further it with their writings and teachings are disconnected from All-Father and too blind to see that. I would further surmise that any such soul has not had the experience of being fully exposed to the trials and ordeals of physical battle and violent environments where lives are taken and lost and survival is the object of the game, for Odin is always present, this I can verify for I have both participated and witnessed as much on many occasion. More to the point, I have met him there face to face!

Hail All-Father Odin! Hail those who 'truly' know him...and hail the Sons of Odin!!!

Odinsdagr 24 Harvest 2255 RE Day eight

It seems at times of illumination, that the knowledge and wisdom we so oft seek, has been right before us and all about us all along. Like some mystical forces, engaged in some arcane and ancient dance which is always occurring in our immediate proximity, albeit just beyond and outside of the spectrum of our mundane vision. It seems so wondrous, if not all together surreal, when we are finally able to grasp the knowledge itself, that it has always been there.

You see, that is just what initiation is all about. Even when we feel as though we may possess a certain, if only vague, understanding of that which we covet, it is the absolute clarity and certainty which arrives through initiation, which affords one the trove of confidence in said knowledge/wisdom attached thereto...A certain mastery if you will.

On day eight of the Festival of Runes, the initiate gains a knowledge, a perception of the divine within, and he/she participates with their own Ørlog and Hamingja in an effort to perceive said divine knowledge and thereby ascend toward an acceptance of this divinity.

Worship me naught says the father of Gods and man, but follow my foot steps and emulate my life long journey in search of wisdom and thou wilst honor me and my gift to you! His finger pokes at my Hugauga, stirs the Wode within my mind and leads me toward higher idealism. Hail All-Father Odin!

Thorsdagr 25, Harvest 2255 RE Day nine

Well, this is it then. The ninth and final day of initiation. When I get off of the tree on the morrows light, it will have been nine nights of silence having uttered not a single word during the span of the holy ordeal. Only the sound of my evening Galdr has pierced the breath of Nótt, the Rune songs alone hath escaped pass thine lips, riding on the stream of my Athem, those holy and all sacred Runes did travel, wending their way tither, unto all the worlds at large!

Transformed shall I re-emerge, inspired further hence by the taste of Odroerir.

Friggasdagr 26, Harvest 2255 RE The morning after

It is just the other side of sunrise and I have now descended from the great tree. The final night had delivered unto me two realizations, one very happy, the other, truly disturbing. The first realization is that, where I once sought only deep and complex thoughts while searching the realm of shadows, in search of greater wisdom, such was my only light in the vast darkness which enveloped and consumed my mind so that my Hugauga may come to recognize and embrace that light. And now, a second light has emerged as well, to stave off the impenetrable darkness, a gift from the Gods themselves, and delivered unto me by Odin and Freya themselves! She is my song, my Nordic Princess, Linda, and wherever my thoughts of her shall wander, my heart dost always follow! I render unto the holy ones my unyielding respect and gratitude! The other realization is neither attractive, or comfortable to embrace. And yet, this knowledge is passed down from Odin himself. It is an inexorable and sad truth, albeit, it is one which must be addressed and with little time to spare...

Where once our ancestors stood upon the sacred grounds, in the lands of our fathers, consumed with dismay at the knowledge that the sacred ways of their fathers had nearly been annihilated and swept from the plain of Jord by Christian marauders and converted betrayers of the folk. We, their descendants now, not only glance back into that long ago time of decline and despair but we too, find ourselves at that same precipice! Consumed with the same overwhelming sadness which accompanies such a reality. I have heard so much talk of the re-awakening which has been occurring since the late 19th and early 20th centuries, of our noble and sacred folkways, but look about with honest eyes and ye shall see a truth much less appealing and way more disturbing! We are standing in this wolf age, at the very place our fathers once stood, surveying the dwindling remnants of what remains of our indigenous and holy ancestral ways. Oh sure, there seem to be plenty of us to protect and defend the flame this day. But we age and wend without pause towards our own departure from Midgard to join our beloved Gods and ancestors. And who then will accept the flame we seek to pass, let alone vow to protect and defend and pass it on?

If we don't discover bold and courageous folk to pass our own knowledge on to, folk not only willing, but worthy. Not merely courageous in word and desire, but in deed as well, then it will perish with us..., ushering in the Fimúlvintúr and ultimately, Ragnarok! Those of us who lay claim to the old ways today bicker too much amongst ourselves and within our holy folk community. Too many Helmsmen and not enough rowers makes the longship's journey slow and perilous and without the means to outrun the coming tempest! Pride is a noble trait, but ego can and will wound. Egos in constant competition with each other will kill until all are defeated. We must learn to assume a mastery over our own egos, control them, not allow for them to control and dictate our actions.

We must place an emphasis on the folk, and not only the immediate survival of our holy faith and folk ways, but the advancement of it as well. The laws of nature dictate that the female quality/gender is required to produce new life. We are currently 90%, or better, male in our folk community the entire world over. We must make our women folk feel honored and welcomed as equals. We must find a way to make the old folk and clannish ways of our ancestors, which we follow today still, appeal to them as well. We muse provide them with the desirability to warrant their return to the old ways of our folk community, lest the old ways of our noble and honorable faith ceases to exist! Our women, better than us, and more suitably so, are more likely and with greater ease, able to teach our kinder, with their inherent maternal instinct. And our kinder are more likely and readily willing to accept what our women folk say and teach them. Nothing has changed in all the millennia of our folk's history. In over 40,000 years, our women and children are still a mandate for our survival and advancement.

We had better stop banging our shields and clanging our swords long enough to address this paramount issue. For there is nothing more epic of importance to the survival of our folkways and faith community, let alone any promise for the future of our folk.

So then, there it is, two realizations, two truths. And I embrace them both as well as the responsibility for which I am charged to defend and bring about a positive effect wherein both are at issue. My time on the tree was most enlightening and beneficial to me and my growth. May it be so for that of the folk as well! Hail All-Father Odin, and hail to those who have stayed the storm and rode it out while hanging on the tree.

Appendix of words and meanings

Athem - *a component of the complex Nordic soul structure, in its most basic sense, it is one's breath of life.*
Dagaz - *one of the 24 Elder Futhark Runes, very basic meaning is twilight.*
Drighten - *a very learned teacher.*
Einherjar - *Odin's heroes, his warriors, the slain, lit. trans. One harrier.*
Fetter Grove - *as used in this essay, Prison, Old Norse trans. Grove of bondage*
Fjolsvidr - *one of the numerous names for Odin.*
Galdr - *the Rune's song, chant, incantation.*
Gebo - *one of the 24 Elder Futhark Runes, very basic meaning is gift, shared or exchanged gift.*
Hamingja - *a component of the very complex Nordic soul structure, basic sense, it is one's store of luck.*
Herjan - *Lord of the Host/Order.*
Holy Tree, the - *Yggdrasil, the world tree, the multiverse, both seen and unseen.*
Hugauga - *the mind's eye. Part of the complex Nordic soul structure.*
Jord - *Earth Goddess, Mother Earth. Jord's plain is therefore the surface of the Earth.*
Kinder - *German for children.*
Laguz - *one of the Elder Futhark Runes, very basic meaning is water, primal waters.*
Laufey - *Loki's mother.*
Loki - *most basic understanding; the God of chaos and mischief. Loki's laughter is employed herein as descriptive of the jarring and unsettling noise of prison once the population is awake.*
Mim's well - *the fountain/spring of wisdom, Odin plucked out one of his eyes and gave it to the well's depths in exchange for a drink of its sacred water which imbues the drinker with unparalleled wisdom. Mimir, the well's owner is a wise and ancient Giant/God far older than even the oldest Gods. Each day he drinks from the well in honor of All-Father's pledge at the well.*
Nótt - *Night. Therefore, Nótt's breath is the night air.*
Odin's Ordeal - *Whereby Odin hung on the world tree, Yggdrasil, for nine days and nights to gain knowledge of the Runes, which he later shared with the rest of the Gods and man so that they could understand the hidden mysteries of the nine worlds, the universal*

truths and realities which are otherwise hidden from our immediate view of understanding.
Odroerir - *the mead of poetry, that which stimulates ecstasy and incites knowledge and thereafter, wisdom.*
Ørlog - *A component of the complex Nordic soul structure, primal layers, simply put in its most basic sense, it is like karma.*
Ragnarok - *twilight of the Gods, end of the world, an extinction level event along the same lines as that of the Christians Armageddon, for a lack of more immediate and concise description.*
Rede - *Counsel, advice.*
Runes - *Lit. Trans. Mysteries, secrets unknown to the uninitiated. Runes are comprised of three key parts, the stave/shape of the rune's sign/sigl, the Galdr which is the song, sound, chant, incantation, and the mystery, the rune's secret, its meaning. Runes are universal truths, manifestations of the divine knowledge made manifest and expressed through the secrets of the runes which would otherwise escape our comprehension of these truths. This is of course the very simplex and vague illustration of the runes which of course are far too complex to address within the allotted space here. However, on another and equally important note, it should be stressed here, that the alphabetical equation and import people today like to ascribe to the holy Runes, was of no real significance, or chief value to our ancestors until the middle of the eleventh century except under the veil of unique circumstances.*
Skraeling - *Lit. ON. trans., Native inhabitant, commonly employed to describe the ancestors of todays American Indians, though erroneously employed by some today to mean wretch, which by definition should be properly ascribed to the term Nithling. There is nothing ignoble about the term Skraeling when applied in the same context as our Vinland forefathers used the word It simply means non-white.*
Storm, the - *As employed in this writing, the storm is descriptive of the attrition of the initiation and the effects thereupon one who undertakes such an ordeal.*
Sunna - *the Sun Goddess, the sun.*
Surtr - *The Fire Giant of destruction. His flame will consume the whole of Midgard (earth) at the time of Ragnarok, hence, Surtr`s fire.*
Thor - *The God of strength, Son of Odin (father Sky) and Jord (Mother Earth). God of thunder, brother of the folk and defender of both Gods and folk.*

Thurisaz - *one of the 24 Elder Futhark Runes, very basic meaning is strength, breaker of resistance and thorn of restriction.*
Thurses - *Giants, forces of chaos.*
Tiwaz - *one of the 24 Elder Futhark runes, its basic meaning as used in this writing, is self sacrifice for higher purpose.*
Urd's Well - *also the Well of Wyrd, or wyrd's well, the well of fate, named for one of the three Norns (fates), Urd = that which has already occurred, the past.*
Valknut - k*not of the slain, should be worn only by those fully dedicated to Odin, both in life and death. It is a visual oath for all to see that its wearer is ready to be taken into the ranks of Valhalla any time Odin sees fit to take him/her.*
Valkyries - *daughters of Odin.*
Ygg - *one of the numerous names for Odin, Lit. Trans. The Terrible, Terror of the Gods. Yggdrasil, the name of the holy world tree, means Ygg's Gallow.*

HANGING FROM THE TREE: A Quest for Divine Wisdom

An examination of the Norse-Teutonic myths, or more pointedly so, the Poetic Edda (*the Elder Edda*), will illustrate the Allfather Odin's relentless pursuit of knowledge and wisdom. No more poignant example of his quest may be gleaned than his discovery of the Runes (*mysteries*) while hanging upon the World Tree: Ýggdrásill. From the Hávamál we glean;

> Stanza 138
> I know that I hung on the wind rocked tree
> nine long nights. Pierced by a spear,
> dedicated to Odin, myself to myself on that tree of which no man knows whence its roots begin.
>
> Stanza 139
> No bread was I dealt, nor drink offered me
> beneath me I gazed; and roaring I grasped
> the runes from there, I returned.
>
> Stanza 140
> Nine mighty runes did I learn from that
> famous son of Bolthor, Bestla 's father, and a
> draught did I gain of the sacred mead dealt
> from Odrerir.
>
> Stanza 141
> Then I began to wax in wisdom, and grow
> and prosper; one word led me to another,
> one deed led me to another.
>
> Stanza 142
> The runes you must find and the meaningful
> letter, a truly great letter, a truly powerful
> letter, which the mighty sage colored and
> the awesome Gods made and Odin himself risted.

Within the language of the Hávamál, and indeed several lays within the Poetic Edda, are great Runes (*mysteries*) concealed, awaiting discovery by those who would "be" and "become" initiated.

Else wise, the stanzas assume a mere poetic quality of literary value; stanzas, kennings and metre. Indeed, few inquiries into the Hávamál and the entire corpus of the Poetic/Elder Edda, are surmounted from a truly Heathen/Pagan theological perspective, rather most, if not all volumes are derived from the very pedestrian vehicle of exoteric academia as are the myriad of translations which in fact are not translations at all, albeit interpretations of the lays. For example, the very word "*the*" in Old Norse is "*hinn*". "*And*", is "*Ok*". "*I*", is "*Ek*". The latter connotation carries with it; "*I am / I'm*" , as well. The meaning and value of these words do not change, nor are they complex in their nature, or form. Thus asserted, I posit my argument for "interpretation" contra translation.

With the afore stated in mind, we must turn to and examine the clues within the stanzas and their value thereafter. Particularly stanzas 138-142 of the Hávamál.

The myths teach us that Allfather Odin consumes no food. His only source of sustenance is mead. That He feeds all food dealt Him to his two wolves, Geri and Freki. At least, that is what most authors would tell us in regard to said myth. However, the myths do in fact have much more to say concerning Odin's appetite. In stanza 139 of the Hávamál, Odin speaks to the fact that no one gave Him *food*, or drink. And in fact when the world of men was young, Odin and His companions, Loki and Hœnir, go traveling upon Miðgarð when suddenly the three become famished! So they slay an ox and endeavor to cook it on a spit over an open fire, but the meat won't cook. This failed roasting of the ox is related in the story of Thiassi and in the story of Iduna's Golden Apples of youth. In the ladder, we may discern that when Iduna and Her Apples go missing from Asgarð, old age creeps and takes rent upon the Gods, Odin included! So then, Odin does indeed eat the golden apples which Iduna bears within Her casket to the Gods each day in Asgarð.

In stanza 138, Odin sacrifices Himself to Himself. That is to say that he sacrifices His base desires unto His "will" to higher ascension. This He does upon Ýggdrásill (*the World Tree*), which supports the multiverse of the nine worlds, and Odin says that no man knows from whence its roots begin. Clearly this is itself yet another rune to be discovered, as the myths plainly elucidate that the tree's three roots are each submerged in, and are nourished by the three wells; **Hvergelmir, Urð's Well and Mimir's Well**. So then, we must either conclude that Odin's Ordeal had occurred prior to man's initiation (or the capacity therefore), or that the meaning of the three wells lay hidden in esoterica from the uninitiated mind of man.

I opine that both are indeed the case in point. While the former wields the property of Odin not yet discovering the Runes until the next stanza, 139, and man would have to thereafter receive the gift of the Runes from Odin, in order to become initiated. He, "*man*", must yet become initiated *runically* in order to see that which is latent only within the esoteric realm. This presentation would lend credence to the latter.

The esoteric value of the three wells themselves are as follows; **Hvergelmir** is the well of the divine creative process as Odin thus "*wills*" creation to begin. The Elivagr (‘*eleven rivers*’), flow forth from this well and commence the divine process. From this flow, Ginnungagap will become full with the yeast and icy waters which create hoar frost and rime which in turn become solid blocks. From these blocks of ice will be born Ymir and Auðumla and with them the chain of life began!

Urð's Well is the beginning of time itself as reckoned by man. All which has been, is contained within the waters of this well. As a side bar here, albeit a germane one, Odin tells us that He spent nine '*nights*' upon the tree. Nights, not days, being the mode by which the Norse-Teutonic tribes had reckoned the measure of time. Additionally, annual time was reckoned by winters. To the Fundamental Odinist, this reckoning of time yet remains.

The third and final well is **Mimir's Well**. The water contained within this well represents all memory, knowledge and wisdom that ever has been or will be! It is at this well that Odin plucked out one of His eyes and dispatched it to well's depths as a sacrifice in exchange for a draught of its prophetic waters.

Odin aged while on the tree during his ordeal. For He consumed none of Iduna's precious golden apples of youth while He hung upon the tree. Conversely, once He had “*discovered*” the mysteries of the multiverse (*the runes*), He no longer required any food, for His vitality is sustained by mead alone and His employment of the runes' magic; specifically in voice (*Galdr*). Though from this point on, Odin is gray of hair and beard.

Stanza 140 informs us that Odin learned nine mighty runes (*spells/songs*), from the “famous” son of Bolthor, Bestla's father. Bestla is Odin's mother, hence Bolthor being Her father would denote that His famous son is none other than Odin's maternal uncle (*the Norse-Teutonic maternal uncle-nephew relationship is well catalogued throughout the sagas as well as history's tomes*). This much the myths are clear on. Alas, no more is ever posited about this maternal uncle who taught Odin these particular nine mighty runes.

Or, is the truth of the matter merely hidden yet more in the runes of the stanzas?

I opine that we, the readers of the myths are all too familiar with this enigmatic uncle. More so, we heathens who are initiated in runic wisdom are. The key lies with the adjective regarding Odin's maternal uncle. He is "famous"! Yet, not readily identifiable by name. He must be a Jötun as He is the son and brother of a Jötun. Additionally, he must be wisest of all beings, Jötuns, Gods or Man. By such a deduction, I opine that Odin's "Famous" uncle is none other than Mimir. This is why Odin loves Him so. Why He preserves and protects His head. Seeks rede (*counsel*) from His head, right up till Ragnarök itself! It too bears fruit as to why He sacrificed an eye at the well in order to gain the power to see with His Hugauga (*'mind's eye'*). And who else is wise enough to teach Odin nine mighty runes, when He had already gained knowledge of the entire elder Futhark? Mimir stands alone and above all others, in my comprehension thereof.

Stanza 139 describes Odin's winning of the runes: "***beneath** me I gazed; and roaring I grasped the runes.*"

Odin's very declaration of His discovery of the Elder Futhark Runes, afford us yet another insightful clue as to who his "Famous" uncle might be. Looking down from his place while hanging upon Ýggdrásill, Odin would see Mimir's Well, where one of the tree's roots is nourished and where all wisdom (*the Laws of Nature*), is contained. The Futhark itself are components of those very laws if they are not themselves altogether, said laws. Yet one more connection to Mimir and His well and further insight into why Odin is so smitten with the wisdom which the well's waters do contain. This too, is "why", the sacrifice of an eye plucked and plunged into the well's depth. That He may see what is hidden in the well's deep... the worlds below! Odin's eyes have assumed many equations by the myriad of mythologists and scholars in their writings. For example, His sacrificed eye has been equated with the moon (*Mani*), in the ink black night sky. A reflection of His eye peering up from the bottom of Mimir's Well. Also, the eye can see into all of the dark realms of the underworld. Conversely, His remaining eye is the sun (*Sunna*), itself, hence the sunwheel also being called 'the 'Eye of Odin'. This eye sees all which occurs in the bright realms of the 'visible' world. When Odin occupies His throne, Hliðskjalf, He has use of both of his eyes' sight, which is how He can see into all nine worlds!

It is the nine mighty runes which the corpus of this study addresses, albeit not prior to unearthing a few more germane clues from the stanzas relating to the runic knowledge won by Odin while submitting Himself to the rigors of His ordeal upon Ýggdrásill.

Stanza 141 relates that once the Allfather began to wax in wisdom and prosper, one Word led to another for Him; meaning one rune led to the next in the rune ring... *Fehu to Uruz to Thurisaz, etc., etc...* The words being voiced as Galdrar.

One work led me to another, He states. This assumes the rune's value in '*Deed*', or action. One leading to the next and so on and so forth. When the ring arrives at Othala, it begins again at Fehu. It is an endless circle, or ring... *Self-transformation on a continuum!*

Finally, for this analogy, stanza 142 regards a '*meaningful letter*'. The letter being the rune's stave (*shape*) with the added property of its song (*Galdr*). We are counseled by the Allfather Odin, to seek this One powerful rune above all others! Which rune is being given such an epic station of importance? Is it the Odinic paradox of Dagaz? Perhaps the mother rune of Hagalaz, which all others may be found in. How about Elhaz as life rune? What about Eihwaz as life, death and rebirth rune, which runs the very axis length of Ýggdrásill? Maybe it is Jera in its cyclical form and function, or Manaz as representative of Aryan man's divine ancestry!

It could be any one of these runes mentioned with good cause. Though I opine that very rune in question, mightiest among them all, must itself give birth to Ansuz in turn. The sound validity which I offer for this is that the rune Ansuz, in and of itself, is the Divine Breath which Odin himself imbued Aryan man with... the Önd... with which we may comprehend all other knowledge and wisdom. Our very awareness of this knowledge is awakened and waxes when we ourselves "become" initiated. When we elect to hang upon the tree ourselves and "be".

Therefore I opine that Nauthiz (ᚾ) is the rune, or letter, in question. Sacrifice is born of need and no cheap sacrifice will do. As with anything of value, one yields what one is willing to invest. The greater the sacrifice, the greater the reward shall be. So then, how great the need (ᚾ)?

When we forfeit our actual voice with a vow of silence for a given period, we are hanging on the tree (the Ýggdrásill Rite); our voices being the one true thing which belongs to each man, and woman. And the longer the silence, the quieter the mind. The quieter the mind, the louder and more clearly we may discern the very voices of our Gods and Ancestors. To hear what they have to teach us as they speak to us from within ourselves. For they live in our blood! Every God and ancestor of our Aryan lineage which has ever existed, yet lives in every single drop of our blood. Their voices travel the highway of our DNA, from millennia past. What an awesome and powerful awareness this is. This *is* the trú way of the warrior. Every Aryan man and woman who has answered the call of Allfather Odin, to serve our Gods, Folk and sacred mission of the 14 Words. When the mind is right, we are right. When the mind is not right, we are not right. We must learn to silence our minds if the voices of our Gods and ancestors we would hear. Fasting from food in concert with voice fasting for periods of time can yield even greater rewards. When we participate in this process for *at least three days and nights*, we begin to understand what it means to become initiated. What it means to "*become*" and "*be*" and then "*become*" again. "**Being and Becoming**". This is what the Ýggdrásill Rite is about. What it means to "*Hang on the Tree*".

After forty years of walking the Northern Road of Odinism, I have yet to see in writing, stanza 140 of the Hávamál properly addressed. More so, when seekers of runic knowledge have sought my rede (*counsel*) at the serious and complex level, none have ever queried about the nine mighty spells (*runes*) which Odin was taught "*after*" He descended the tree... "*after*" he took up the knowledge of the entire Futhark Runes. Instead they concern themselves with Odin's Rune Tally (*Rúnatals Þátter Oðins*), as did the rune sage Guido von List. I do not mock nor discount the Listian work, albeit I find it rather disconcerting that few, if any have placed much stock, or curiosity, into the nine mighty runes. To be certain, Odin's Rune Tally is of paramount import, albeit there is an equally, if not greater urgency for the runically adept man, or woman awaiting in the mighty nine! Perhaps this is why they are so under appreciated, or why they are so unnoticed beyond their stanza context within the Hávamál itself. Why they yet remain so obscure.

On one hand these nine mighty spells (*runes*) describe Odin's own quest for wisdom and thereafter His ordeal upon the tree. They too are the blueprints, if you will, for our own quest and ascension via the vehicle of Odinic paradigm. And yet, on the other hand, they are the laws of which no law of man may alter or manipulate. This is why they are so mighty I opine.

These nine mighty runes may be found within the Elder Futhark, albeit they stand alone as well. These nine runes, each one, are non-invertible. Their staves (*shapes*) are the same up or down. In fact, to assert their stave value in such a way is an oxymoron, for there is neither up nor down where these rune staves are in regard.

The Order of Odin's Ordeal

The Nine Mighty Runes are as follow:

ᚷ, ᚺ, ᚾ, ᛁ, ᛇ, ᛈ, ᛊ, ᛟ, ᛞ

This is of course the chronological order in which they appear within the three Ættir of the Elder Futhark. The order in which they appear in concert with Odin's Ordeal, are thus:

ᚾ, ᛊ, ᚺ, ᛁ, ᛈ, ᚷ, ᛟ, ᛇ, ᛞ

The process is described thusly…

> **Nauthiz (ᚾ)**, the Nauthiz (*need*) which Odin feels is the engine which moved the Allfather into action. His very desire for uncommon wisdom is the catalytic agent. This need (*Nauthiz*) initiates the entire process Need and necessity are indeed fundamental truths in nature's law: Winter *needs* spring, spring *needs* summer, summer *needs* autumn. Dark *needs* light and light *needs* dark. Chaos *needs* order and order *needs* chaos. I could continue ad nauseam; albeit, I feel the point has been sufficiently illuminated. Wherefore our own quests are concerned, the very frictions we encounter in our lives, be they deliberately created and submitted to for the purpose of "*being*" initiated, or whether they arrive naturally accompanying the day, are in fact necessary opposing forces which bring about changes. Of small wonder is it, that the Nauthiz stave resembles two twigs one would rub together to create fire. Nauthiz is the need-fire from which we may benefit.
>
> **Sowilo (ᛊ)**, Sowilo is next and is itself necessary (ᚾ) to facilitate the need (ᚾ). Sowilo is the *"Willed' force"* or action applied. The 'will ' and 'willed" action of Odin to ascend Ýggdrásill. In our own quests to "be", Sowilo is the mode by which we shall or shall not attain thus. Or more accurately, by which we "will" or won't! We employ our will every hour of every day. And yet, people with addictive personalities seem to believe that they just somehow cannot harness the energy of their will to cease whatever addictive malady that they have allowed to control so much of their lives be it substance abuse, over eating, gambling, shopping,

pornography, etc… But the reality is, *they **ARE** employing their will*! Just in a negative and counter conducive fashion. If one sticks a needle in one's arm to get high, they employed their own will to do so. The syringe did not magically appear with narcotics in it and then plunge itself into one's arm. *Of course not.* Will is the act of doing or committing the act. Positive or negative. However, Will as defined as will power (*Sowilo*), is the fortitude to act in accord with one's own desires. When you form a thought in your mind, it thereafter requires an act of will to make that thought tangible. When Odin *thought* to mount Ýggdrásill, it took His will to make it so thereafter. This paradigm and law of nature applies every day of our lives and it is inescapable.

Hagalaz (ᚺ), Hagalaz (*hail*) follows Sowilo (ᛋ). It is the necessary (ᚾ) hardship which will yield the reward (ᛟ) sought by Allfather Odin. This truth applies to every one of us as well, as does it remain yet another inexorable truth in nature's order. We all succumb to myriad of hardships in our lives. Indeed, I've heard tell that when sorrows come they come not as single agents. But in battalions instead. This may appear to be the case indeed to those in possession of a victim's perspective. To such folks, every downturn is a personal attack upon them. A conspiracy of nature at work against them! They fail to discern the opportunity which Hagalaz presents to them. For sure our hearty Viking ancestors shunned such a 'woe is me ', perspective in lieu of the 'cup is half full' perspective. Every day was an opportunity to them. And so it remains so today, for us, their descendants! Self pity always blinds folk and robs them of their otherwise stalwart dispositions. Whenever I experience this condition myself, I am reminded of a poem on self-pity by the author, D.H. Lawrence:

> "I never saw a wild thing sorry for itself. A small bird will drop frozen dead from a bough without ever having felt sorry for itself."

It has served me well as a swift kick in the seat of my pants to rid me of any pity which may blind me to the opportunity before me which Hagalaz so often provides.

Isa (ᛁ), Isa is the necessary (ᚾ) self-imposed static posture Odin assumes as He hangs from Ýggdrásill. Once again, Isa (*ice*) and its contracting force, is an immutable law found within nature's design. And so it goes, that for the one who can harness the knowledge of this agent of nature, one may thereafter employ said knowledge towards one's beneficial ends. At times, we must force ourselves (ᛋ) to slow down and take notice of what is in our lives and going on around us. Lest we pay the consequences for failing to notice such qualities. To turn inward into one's mind and to calm one's mind long enough to really consider the epic runes (*mysteries*) of our lives, requires that we *become* as Allfather did upon the tree. To move through time, but not through space! This is Isa at work as employed by the individual who has learned how to move as one with nature rather than against it. This is the key to mindful meditation and the success it may afford us. Just like Odin's example to us from the tree!

Eihwaz (ᛇ), Eihwaz is itself the very axis which vertically runs up and down the tree's trunk and thereby supports the nine worlds. Furthermore, it is the very vehicle which provides Odin access in and out of the world of the dead. It is necessary (ᚾ) for Odin to die willingly, to submit to death in order to learn the runes, (*the very laws of the nature which He himself 'willed' into creation*), and then return to the realm of the living with them. A rebirth! In nature, Eihwaz is the axis which penetrates the up and down corridor of the unseen world in which we live as well the components of it in which we do not. Subjectively, the same is true of Eihwaz on a microcosmic level which travels the breadth of our consciousness. Eihwaz is necessary (ᚾ) for us to effect changes in our lives. To kill off some negative aspect or circumstance within our lives and then revisit it long enough to learn the lesson, or gain wisdom from it, that we then bring back into the positive aspect of circumstance, so as to benefit from the very experience. To own it! As Odin did to win the runes.

Gebo (ᚷ), Gebo (*gift*) is the willing exchange which is necessary (ᚾ) betwixt Odin and the source from which He is initiated by, whereby the runes are revealed to Him. Mimir perhaps? We learn from Allfather Odin in the Hávamál, that *a gift always calls for a gift* in return. This is the power of willful exchange of energies in nature. Not merely to give and to receive. But on a continuum, that is one of nature's primary lessons, to be certain. And so it should be so with us as well since we are a part of nature and not apart from it! This law of natural order also harkens back to my earlier asserted point that we may only yield what we ourselves are willing to invest.

Ingwaz (ᛜ), Ingwaz is yet again a necessity (ᚾ). The very process of gestation is required of any and all potential, if it is ever to realize actualization. Any birth, idea, desire and yes, wisdom, must submit to the very process of gestation. This Ingwaz (ᛜ) is where Odin places the fruits of His labors and thereafter awaits the potential birth of reward. This very paradigm itself is self-evident within both the realm of natural order as well as in our own lives! It is not unique to anyone or thing within nature's realm. It simply is the rule.

Jera (ᛃ), is the harvest. It is the yield, but it is a yield which requires the effort of harvesting, just the same. This required effort is yet another necessity (ᚾ) in order to receive the reward. This is a revolution of a process completed. And it is cyclical. So long as we are willing to put forth an honest effort, the seeds we have sown we shall also reap.

Dagaz (ᛞ), and finally, the illumination occurs… the very wisdom which Odin had sought, and sacrificed Himself to Himself to gain! This Dagaz (*Day*) is the reward (ᛃ). It is a trip to the realm of the dead and back to the living with the numinous knowledge of the runes… the wisdom of the multiverse revealed to Him. This divine journey itself is necessary (ᚾ) for Odin, in order to descend the tree and meet up with the "Famous" son of Bolthor (*Mimir*), from who He learned the Nine Mighty spells (*runes*)… the very truths of the laws of the multiverse, *the laws of nature,* which are non-invertible! What a marvelous and courageous display by Allfather Odin, for us to employ in our endeavors towards willful sacrifice of oneself to oneself.

There are three wells at the three roots of Ýggdrásill. Only **Mimir's Well** contains all wisdom of past, present and future! While the Nornir (*Norns*) themselves assume the very stations of past, present and future, **Urd's Well** itself contains only that which has "*been*", up to the present time. Skuld (*Future*), alone among the three sisters, knows the future fate of man. And **Hvergelmir** is the source of the Elivagr (*'Eleven rivers'*) flowing forth. Once again, a past to present correlation. This leaves only Mimir's Well. A place where Odin will return to again and again, for rede from Mimir. All the way up till Ragnarök!

Yes, it is old Mimir's head which awaits Odin's descent from Ýggdrásill. It is He who will teach Odin Nine Mighty Spells (*runes*). And it is he who is Bolthor's "Famous" son! And in stanza 142, the truly great letter (*runestave*), truly powerful letter regarded therein can be none other than Nauthiz (ᚾ); the very *need* and necessity which recurs in all nine mighty runes. One need leading Odin to the next (*One word leads Me to the next*). One necessity leading Odin to the next (*One work leads Me to the next*).

With this wisdom, Allfather becomes aware that He alone may bequeath the divine breath (*Önd*) to Aryan man via the very act and vehicle of Ansuz (ᚨ)! This great necessity (ᚾ) (*a work*) to imbue Aryan kind (*his progeny*), with the Divine Breath, Önd. This is how and why the Gods and Aryan man are interdependent upon each other… the Gods of the North exist as they have from the dawn of time. But they exist upon Miðgarð in the blood of Aryan kind. So if we perish from Miðgarð, so too shall they perish with us! An honest survey of this truth reveals the genuine essence of Nauthiz (ᚾ) at work in reality.

I hope that this work will provide you with some valuable food for thought and that it may guide and assist you in your own quest for divine wisdom.

Oðin með oss

(*Odin with us*)!

The work you have just perused was composed by the author during the period of his Ordeal of Ýggdrásill Rite which spanned the breadth of 32 nights and 33 days without a single word uttered. This work is the fruit of that meditation

THE DAILY MEDITATIONS

Set honor in one eye and death in the other
and I will look on both indifferently;
for let the Gods so speed me, as I love
the name of honor more than I fear death.
- Shakespeare, Julius Caesar

1 At what point does one stop denying one's own existence, or more so, one's purpose in life? More again, when does one stop denying one's own true Gods... those of his/her own blood/ancestry?

When one ceases one's denial of the laws of nature, ergo, Odin's Law, one shall then, and only then, begin to appreciate the delicate balance that is our human existence within the greater scheme of the universal law of nature, and thereafter, our divine purpose in accordance with Odin's Law. The Judaic-Christian's Bible declares to all that the meek shall inherit the earth. But such a proclamation defies both the very laws of nature, as well as man's majesty, thus reducing him to an ignorant life form whose only purpose in life is to serve a Judaic god as a thrall (slave) and ultimately as fertilizer for the earth. More accurately the Bible should have stated; "The earth shall inherit the meek." For it is the laws of nature which demands that the weak fall while the strong rise. The meek shall inherit the earth???...Such an ignoble declaration is mere Zionist subterfuge designed to reduce the unsuspecting to a herd of docile cattle (Goyim), to be easily led to the slaughter. The earth belongs to none! Rather, Mother Jörd (Earth) is in the care of her Kinder (children). Where the meek/weak are in power, she suffers for their greed. And all who are disconnected from the wisdom of our ancestors are helping them to bring about our very demise.

2 The unworthy always exclude themselves - the Teaching of Heimdall

I tell you now; beware and remain cautious in the halls of fellowship... for weakness within our ranks poses the greatest threat to both our ancient way and our noble Folk! Self-accepted weakness often blinds its owner. Pride and ego prohibit such men and women from acknowledging this malady and thereafter setting about to correct thus. Rather, shame of such weaknesses and behavior associated therewith, should motivate one toward ridding one's self of such maladies. These may include substance addictions, fratricidal gang activity, lack of personal accountability, etc., etc., etc... While it is true, that to err is human - It is even more true, that to recognize such errors and thereafter, resolve to correct them, is to live like Gods!

More so, to take such measures not merely for one's own sake, but for the sake of serving Vor Forn Siðr (our Ancient Religion) and Folk, and in doing so with awareness... This is the providence of the Living Einherjar and the Code of the Trú Northern warrior. And as such, it is the teaching of Tyr. How many of us have known or witnessed such men whom don Odin's sacred symbols, or tattoo them on their bodies, without ever having subjected themselves to the very sacred initiations attached to them? How many have betrayed the sacred oath of the Valknut, by first putting it on their body or wearing it, and then one day deciding to quit following Vor Forn Siðr of Odinism (Our ancient religion of Odinism) and that such symbols are now just mere superstitions?

An oath made to Odin is an oath that one is bound by. And one way or another, he shall see that oath honored, this does he vow!...

> "A hall she saw standing far from the sun,
> on Nástrond*, its doors look north;
> drops of poison fall in through the roof-vents,
> the hall is woven of serpent's spines.
> There she saw wading in turbid streams
> men who swore false oaths..."
> Voluspa 38 and 39

Allfather will make good on his vow. The Valknut is a true blood oath whereby its wearer has sworn an oath to serve Odin, his way and his Folk, both in life and death. When one dons the Valknut, he/she is telling Odin that in return for victory in facing life's challenges, I am prepared to be gathered up to Valhalla at any time that Odin sees fit! For those whom don this most sacred symbol without having performed the proper initiation, a myriad of hardships and difficulties shall arise and remain present in one's life until one correctly performs the initiation. For those whom have donned the sacred sign and then either disregarded it, or changed their mind...they shall surely lose their mind, or suffer a violent death and then be cast out by Allfather Odin, to dwell in Nástrond, in Hel's darkest quadrant...

> " That I advise you secondly,
> that you do not swear an oath unless it is truly kept;
> terrible fate-bonds attach the oath tearer;
> wretched is the pledge-criminal."
> Sigrdrifumal 23

Such is the price such oath breakers shall pay for betraying the oath to serve Odin, his way and his Folk!
*Nástrond (Corpse-strand)

3 Perseverance in the face of real adversity is the measure of genuine courage. So many seek to join the ranks of the Living Einherjar, the current incarnation of the Männerbünd of the Aryan Tribes; Yet most fall short by leaps and bounds once the journey becomes difficult. For no journey of self-realization is without its demons. How can one hope to face an enemy's onslaught when one turns and runs from one's own demons?

The desire, by most who aspire to join the Living Einherjar, is born of some romantic notion rather than an authentic sense of duty and call to service. Their true desire to "BE", is one of selfishness, whereas the true Einherjar harbors not a personal desire, but rather, an obedience to a call to serve something greater than self-interest. The "would be" aspirant hears only the call of a glory which serves only his own self-interest. But the true Einherjar hears the call of the Gjallarhorn. He is willing to persevere in the face of all, out of his sense of duty and his true conviction in his noble and sacred duty. All others fall by the wayside, unwilling to yield to reality yet!

4 If ever the Sons of the North would sit in his hall, then Trú must their hearts remain ever more. For little do men know about the nature of their being.

But Odin knows what lies in the Einherjar's heart and he sees all that they do. Even when others do not. It is not enough to possess the courage to do the right thing when others are watching. But to employ that courage to do right when no one is looking... That is the hallmark of the Living Einherjar! For it is just such noble souls who carry out that which the Norns decree and nature demands. Not for their own glory, but for the glory of that which they serve... Their Gods, Folk and the 14 WORDS! Such is the Trú way of the Northern Warrior; the Living Einherjar.

5 He is no true leader, that man who cannot lead himself first. A man who cannot command himself is not fit to command others! For many is the man who speaks in a fair manner though acts in false fashion. His deeds in action belie the very nobility of his words. Simply are they spoken, though more difficult are they to embrace for the man who talks North while he walks south. Better off are they whom speak fewer words, yet honor them in deed. For from such noble souls do the heroes arise...The leaders of the din of battle, those fit to command others in the host.

6 Know well his ways and stand Trú in them. For tested oft by him shall they be, those who don his sacred knot, the Living Einherjar. Know his words well, and know them true! For long and hard shall be the woe and misery for those who fail to read the runes aright. Many are the tests of Odin. And as such, these are not slights. They are opportunities for glory and victory. For the truly chosen ones know this truth well. And always they rise to the challenge with laughter in their eyes and a smile in their heart. Heil All-father Odin! For he blesses his sons and daughters while he blinds the Níthlings, those who falsely and wrongly wear the Valknut. For such wretched souls whom sought glory cheaply will never see the signs clearly. And woe shall be their lot and for those who freely seek union with them, as well.

7 Long are the nights when the sons of men search the heavens for answers. Craning their necks skyward, they take in the stars enchantment... waiting. Always waiting for an answer not forthcoming. But short and straight is the journey for the sons and daughters of Odin, Kinder of the Gods. For the answers which they seek vex them not. They know to look within, for that is where divinity resides. The way of the Northern Warrior is to return to the place where his/her soul dwelt prior to his/her physical birth. That is,

the Folksoul that is the Gods. And to the very first thought, which is Odin himself. In such a return does one achieve a divine union with Allfather Odin. The Rune of Mannaz (ᛗ) is realized. Such is the purpose of those whose line began with the Gods... The sons and daughters of the Aryan Tribes.

8 To be able to distinguish what is truly essential from what is not. What is important from what is not. What is germane, from what is not, is an essential component in achieving genuine peace of mind. And in acquiring such a quality, one may better fulfill one's purpose. For the Living Einherjar courage is ever needed and thereafter, conviction in that which we serve... our purpose. Without the quality of peace of mind, our purpose may lack the needed conviction to sustain our focus. Thereafter, our meditations become less than clear. Ever needful is the might which accompanies rectitude. The peace of mind which accompanies our sacred and ordained mission to serve something higher than ourselves...The Gods, Folk and the 14 WORDS. For that is what is essential, truly important. And such a realization may afford the Einherjar peace of mind.

9 Place thy troth in Gods of your own blood. From foreign gods, no good can come for the people of the Aryan Tribes. Long have many a lost soul wandered about devoid of aim and purpose. Like some half dead form of life moving about in Ginnungagap, the great abyss, all the while groping in the perfect darkness for something to anchor themselves to. There, in their lack of belief in themselves, and born from an awful desperation to comprehend and know that which is truly divine, they have taken hold of the swarthy hand of a Bedouin god from the Land of Semites. There, upon bent knees with outstretched arms reaching empyrean, they forsake their own divinity; the blood in their veins, and they call out to him in a beggar's tone, to the one who forbade them to eat of the fruit of knowledge and wisdom! And under penalty of his vengeful wrath, they cringe and cower. Having forsaken the Gods of their own blood without having thought twice about it, they now point their self-righteous and accusatory fingers at us, we who remain Trú! Smote as the damned by them for our having the strength and courage to boldly stand erect with pride in our Gods, our Folk and ourselves. Yet their indictment against us is as empty as their wandering souls are, always in search of a spirituality that is never any farther away from them than the blood which courses through their veins, and the voices of the ancestors and Gods which call out to them. In time,

they shall all come to know an awful truth. For no heaven awaits them as they have been led to believe and so eagerly chose to trust in. You see, in a religion (Abrahamic/Semitic) where the chosen people of god are Jews... Only Jews shall benefit from such a theology.

Seek to know the Gods within, the Gods of our blood, and you shall always be richly rewarded with the truths of nature's law, the very will of Odin.

10 So few... Too few, are willing to assume the station of genuine leadership. Yet, so many are intent upon defaming those who are willing to sacrifice so much in service to others. For anyone who harbors designs of self-styled leadership always learn swiftly, of the taxing demands which await thee. For if such demands are disregarded, then one has merely assumed the station of a despot/tyrant, and nothing more! Corruption replaces genuine conviction and the sincere call to serve others. Of course, such corrupt souls never glean the reality of their own corruption. For such corruption creeps into their lives slowly, so that it begins to assume an erroneous quality of normalcy. One may not descry an error when such errors seem normal. It is only after the fact and in retrospect that one may glance back whence one has come, to see the reality of such errors. Only when one's self has broken free of the fetters of corruption may one clearly discern the very real and detrimental effects which such corruption had upon one's own welfare and even more importantly, that of those he/she had sworn to serve! Let those among us whom answer the call to serve our Gods and Folk, refrain from pointing the accusatory finger at others, nor advocate their defamation. Rather, let us employ their errors as a compass, that we may avoid committing such errors ourselves. Let their poor aim serve to inspire us to make sure that we always hit the mark. Let us never contribute to the already damning lack of unity amongst our Folk, but instead, seek to establish rapport and unity with our Folk of the Aryan Tribes.

For this is a hallmark of genuine leadership and as such, this is what is ever needed in the character of new and meaningful leadership. If you would truly be of the Living Einherjar, then truly a leader you must become in service to our Gods and Folk! Slay the ego, save the id, suppress the urge for individual self-recognition and serve the needs of the 'all' which is our noble Folk. For therein lies the requisite for the success of our sacred mission.

11 Many are the Sagas and lore of the Aryan Tribes. Many too, are the corruptions of them by those whom serve foreign gods.

Certainly great wisdom awaits the student and seeker upon the Northern Road, in the many volumes of sagas, myths and lore. However, great slants and influences of Bedouin faith have been inserted within many of them to serve such ends as was intended in some instances, while in others, it was merely an inevitable, albeit innocent occurrence at the hands of Christian educated chroniclers. Yet, within these many texts, great and hidden runa remain, awaiting discovery. It then becomes a matter of great care and importance to bear this in mind while perusing these volumes. Proper meditation and communication with our Gods prior to your studies should help you navigate your way through the murky waters that is our corpus of sagas, myths and lore. That you may successfully discern what is Trú from Vor Forn Siðr and what is from foreign influences.

All becomes a mandate on the wondrous journey North.

12 Thralldom may be measured by how much self-command one has forfeited at the altar of self-accepted weakness, vice and addictive behaviors. Even more so, by how little one is willing to do in an effort to eradicate such pernicious behaviors and correct such voluntary enslavement.

Once, is a mistake, while twice becomes a habit. Such is the simple nature of truth. We have all made errors in our lives. But as Allfather Odin informs us in Hávamál 133; "...no man is so good that he has no blemish, nor so bad that he can't succeed at something." If one would be free within, then one must slay the dragons which threaten to rob one's soul of such freedom. That which holds one down or back, will not depart one's life of its own volition! But rather, such an agent of sorrow shall wish to reside in one's life as a permanent guest when left to its own device. One must consciously own the effort to wrest back control over one's own affairs by exercising self-discipline and will!

Such command of one self is a requisite for any/all Living Einherjar.

13 The truth is 'always' the truth. Not simply when it seems to work for, or fit the desires of our ego or vanity. Those Trú to this wisdom, advance, while the mere dabblers 'mouth smith' many words which they pander, albeit failing to live by and therefore failing to truly believe in themselves. Though this does not stop them from forming, or offering an opinion which they are not qualified to offer. They may learn to mimic, memorize and recite truths, but their actions and failure to abide by those truths render them empty and of no account when and where they escape their lips. Before the alter of experience they are moot. For one who lacks both genuine conviction and the self-discipline to abide by it, his/her ego shall never serve them well, let alone anyone else. Ah, but one's fault is another's virtue within his/her own heart. Seek not to assign fault to any other. Rather, seek inspiration from another's faults to correct your own. Let others weaknesses serve to fortify your own strengths. Let others doubt enrich your conviction. And let others lack of resolve serve your own will to hold fast to your own self-discipline.

14 Treason is what occurs when cowards trade courage and conviction away in order to save themselves! Such souls seek often to justify the myriad of weak reasons which they offer for their cowardice. If they are able to secure a sympathetic audience, they themselves begin to believe their own lies as new truths.

The true Living Einherjar know that the Norns came to them while they were still in their cradles and sang to them/us, the song of their/our fate. Such a truth and realization affords solace, peace of mind and sureness as one moves through this world we color Midgard. True Einherjar shall not blanch in the face of adversity or sacred duty when the hosts and hordes of popular opinion call them monsters and seek to judge them as if they were peer to the holy Einherjar. The genuine Living Einherjar are peerless! When we are labeled ruthless and callous, we shall not capitulate before the rabble and the craven. NO!!! And we shall stand inexorably in service to the mission of the 14 WORDS as the very defenders of both Asgard and Midgard (Gods and Folk), secure in the knowledge that Valhalla beckons to us with the greatness which accompanies victory and the valiant heart! As for the wretched and craven traitors... Nástrond awaits their reception. Heil the day of the rope and heil the Lord of the Gallows... Heil Odin!

15 Conscience displaced will always make cowards out of otherwise courageous souls! The same may be asserted regarding unwarranted compassion or guilt. Such noble qualities of conscience and compassion become ignoble in the forum of war. Many great warriors, Tribes and Clans have perished from the face of Midgard due to their failure to heed this fundamental truth of nature and her laws regarding such affairs. One should never have any feelings of guilt or remorse, nor any misgivings wherefore the survival of oneself and one's race and Folk are concerned. Those souls whom cannot grasp this truth are weak and weakness only breeds greater weakness. If one is not willing to fight that which seeks the very destruction of one's Folk, culture and heritage, then such a soul does not deserve to live at all. Such are the laws of nature... Odin's Law.

This should not be taken to imply the promotion of acts of violence towards others. For it is no such license. However, if a foe seeks to act violently toward you, your family or your Folk, you then not only have a right to defend against such an attack, you have a duty to do so with such extreme prejudice and even greater violence than your attacker employs, so as to set the loud and clear example to all others with designs to trespass against you with acts of violence, to reconsider their ill intentions. Approach us with peace and you shall pass by in peace.

16 "A man is what he honors." - an Odinist proverb

A meditative observation regarding religion; Religions are in fact places in which we anchor ourselves to. Perspectives from which we view life and our world as we seek to comprehend our place within it and the myriad of mysteries which surround our lives, from day to day. Gods are those voices and inspirations within each of us that guides us to those places which we have anchored ourselves to...religions. The myths, Folklore, culture and heritage of any indigenous people gives rise to that race's indigenous religion. Therefore, if one elects to honor a foreign religion and its god, one is then dishonoring that to which he/she owes his/her very existence to; one's myths, Folklore, culture, heritage... One's race!

17 The warrior is the mind, the discipline of the mind and then thereafter, the expression of said discipline through the exercise of that mind's will. When the mind is right, the warrior is right. When the mind is not right, the warrior is not right. One who would study

the way of the Northern warrior, the Living Einherjar, must first study the way of the Aryan mind, one's own mind and the mind of man thereafter. For this is the way of the Living Einherjar. Furthermore, to conduct an honest survey of one's own mind and then connect with it - is to connect with Allfather Odin. To resource the mind's power and learn to exert one's will, is the way of Odin's warriors.

18 "Without the Gods, a soul wanders but is not free." - an Odinist proverb

To be free in the pursuit of one's purpose, one must follow the path which leads to the place where one dwelt prior to one's physical birth... The Folk soul/consciousness. An honest reverence for our ancestors and Gods, and communication with them will lead one to that sacred place and to the wisdom which awaits one there. For there one finds Mimir's Well, Urd's Well and the Well/Spring of Hvergelmir, where the journey of our kind began at the very will of Allfather Odin's bidding to "be"! All else follows. It is beneath the great Ash Tree Yggdrasil, which is rooted in the Nine Norse-Teutonic Worlds, that these three mighty ancestral wells are located, beneath its roots. It then is in the very recess of our Folk soul/consciousness and ancestral memories, that we may find the knowledge and wisdom contained within the waters (Laguz (ᛚ)) of these all sacred wells. By delving deeply into the waters of our primordial consciousness, we ascend the cosmic tree of life, Yggdrasil. For in such an ascension, we are able to follow the path which leads us to that holiest of places where we existed before we were born. Before we, as pure spiritual beings, devolved into carbon based physical life forms.

19 The Living Einherjar must always strive to adapt to life's circumstances and strange surroundings, while ever holding fast and true to one's convictions and reservations. If one cannot adhere to such a simple truth, one shall not achieve success at one's objective. As the old saying goes; "When in Rome, do as the Romans do." Many have taken this wisdom from our ancestors, as a license of sorts to engage in hedonistic or even odious behavior. Such thinking is not only pernicious, it is erroneous all together. First of all, no Odinist man or woman need require any such license in order to ease their conscience for their acts. Their own moral and noble cause and conscience shall ever be a faithful friend and compass as they wend

their way North. Equally as important is the intended implication of the axiom in question.

When in Rome, do as the Romans do, comes to us from the example of the Vandals who sacked Rome in 455 CE. In order to achieve thus, it was essential for them to infiltrate the very city. For they could not simply lay siege to Rome by just walking up to her ramparts, arms in hand, without meeting any resistance, prior to achieving their intended objective. Therefore, Gaiseric, the Vandal Chieftain, had dispatched scouts to reconnoiter Rome's strengths and weaknesses. In order to achieve this, the Vandal scouts had reverted to acting like the Romans so as to fit in. Having been successful at their mission, they returned to Gaiseric with their report. The Vandal army/navy attacked from the sea with overwhelming success and Rome lay in ruin. While I cannot verify the authenticity of the correlation betwixt the old saying and the actuality of the Vandals' siege of Rome, the example serves the purpose for illuminating the paradigm at hand, just the same. For the lesson of primacy is this: One's effectiveness and/or success, lies in one's ability to adapt and overcome. Such are the teachings of Odin, Tyr and Thor.

20 Being and becoming... We "are", but yet, we seek to "be", as well. The process of being is always 'now'. While the process of becoming is the seed of potential, the hailstone of Hagalaz (ᚺ). To be one of the Living Einherjar, one must evermore experience this cycle of becoming, being, death, and becoming, being, death, over and over without end. Simply put, self-transformation on a continuum: "being and becoming". It is the constant state of struggle throughout the whole of our lives. Each day we awake in the realm of the previous day's 'being'. We then proceed to kill that being, sacrifice our self, to our self, in order to 'become' anew for this day. This is the divine process of the Einherjar, both living and in Valhalla. If we are truly blessed by our father, Odin, we are afforded an endless stream of struggle for which we may overcome in order to "become".

Where the weak moan and complain about such hardships, we embrace them with a wolf's knowing grin in our hearts. For in this place of 'becoming', we come to know genuine self-worth and our true and divine purpose within the scheme of natural order. Yes, indeed...the struggle brings victory to those strong enough to 'be' and yet intelligent enough to know that we must always strive to 'become'! Heil Odin!

21 It is an unfortunate truth, albeit a truth all the same, that the overwhelming majority of the living Einherjar are now, have been, or will be incarcerated for crimes, not against the laws of nature, but rather, the laws of man. To be certain, some of man's laws are indeed necessary in order to maintain a functioning healthy civilized society. However, to be equally as certain, all healthy societies within the parameters of western civilization have ceased to be long ago. Indeed, here in Vinland (the U.S.A. part), over 190 years ago! Many a crook preys upon society with government license to do so and with little or no consequences at all when they are caught with their hand in the proverbial cookie jar, as it were. But since such types support the sick society of big and corrupt government, they may enjoy leave of prosecution for their errs, while those who resist (as our patriotic Fore fathers once had), are held accountable in an effort to minimize their threat to the sick establishment which forcibly killed off healthy Folkish society. But I declare to you all, live well by these ageless words, "Tu recht und scheue niemand!" (Do right and fear no one!). But where those do wrong to our Folk, without fear of society's police and courts, teach them well to fear us... Teach them well to fear Norse Law, the Laws of our Aryan Gods and Nature's decree!

While such Nithlings may enjoy some twisted privilege of being above sick society's laws, they are not above Odin's Law! This must all learn whom would have any contact with us. It falls to us, the Living Einherjar to enforce and carry out Odin's Law wherever his Folk/Kinder have been legitimately and deliberately harmed. Do Not take this as some license to harm innocents for your own satisfaction. But by the same rule of honor, do not seek to justify any excuse for allowing a genuine trespasser against our Folk to escape justice under Odin's Law. Heil Odin!

22 "From his weapons on the open road
no man should step one pace away;
You don't know for certain when you're
out on the road
when you might have need of your spear."
Odin's Law / Hávamál 38

The law of nature; Odin's Law, does not recognize the inferior and anti-nature laws of man which would separate the Living Einherjar from their weapons!

With wits and weapons shall the Living Einherjar tread forth upon Midgard in defense of our Gods and Folk. For this is the supreme Law of Odin. Today's "Spear", as it were, may be an AR-15, Ruger Mini-14, AK-47, Mossberg 12 gauge, S&W .38 Special, .357 Magnum, .44 Magnum, Colt M-1911 .45, etc., etc., etc.. Let any who would willfully trespass against our Folk and Odin's Law, be dealt with harshly as a foe of the Aryan Tribes. Extend neither mercy nor compassion to those who would seek to destroy our Gods and Folk. For this is nature's imperative, Allfather Odin's divine Law! And let not any among us feel pity, remorse or guilt over dealing with such ignoble fiends. They surely feel not toward us!

23 He is a fool, the one whom seeks the approval of others, wherefore the defense of himself, his family or his Folk hangs in the balance. Many are the corpse, which litter the plain of battle. Their bleached bones are a testament to their indecision in the theatre of war. A reminder to us all that nature's law does not always favor the most able or deserving warrior. But rather, those who do not hesitate! The theatre of battle may be the living room of your family's home at 3:00 a.m. in the form of an uninvited intruder. Or the parking garage outside of your place of business. At the ATM machine, the street in front of your home. Or it could be the gang warfare-combat zone which your once peaceful neighborhood has turned into! It could even be an attack against you in a prison environment.

Wherever it may be, hesitation could spell the end for you or your family. While empathy and compassion are noble qualities where they are warranted, those very qualities misplaced will make cowards out of otherwise courageous souls.

Just as much, invalid guilt is always a poor compass, it shall never point North! Better served are those without remorse wherefore duty and service in defense of our Gods, families and Folk are in regard. The voice of Odin is ever more the conscience of the true Living Einherjar. Heil Allfather Odin, And heil his true sons and daughters, those secure in their purpose, certain and confident of their lot in this life as the defenders of the mission of the 14 WORDS.

24 Let us consider nature's law, both fluid and inexorable. The elk on the plains, when confronted by the hunting wolf pack, will be swiftly separated from the herd and thereafter becomes the focus of the pack. If it hesitates for even the briefest moment, all else matters not beyond that moment of hesi-tation. For the elk, death now in the moment becomes inevitable. For the pack, they eat and live on to see another day. And so too must the pack be fleet of foot if they would evade the hunter's shot. Likewise, the lone wolf, wandering the route alone, must remain ever vigilant and be quick to act in the face of danger to either him, or that which he serves.

Consideration of all available options is the hallmark of the wise. But too much consideration may quickly dull the sharp blade that is the mind, and thereafter, ill reason one's self into submission and capitulation. Such are the rigors of hesitation's firm grasp!

Odin's Law: "He should get up early, the man who means to take another's life or property; the slumbering wolf does not get the ham, nor the sleeping man victory." - Hávamál 58

25 The true warrior is always a warrior. That is to say; one must not simply believe it to be only necessary to think as a warrior when the battle is at hand. Rather, one must think as a warrior in all that one does. Whether one is meditating, gardening, or preparing a meal, one must think as a warrior. Many are the students of martial science, whom study and spar quite devoutly. But when the chaos of authentic battle confronts them, many are lost! All the years of devoted study to their martial discipline is of little or no assistance to them for their lack of "thinking" martial science and engagement in all that they do throughout the days of their lives. Sparring is fine, it keeps the body agile and the mind sharp. But it falls short in follow through urgency. The practice of mixed martial arts training and competition are a sound means for correcting such a malady. Even better yet is considering any and all combative scenarios on a continuum. It is a constant chess game, if you will, in one's mind. Always seeing and thinking in terms of three or four moves ahead. The Living Einherjar, if he can avoid unnecessary confrontation, he will be victorious towards the purpose of his service and being. If he can avoid physical combat in a confrontation with his honor intact, then he will be the victor. However, wherever physical employment of violence becomes necessary, one should engage one's enemy, with one's full force and without remorse. You see, the mind is the

warrior! And when the mind is fluid and just, so too is the physical Einherjar.

26 When we consider the model of what may constitute that of an honorable Aryan warrior, we must consider those in our past whom possessed that quality of Aryan chivalry. For history teaches us when we pay heed to it. But honor arrives when we too become those very examples ourselves. Consider the example of Manfred von Richthofen, otherwise known to history as WWI Flying Ace from Germany, the Red Baron. His idea of battle was truly noble and beautiful, based upon the concept of Aryan Chivalry (Compassion and fair play "where" it is warranted), as opposed to wanton and unnecessary violence. Other such men are Otto Skorzeny, Robert J. Mathews and G. Gordon Liddy.

These men/warriors of Aryan phylum, are the very epitome of those warriors in command of their will, compassion, service to noble ideals and of course, chivalry. It then must become the task of every Living Einherjar to endeavor to make this quality of the noble elite, his own as well. To know when to be compassionate and when to be ruthless... Such a distinction is a hallmark of Aryan Chivalry and the Living Einherjar.

27 By serving our Folk and their spiritual welfare, we too are serving our Gods and the very will of All-Father Odin. Toward such ends, the Living Einherjar must pursue the mechanics of martial science and discipline and the study thereof. Every martial discipline that is available to the Living Einherjar should be considered. And at least one form should be mastered for employment. Fusion, of several disciplines is always advisable. Always remain fluid in your seeking of knowledge and the application of said knowledge regarding your martial discipline. Always remain aware, as awareness is the source of all wisdom. And always remain in motion, both physically and mentally. A hammer at rest is merely a weight, devoid of its own design and purpose. To fulfill its purpose and destiny, the hammer must remain in motion. The mind is the hammer! The physical exertion of the will, is the function of that hammer. To abide by our principal purpose as servants and defenders of our Gods and Folk, that is the way of the Living Einherjar...the Code of the Northern Warrior. There can be no spirituality, save for the means of defending that spirituality against all threats!

28 "The supreme form of courage is the one against the all." - An Odinist Proverb

The supreme form of courage is the one against the all. This too, is the very essence of the Living Einherjar's nature as "One-harriers", that is to say, the one/ones who fight alone. When one must fight, it would be nice to be accompanied by one's brothers-in-arms, for truly the Einherjar proper in Valhalla, prepare daily, for battle side by side with each other and our Gods, against Loki and his wretched lot at Ragnarok! At such a time, Odin's heroes shall exit Valhalla's 540 doors, shoulder to shoulder and 800 at a time. Off to Vigrid plain shall they wend to face Loki and his host of damned and dishonorable souls! However, where the Living Einherjar must, he shall stand alone against the ranks amassed against him. He shall face what the Norns have decreed shall be his fate/destiny. And he shall face what he must with courage, honor and rectitude in his heart. He shall hear loudly, the metal's song as his warrior ancestors clash and clang their weapons in Valhalla as they cheer him on in his noble and valiant deed! To bravely and boldly face one's foes, alone and vastly outnumbered if necessary. This is the way of Odin's true heroes.

Sometimes, that means that one must walk alone as well. Resigned to whatever one must face, alone. Even though one may be surrounded by others like him in appearance, it is the noble character and conviction to walk Trú North, which dictates their worthiness to walk with you, not how they look or what they say. But by their deeds. Where one has been blessed by the Gods to have another to stand with, he is truly rich. Where they are blessed with others of their metal and character, they are wealthy to be certain. But when one has only the Gods and the spirit of his ancestors to accompany him, he knows yet of his fortune and genuine wealth. For the promise of his descendants yet to come, he serves his natural purpose as defender of his Gods and Folk. And this he does alone if/when need be. Secure in his sound conviction of his service to something higher than himself. And certain in the knowledge that his lot in life has been preordained by both the Norns and Odin himself! Heil All-Father Odin! And Heil his heroes, the Living Einherjar!!!

29 Aggression unchallenged is aggression unleashed! In this, be certain. If you are attacked by another/others, do not expend valuable time seeking a reason for thus, in your head. For it is a moot issue.

All that matters at such a place in time is war! The neutralization of the source of the attack. If such an encroachment against your safety/welfare, or that which you serve (Gods, Folk & the 14 WORDS), is permitted to occur without defense and counter attack, it will be a betrayal to yourself and your honor. It will constitute a failure of your avowed duty to protect and defend that which you serve.

And it will invite further attacks against you and your cause. Odin's Law (the Law of Nature) dictates that where aggression is employed against us, even greater aggression shall be dispensed in response thereto, and without guilt or remorse. This is the Code of the Northern warrior, the Living Einherjar.

30 Regarding the virtue of strength; perhaps it is when we are at our weakest, or feel most vulnerable, that we must be strongest. For if not, we may survive the moment and then think ourselves to be strong. Only to find out just how weak we have become whilst we had believed ourselves to be at our strongest. Such unkind realizations always arrive as the light fades to black! Better are we served daily by honing our fortitude, than to perish on the eve of genuine weakness. For, from this malady there is no recovery.

31 Courage, legitimate courage, is doing the things that need to be done, but that no one else wants to do. Honor, genuine honor, is doing those things when there is no one there to bear witness to your devotion and deeds.

Fret naught over fame won, my brothers... For our father Odin sees all that we do. And he shall reward each one of us accordingly.

32 We as a Race/Tribe/Folk, have been displaced in our own Odal lands (Home Countries), by our own penchant for disunity as a people and diplomacy toward those who would/do deny us our own living space, institutions and self determination to fulfill our own racial destiny. We must accept reality as it pertains to Aryan man and resolve to correct the pernicious behavior. Say "NO!" to those who would seek our very destruction. Say to them; "Keep your hands off of our weapons and our women and keep your feet off of our land!" Place no allegiance in a ZOG Government of today. For no such government in existence at the time of this writing (2012 CE) is loyal or sympathetic to the enrichment, survival or advancement of the

Aryan people. Our Race Is Our Nation, O.R.I.O.N.! This truth, must the Living Einherjar embrace in our service to the sacred mission of our father Odin; the Mission of the 14 WORDS.

33 So many today among us seek to assign the lack of Aryan advancement, to one of the eras of the past century and a half, as it were, as they apply to political programs in the western world. But politics are by-products of systematic constructs based upon the racial makeup of that system's people, or groups of mixed races, etc... More so, said group's culture and heritage. If more than one people/race comprises such a system, the system will eventually suffer a breakdown, as it contradicts the laws of nature. Such are the facts. When a people/race abandons its own ancestral traditions, rituals and culture, it too is forfeiting its own heritage and thereafter, and ultimately, its right and desire to live as a unique race. When the people of the Aryan tribes traded away the traditions of our ancestors and their (Our) Gods, for the new Judeo-Christian mono-god, they ushered in the "Wolf's Age;' and created all of the chaos which plagues our Folk today! As a rudimentary point, it is not even necessary for an Aryan to actually espouse or believe in the traditions, myths and lore of our ancestors, as they are presented today. Just honoring such traditions is essential to keep the flame of ancestral memory alive! Fundamental Odinism is a "Living and Evolving" religion. To keep the ancestral traditions of millennia ago, alive today by honoring them. Of course, we also honor it by adding to it in a progressive and conducive fashion, in the same manner as Ørlög and Wyrd are comprised of many primal layers of the deeds of our ancestors. It then falls upon us, the Living Einherjar, to keep the wolf at bay by ensuring that the traditions of our Aryan ancestors (not Judaic Zionists), not only survive, but advance to our posterity.

We must assume our sacred duty as the men and women whom comprise the very bulwark that shall deny Zionism any victory over our Folk! As we find ourselves at the edge of Idavoll Plain, we may spy the field of Vigrid and feel the bite of the icy mist of decadence as it prepares to let slip the minions of Loki's host from their fetters. We must not fail in our service to our Gods and Folk! The truly ancient ways of our ancestors are yet our best hope for victory. Vor Forn Siðr (Our Ancient Religion) is timeless. Its wisdom is applicable to our Folk throughout all epochs of time. If we study the Lore, myths, Sagas, traditions and rituals and apply the very truths within them to today, and add our own constructive element to them as our contribution to the Aryan phylum...victory shall be ours. And when our posterity gather around the hearths of millennia from now, they shall sing of the songs/sagas of us today, along with those of our own elder days gone by, which we defended and fought to advance and pass on to them. Heil Allfather Odin! And Heil the Gods and Folk which descended from his will to be! May we today, the Living Einherjar, 'will' that our descendants too shall be, for millennia yet to come. O.R.I.O.N.!

34 A life of activity suggests a life of purpose. So then, let our purpose be loudly clear...The 14 WORDS!!!

Let our activities be creative towards such ends. Let us become the very vassals of Odin's will, the very vanguard of this sacred duty to serve the greater good of our Gods and Folk. The defenders of blood which Odin himself has passed onto us, and yet lives within each one of us!
Let our holy endeavor be that it shall course through the veins of our posterity. For it is his divine will, and nothing so noble exists as serving his will, that we as a race/people, shall always be! Heil Odin!!!

35 Dogmas, doctrines and theologies are nothing but words. They are the constructs of man. And as such, they constitute mere words composed and structured into phrases and what appear to be witty axioms. Thought is the closest mortal quality to that which is divine. While the flesh/body is the farthest from it. While it is true, that words are born in the cradle of thought, they are yet just that; words based upon such thoughts.

Deed is truly divine. For it both mirrors and echoes the divine communication betwixt man and that which is divine. Words are empty of any volume or value if they are not substantiated with deeds. Conversely, deed does not require word in order to be realized. Self-transformation via gnosis and converting divine thought into noble actions/deeds, that is the true way of Odin. Membership within the ranks of the Living Einherjar in service to Odin, our Gods and our Folk, that is Vor Forn Siðr.

Meditation is the way to commune with Allfather Odin. Thought from said meditation is the fruit of that divine communication made manifest. Deed in concert with such communications are the divine will of Odin and the purpose of his progeny; The Folk of the Aryan Tribes.

36 It is a rudimentary Thew (principal) that any genuine Living Einherjar, or the candidate whom aspires thereto be, must be a student of history as it truly elapsed and existed, not as is more oft than not, erroneously presented, today. We must study its truths and lies, that we may come to know where and at what place in time and in history that certain lies became the new truths. We must seek to correct such lies and reveal them as such...

> "I advise you Loddfafnir, to take this advice,
> it will be useful if you learn it,
> do you good, if you have it:
> Where you recognize evil, speak out against it,
> and give no truces to your enemies."
> Odin, Hávamál 127

Our quest for historical facts must be traced all the way back to not only recorded history, but oral history as well. And when we seem to reach the journey's apex, we must call upon our ancestral memory, for there will we find the Hyperborean origin of our Allfather Odin, Yggdrasil and our first human Aryan ancestors; Ask and Embla. There will we find the truth of our nature and being, and of the very blood/DNA which flows through our veins. The origin of the Aryan Tribes. This we must teach our progeny and pass on to our posterity, for it contributes to a majestic and glorious past and a foundation which is worthy of respect and elicits honest pride and shall awaken the desire within our Folk to serve, defend and fight for our very survival and evolution back to that which we devolved from...a divine state of thought/mind and being.

37 We must pour over all available texts. We must seek out that knowledge which now seems obscure. We must retain that which is essential and thereafter seek to experience and apply said knowledge, thereby converting it into wisdom, and we must discount the non-essential and nonsensical and all which is contradictory to the Law of Odin (Laws of Nature) and the noble character of our Folk. Herein shall we find our father, Odin, speaking loudest to us.

38 As the Living Einherjar, we must not allow those who trespass against our Gods and Folk, to go unpunished, anymore so than the

Catholic or Jewish religions respective security forces, would allow, nor that of the Islamic Jihadists! Let those who commit crimes of malice and violence against our Folk and Vor Forn Siðr of Odinism, be held fully accountable so that all would be trespassers will come to know... If you meet us with peace and honor, you shall pass by in peace (Frith) as well. But if your designs against us our ill-natured and malicious, you shall suffer the wrath of Hinn Hammar (The Hammer), and be held to answer for you crimes against us!

This is Odin's Law, and we, the Living Einherjar and Valkyrjar are his holy army of enforcers of that divine law. Heil Allfather Odin!

39 The only fingerprints which character leaves in its wake are the memories of one's deeds. The noble actions of the Einherjar and Valkyrjar are the indelible fingerprints left upon the very face of history for us today to employ as the very models of Aryan chivalry. A compass which always points North and guides us to heroic and noble deeds which benefit not our own egos, but rather, that which we serve; "Our Gods, Folk and the 14 WORDS.

> "Cattle die, Kinsmen die,
> the self must also die;
> I know one thing which never dies:
> the reputation of each dead man."
> - Odin, Hávamál 77

May our descendants recount our deeds one day with honor on their tongues.

40 Hold yourself up not to mockery, judgment, or sneers of lesser men who insist that they are your equal, peer or better. For such delusional souls are inferior to the Einherjar's superiority. From such men, praise for your selfless devotion and service to others will always be absent. In its place, you shall find only scorn, contempt, jealousy and envy in the hearts of such men! Be not dissuaded from your mission by such ill noble characters. Hold yourself accountable only to our posterity.

So long as even a single Einherjar lives, Ragnarok is stayed. Begin and end each day with this Galdr; "Ek Einherjar, ok Ek hinn Hammar!" (I am the one harrier, and I am the hammer)!

Let this be our mantra in service to the mission to our Gods, Folk and the 14 WORDS. Heil Allfather Odin! And Heil his holy warriors!!!

41 As stated previously in this work, genuine honor is doing the right thing when no one else is looking! As the Living Einherjar, we do not serve for the sake of praise. Rather, we do so in concert with the duty of the oath which each of us have sworn. The call which we have answered to serve and fill the ranks of Odin's holy army.

From those souls whom seek praise, fame and attention, do not seek companionship. For they will cloud your judgment, alter your divine purpose and rob you of your desire to serve honor, as opposed to ego!

Keep your feet on the road North my brothers and sisters and your hands upon the hilt of the sword named honor, and Wunjo (ᚹ) (Frith & Harmony) will accompany your Ørlög and Hamingja.

The way to your destiny shall remain ever clear in both your heart and your mind. Such is the teaching of Baldur and the true cradle of renown fame awaiting thee!

Fara Með Oðin, minn broðirs ok systirs, ok megi Goðanum blessi þig allur. Heil Alfaðir Oðin! Ok, Heil þig allur!

42 It is just amazing how easily our western civilized society, once the mightiest in the world, has succumbed to mediocrity and settled for inferiority. Talk about your anti-hero!

What was once a grand quest toward creating the übermensch which Nietzsche had unveiled to the mind of western thought, has been reduced today to a society plagued by a surplus of human waste, content on being the üntermenschen, instead!

I am reminded of Nietzsche's, "The Hammer Speaks", from Zarathustra... If destinies you would create, then you must become hard, he had written. Only the noblest is altogether hard.

Heil to the genuine Odinists, those who seek to become hard and create destinies! Heil Allfather Odin!

43 If one seeks to see the face of divinity in this mortal life span, then one must approach the Stalli (Alter) with such honesty that allows for one to empty one's mind of every active thought, image or preconceived notion. One must strip away and disregard all of the debris which one accrues; all negativity, all hate, all love, all emotional clutter. One must be fully present in the moment and approach the alter of life with a complete understanding that one may not slip through the veils and portals which separate worlds and dimensions, so long as they remain anchored to a myriad of social and emotional burdens. The Sál (Soul) must be naked and lighter than air itself. It must be pure and unfettered consciousness. All imbalances must yield to balance. All light must cede to darkness, and all darkness must turn in on itself and transform to create new light. In this place, this state of "Being", one "Becomes" the Dagaz (ᛞ), the divine synthesizer of all bipolar energies.

Matter and anti-matter. Light and darkness. Positive and negative. Love and hate. Life and death. It is here that we meet and merge with all that is divine. We meet our beloved Gods unmasked! All lies perish beneath the crushing blow of Thor's mighty hammer of truth. Wisdom flows freely as the dam of ignorance is violently destroyed. Zion crumbles back into the Bedouin sands whence it came. The shackles of thralldom slip loose to free the Aryan soul!

Allow yourself to drown in the sea of wisdom, taste of Mimir's cool water. Sink to the bottom of his well that you may be born anew, free of all self-doubt, and imbued wholly with the divine spirit of Odin! Heil Odin!!!

44 I shall not reward disrespect with respect. Nor shall I address aggression with peace! I am not Gandhi, nor am I a man who disregards the supreme laws of nature in lieu for man's inferior laws of the land. If the laws of the land are in fact compatible with the laws of nature (i.e. the Gods), then I too shall abide by them; but where they take their leave from nature's wisdom, so too shall I disregard man's ignorance and remain true to natural order. For I am a heathen, a son of Odin! And hostile acts against myself, my Folk, or our sacred and indigenous way, must be avenged whenever and where ever they occur, or we have no right to "Be" at all. Such is the law of nature. Such is Odin's law… Heil Odin!

45 We have the best religion/way known to man! For it IS indigenous, it IS ancient and it IS a free Siðr (Way – Religion). While racial fundamental Odinism is not for all of our Folk, that is its very appeal. Not all may assume a place among the Living Einherjar, even if they exhibit an outward desire. Still, others are too weak or meek, to aspire at all. In which case, they are no genuine Odinist to begin with!

Odinism is, nevertheless, truly a 'free' religion/way. We are free to assemble and associate with those whom we desire to, and disregard the rest while maintaining a state of Frith when and where it is warranted with others whom follow the way/religion in some form.

Anyone who is not seeking to serve the Gods, Folk and Siðr of the Aryan Tribes and our posterity, when they owe their very existence to thus, is neither friend nor faithful of our sacred way!

46 It is easy for the soul of common character to be swept away within the mainstream rush of current events. What the uncommon soul must diligently consider is this; If this or that government representative, senator or agent is serving ZOG and Israel`s interests, how then, may they serve the people of the Aryan Tribes, with any legitimacy? More so, why would they desire to? The honest answer, of course, is that they would not! Nor do they.

47 Respect and common considerate behavior are oft charged with the same quality these days. Actually, one is fused with, or superimposed over the other, thereby affording both the illusion of assuming similar quality. However, deference, as respect, is that courteous and considerate, albeit common enough gesture. Conversely, genuine respect is the quality of great esteem or high regard beyond the pale, or standard, if you will.

To respect others in command of admirable faculties is an appropriate gesture. But to respect oneself, I mean truly respect oneself, is indeed a noble virtue of its own accord. You understand that with genuine self-respect arrives an awful realization. That is, that the field of others worthy of your respect narrows considerably. Emphasis upon considerably!

48 Genuine Odinism/Wotanism, as all genuine heathen/pagan religions are, is rooted in the laws of natural order. Nature is no

moralist; she neither recognizes nor affirms wrong or right. No good or evil, only chaos and order; balance and imbalance. All notions of right or wrong, or good and evil and the like, are derived from the human condition which we comprehend as morality. Of course, I am not making a case against the sound and orderly civility of morality whereby western civilization doth prosper and wax. I do however, find err in the over-zealous moralist, more oft than not, associated with the Abrahamic faiths. Their moral codes are in fact based entirely upon the allegation of Jesus' actual existence and the anti-natural concept of blind faith thereafter. With the likes of great and respected historians and chroniclers of their time; Tacitus, Pliny the Elder and Caesar, whom were all prolific writers whom were committed to great detail to which we may attest by perusing their many works left for us to study, no mention of the name of the Jewish Rabbi Jesus is mentioned. In fact, his name does not appear anywhere in history's annals prior to the first four books of the New Testament bible otherwise known as the Gospels of Jesus and his Apostles. But that's a meditation for another time.

Blind faith is merely a buzz word, or Zionist catch phrase which in reality translates to willed ignorance. Devoid of any legitimate facts, it is designed to rob man of his majesty, true purpose and his relationship with nature. No matter how civilized western society purports itself to be, the supreme truth yet remains inexorable...no law of man trumps nature's law!

Those 'whom' grasp this reality, fully espouse the most genuine of all moral codes. We call such souls heathens/pagans. A soul imbued with the audacity to honor something which he/she can actually see, feel and experience. A genuine spirituality, which fails to seek or require permission to live, and the courage to do so, without apology... This is the measure of a true heathen/ pagan. It is certainly a requisite of any radical Fundamental Odinist/Wotanist.

49 The maxim; "The enemy of my enemy is my friend." does not hold true in all scenarios. Nor is it compatible with the reckoning of Odinist/Wotanist thews (virtues). I have heard some say that the perpetrators of the 911 attacks upon ZOG targets here in Vinland, are somehow our friend. This is ludicrous!

To begin with, one must consider the full breadth of those whom were responsible for said attacks, including those cloaked in red, white and blue as well as blue and white. Not merely Bedouin Muslim radicals! Next, let us survey those radical Muslims... they certainly are no friend to the "Aryan Devil", or our heathen and "Infidel' religion of Odinism/Wotanism. As far as they are concerned, they'd desire to see our heathen heads severed from our bodies in the name of Allah, point blank reality!

The only commonality which we share with the radical Muslims, is an unabashed abhorrence for any and all Zionist Occupied Governments, which are those controlled by Israel and their Holocaust industry which they employ to extort billions of dollars annually, and their myth of six million which they apply to guilt otherwise healthy Aryan men and women into thralldom and acceptance of passive genocide of the people of the Aryan Tribes.

So then, while the enemy of my enemy may serve as a potential ally, one would be well served by holding in reserve, those whom one may willingly regard to be one's friend.

50 There is much to posit regarding the "dabblers" associated with our sacred religion/way. The ones who levy the claim that they are "real" Odinists; while they profess the merits and allure of Satanism. I tell you now that no part of Judeo-Christianity, inverted or otherwise, is compatible with any heathen/pagan religion/way, including Odinism/Wotanism. Nor is any such corrosive theology which seeks to hold the human soul in bondage, conducive to any genuine Odinist/Wotanist ideology. The mere suggestion by those whom would extol such hybrid teachings under the guise of some true quest for Oðinic wisdom, merely reduce themselves to the office of new age dabblers, no matter how intellectually gifted or academically endowed they may be. Truly Hermetic, they are not. And yet, they suffer in their belief that they somehow are! And so shall those who adhere to such teachings.

51 Comprehension of the divine as it expresses itself within the scope of the multiverse of existence, occurs in various manifestations; numbers, colors, celestial bodies, symbolism, imagery and vibrations, to cite the most obvious. For those of us whose lineage belongs to the phylum of the Aryan Tribes, this all exists within the breadth of our collective myths, sciences, philosophies, architecture, and art and of course, our indigenous Gods (Goddesses included therewith.)

The vibrations are their voices which are expressed in the Runes (mysteries) and their Galdrar (songs), as the very echoes and reflections of natural order... nature's law writ large upon the Folk soul/Folk consciousness. This divine energy rides (right action & rhythmic motion i.e. Raido (ᚱ), the very stream (Laguz (ᛚ) of ancestral memory which exists within our blood and flows forth from the beginning of our racial line. It resonates from Allfather Odin's first thought and will to "Be", and his will that "we shall be!" To this day it continues to resonate within each and every Aryan, whether they are able to grasp this or not. It exists. It then becomes our spiritual journey to reconnect with the Folk soul/Folk consciousness, so that we may come to know the truth of our Gods and appreciate the wisdom of Odin and the Runes (mysteries) within and without. And that this wisdom not be sought or coveted for merely selfish gain! But rather, selflessness and service to our Gods, Folk and ancient holy way as can be applied in the immediate sense of now. But more so, as well, in the future of our progeny; these very ideals must we defend and preserve for our posterity, at all expense. For this is the way of the Northern Warrior-Priest-Teacher. Heil Odin! Heil those true to his holy ways!

52 Noise pollution defined: The emanations of human waste, and then some! Opinions postulated while lacking in the experience thereof.

53 Courage defined is manifold. However, reduced to its rawest form, courage must be defined as an exercise in the power of one's will. Additionally so, will and courage are ever faithful companions. The vehicle in which they move about, are the men and women who possess noble character and the fuel which powers such character is called fortitude.

54 The myth of equality exists nowhere within the broad scope of nature, or the tapestry of natural order. Only man declares such a state of existence, with his inferior law which, for the moment, has usurped and supplanted that of nature. But sooner or later, as history has illustrated time and again, somewhere, men of superior nature, substance and character find the courage required to shrug off the shackles of political correctness and disregard that which is contrary to nature's law. And they respond with greatness and shed light upon nature's truths which weaker men had sought to keep concealed in

darkness from seekers of the truth! Such men and women of superior nature and character have been hated in life by the meek and the weak, albeit, they are revered in death by those whom their deeds had inspired. For such, seems to be the decree of nature in any society, which is so far removed from the superior and inexorable laws of nature.

55 An inflated ego serves none well, least of all its owner. Narcissism creates only deception and destruction.

56 Some willed action. That's what is called for when the state of nothingness has overstayed its welcome! If there is no wind to fill the sail and you desire to move the boat, you start rowing! That's what to do. The power of SOWILO (ᛋ), "Willed" action.

Ever are my thoughts my friend; ever are my dreams my foe! For my dreams entice me to lay down my weapons and take in the breadth of desire. Conversely, my thoughts advise me well to hold fast to my weapons as I wend my way across the plains of reality. So that I may always be prepared to slay any unwelcome intrusions upon fact and truth, which might otherwise blind my vision, dull my senses and thereafter deprive me of what is good in this life and what potential awaits those whom are fully grasping the sword named SOWILO (ᛋ),... Willed action is ever a sharp blade!

57 To sit entirely still, and move through time, but not space, and empty the mind of all thought. So truly divine! Within the Hugauga (mind's eye), the eye of Odin appears...the face of all the Gods and Goddesses are there, "Augenblick" (In the blink of an eye)! It steals one's breath and speeds the pulse. And if you let them have you, allow them to take you over, it will consume you wholly and fill you with the spirit divine.

58 Insatiable hunger and thirst for wisdom from Mimir's Well. Like a great beast deep within me, it emerges. It respects no limit, no bounds. It knows only the quest; the quest for ancient wisdom. The kind of Rúna (mysteries) which are revealed only to those whom are willing to pay the FEHU (ᚠ)/fee. For twenty-three days now I have been completely silent, not a single word spoken. Twenty-three days have purchased me a small albeit precious drink of the cool pure water from memory's Well.

59 If the source of all wisdom is awareness itself, then one must be present in the very moment in order to exercise awareness. Additionally, in order to access said state of fully conscious awareness, one must not only be present in the moment, but be fully submerged in the experience of the moment. Here, in the most sacred of places; the totally aware "NOW" moment, may one merge with the divine and the very wisdom which flows forth, therefrom. Here, one might meet Odin at the edge of Mimir's Well.

60 There is an ancient proverb which states; "Pain can be a source of illumination." To be sure, it led Allfather Odin to great wisdom. Pain is nature's way of letting us know that while something is wrong, we are still alive. And yet, pain is weakness leaving the body! It is the fortitude and courage to forge ahead through the pain. Such is the measure of genuine strength and the teaching of both Thor and Tyr. These two Gods epitomize in mythical writ, what it truly means to serve something noble and greater than one's own self interests.

I conclude for now with this quote; “If one does not work hard to earn the heritage, one will perish in the end, or at best hold the stirrups for those who are on their way up.”
--the voice of a German Ancestor

Reyn til Rúna! (seek the mysteries!)

PART III

Prose and Poetry

BEFORE FIRST LIGHT

Just East of the Black Sea -913CE

He stood there facing his would be assailants, the warrior mocked the not unworthy, if somewhat reckless adversaries as they formed ranks in a circle around him. The night was black as soot, but he could descry the features of each man's face, albeit the long shadows cast by the torchlight hath indeed twisted and contorted each face so as to assume the gruesome quality of the living dead!

The warrior tensed his body as the first of nine Khazar warriors rushed head-long at him, swinging with deadly accuracy, the strange and foreign sword which he wielded. The Northman felt every muscle in his thick muscular body tense with the electricity of adrenaline as he met the other combatant.

The Eastern warrior swung his steel at the Northman's hamstring, but Rúrik countered with a swift debilitating downward stroke of his broad sword which separated the Khazar's head from his lifeless torso. Two more of the Khazars flanked Rúrik from either side and he let loose an inhuman sound at them! Were you able to ask the two Khazars, they'd have told you, just prior to their expirations, that the Rús warrior appeared to resemble a monster of sorts. Half human and half wolf, or bear.

Rúrik, having dispatched three of the nine's host, grinned at the remaining half dozen horse warriors whom were clearly out of their element as they stood their ground. Each man wishing that they had not accosted the wandering fierce berserk Rús warrior which they now faced. The falling rain began to pound out an eerie beat upon the hard soil of the steppe lands where the lush grass was sparse. The Khazar warriors had considered making haste for their mounts and fleeing this mad barbarian but their steeds were scattered hither and thither, grazing upon the tall steppe grass, oblivious to the violent battle playing out. The sound of clashing steel sang out loudly, splitting the silence of the crisp night air and joining in with the soft chorus of the wind blowing through the tall wispy blades of steppe grass. Rúrik brought the battle to them this time, gutting his nearest opponent with a swift and fatal short upper thrust. He turned and parried to face another of the horse warriors just as the last one's innards spilt upon the ground, from the split open gut whence they had come, now lying in a steaming and spent heap. Blood makes the grass grow and Mother Jörd fertile, mused the Rús warrior inwardly as he fought off the advance of the next Khazar.

A flash of white hot pain sent Rúrik 's head reeling momentarily as a Khazar's sword cleaved the flesh open on the Northman's broad and battle scarred chest.

Rúrik grabbed the blade's owner by his garments and drew him in close enough to cut his throat from 3 to 9 with his long knife. The mighty Rús threw his head back and gazed empyrean and shouted a single word... 'twas a name really, "ODIN!"

The remaining four Khazars dispersed into the recess of the black night's ebony shadows with great haste! As the moments elapsed into an hour, or better, the Khazars began to shout at Rúrik from the cover of the night. Their eerie taunts having less than the desired effects upon the Northman who was now crouched over one of their fallen comrades. Motionless for the better part of the last hour now, the four conferred with one another.

Was the Rús dead? Why had he not sought the refuge of the dark night beyond the torch light's eerie glow? Surely he was badly, perhaps mortally wounded if not dead altogether.

A long mournful howling pierced the still night air! Other howls from in the night seemed to be answering his call. The Rús man howled yet once more. He had made his peace with his Gods, and now, but only howled.

The Khazars reappeared from the cover of darkness, drawn out by Rúrik's odd behavior. When they stood at the torch lit parameter, illuminated once more, the Rús warrior wrenched the head of their recently departed companion so that each man would meet the grim and empty stare of the death mask as Rúrik shouted to them. "You have fought valiantly this night, yet many of your kin have I sacrificed to old One Eye! The rest of you shall join them soon. Though I may sup with Allfather Odin in Valhalla this very night myself, I embrace my fate!"

Then Rúrik stood fully erect with broadsword and long knife in hand. He stood in the stadha of the Elhaz Rune and called out for his God to bear witness... "ODIN!"

The Khazars looked on in disbelief at the crazed warrior from the Northlands, his face painted with victory runes in the scarlet blood of their dead kinsman. His beard, red and dripping with blood, he bellowed a hearty laugh! "We shall all find our destinies before first light," shouted the Rús as he advanced upon the remaining Khazar host and they moved to meet his advance, each man knowing that they were about to die.

Just prior to the final clash and clang of steel biting into steel and flesh, Rúrik the Rús from Chernigóv loosed his battle cry... "ODIN, Victory, or Valhalla!!!"[4]

[4]Short Fiction based on dated history

RED
(913 Common Era)

Look now before me, spy then the wasteland of war torn bodies, strewn like boulders across a rocky hillside.

Blood stained snow melts b'neath the warm weight of severed limbs and spilt bowels.

The carnage is great and the stench of spent lives is the odor of the newly departed... those gone to Har's hall: "Valhalla!"

Swords raised high to the God of war and death, Allfather Odin, leader of the wild hunt.

Clashing thunder of sword, axe and shield heightens in the frenzy of war, as bone and blood are offered up.

Allfather roars with glee from his high seat, Hlidskjalf, in the hall of the host. The joy of war warms his heart as gore and guts litter Mother Jörd, fertilizing her womb... for blood makes the grass grow!

And victory makes the kindred strong.

For Allfather Odin smiles down upon his loyal sons and daughters and keeps them well till he gathers them up to his holy hall.

Listen now to the howl of the wind, as it blows ‘cross the now fertile field of immortality.

The pack’s mournful song is long and loud as it wends upward to the High One’s ears.

His reply is a single statement spoken through his raven’s caw: “Victory, or Valhalla!”

Hence, the battle this stormy day will rage on till all is red.

THE ROAD TO VALHALLA

Lamp of Odin crosses Father sky,

from Asgard to Midgard it shines on our lives.

From Deutschland to Vinland may our Hammers strike Trú,

for the Gods are amongst us, with me and with you.

Great Kindred spirits show us what's Trú,

so our deeds and our virtues are worthy of you.

Tradition and honor our Ancestors would say,

are a warrior's hallmark and the Aryan way.

So stand by our Gods and heed what they teach,

to fight for family and kinfolk keeps Valhalla in reach!

MASTER AND COMMANDER

Ye of noble heart, hear me well and mark my words,
go naught quietly into the night, nor recede gently
with the ebb and flow which marks the time.

Pity not the coward or his craven lot!
For misplaced guilt will always make cowards of the brave,
and steal majesty from the noble.

For he is no commander who is naught first his own master.
No man is fit to command others
if he first cannot command himself.

Let naught even black of darkness bear witness to your
anguish and pain.
Give no thought of remorse to your acts of righteousness.

For often such acts will be judged and condemned by those
lesser men whom claim to be your equal, your peer.
Forfeit naught your will to those agents of ignobility.

Face the day boldly my brethren of the stalwart heart,
yield naught to the night as you exhale your last breath
no matter the pain, and may your name always be listed upon
the banner of honor and that of Master and Commander.

BALDUR RETURNS

Electric sensations excite the soul
as something ancient returns from the old.

Fire burns in Father Sky so bright, 'tis the Lamp of Odin's eternal light.

It heralds the coming of a presence so trú,
as the return of hope paints the dawn azure blue.

Yes, the rapture of summer brightly burns;
now behold this glory as Baldur returns!

EK HEITI ULFHETHNAR

(I am called Wolfskin Heathen)

Lurking in the grove of asps, like some ghostly mists which
elude the unsuspecting eye.

The solitary wolf waits and watches with the tempered patience
of a skilled hunter.

He lies in wait, eyes of gold fixed steadfast upon the unsuspecting
prey, oblivious to the fate which awaits him.

Ravens wheel above in the steel gray sky, eagerly awaiting the
hunter's assault... Bloody runes splatter 'cross the canvas of icy
white.

The heat of spilt innards melts the snow as the frenzied attack
reaches its zenith, the stalked and the stalker entwined in some
macabre dance of life and death, orchestrated by nature's law.

The Ravens, now grimly assembled upon the boughs of barren trees,
begin to caw the songs of victory.

The light of life expires in the glassy black eye, as razor sharp
teeth stained crimson, rip and tear at the flesh which was
living only moments ago.

Sated now, the wolf breaks to run through the snowy woods,
dashing through the trees, reeving as thread through the
eye of a needle.

In the distance, the mournful howl of the pack may be heard and
suddenly,
the great wolf is slow of step and falters!

Great is the pain as his hind quarters and jaw retract and constrict.
As he begins to morph, an eerie howl escapes his snarling lips.
The howl becomes a word and the word a name; "ODIN!"
"Odin!", I shout as I stand erect now, draped in the hide of a wolf!
There, in the snow laden woods, bathed in blood and gore,
I glance about only to spy the carnage of the long
day's battle.

Spent and lifeless bodies litter the icy plain.
Severed limbs strewn about here and there.
The blood stained snow now gives way beneath the weight
and warmth of severed and spilt bowels, congealing in small pools
of sanguine offerings.

Others do I spy, men of my own Clan. Garbed in wolf furs
and two dawn the Bear shirts!

Acknowledging one another, we raise our blood drenched swords to
the sky and begin to howl the morbid songs of victory.

Offering up to Odin the souls of those valiant slain whom adorn
the sacred field of honor!

This day will mighty Hár receive well so many in Valhalla.

Gazing empyrean, I hear my own voice, raspy and distant as that
of a stranger, escape my throat:

" Father, Ek heiti Ravenulf. Ek heiti Hárulf. Ek heiti Othinns Sonr,
ok Ek Ulfhethnar!"

SEEKER

So now, as I lie down this eve, to sleep the sleep of the dead,
I'll take my final breath and journey to Helheim to walk among the dead.

To learn their hidden truths, I must travel the road of initiation,
and give myself to myself, and unto Odin!

But for the glorious God of hope, Baldur now reaches out to me!

Dare I touch the burning ashes of his smoldering pyre?
Or will the embers burning, kindle the fire in my heart?

The winds of Hel blow like a tempest fury 'cross the land of the dead.
See now, the wind, this night, will stoke the flames of Kenaz, the great
fire storm which the holy Gods hath created within me.

And with new meaning, I, the seeker,
will be born forth anew with the morn,
as the Lamp of Odin crosses Father Sky…
Hidden truths will I know
on the morrow!

WHERE IS YOUR SOUL?

Where is your soul, proud Aryan man?

Does it run with wolves O'er icy plains?

Will you give of your all for the Folk's forward gains?

In a Long Ship will you sail with your forefathers of yore?

Will your soul brave the fjords to far unknown shores?

Will you answer the call of the Gods all and one?

Will you pick up the sword and see their will done?

Or will you look at white children without so much as a care,
of great sagas once told, will their ears ever hear?

Are you so selfish and lusting for outlander's gold
that you care not if our children hear the tales of old?

Will it not haunt your soul and heart to see? A greater crime will
never be!

So where is your soul, proud Aryan man?

Has your fire burned out? Or with the Gods do you stand?

VICTORY or VALHALLA

Heil the holy dawn this day and Heil the mighty Gods!

Stand up to defend their honor, for Faith and Folk,
let our swords be drawn.

Berserkers we are called, Bear spirited warriors
fiercest Vikings of them all!

Sons of Odin, loyal all the way to Allfather's hall,

Nomad warriors proudly answering the call.
And when the battlefield is set and our swords are raised in honor,
to Asgard we shall look and shout, "Odin, Victory, or Valhalla!"

KINSMEN

K Keep strong your bonds of love and Troth.

I Inexorably remain Trú to each other and the beliefs you hold sacred.

N Noble, the true definition of the Sanskrit word; 'Aryan'.

S School your folk! Education is the way to our folk's survival and
higher evolution.

M Many have died, or been imprisoned for preserving the ways of faith
and folk. Never forget that, or those 'whom have paid, or are
paying that price for your rights!

E Enemy. Our enemy is anyone who threatens the welfare of our faith
and folk, no matter their color, or race... An enemy has no color,
or race.

N Now take these words of prose to heart, for I scribed them just for
you, my Aryan Kinsmen.

VINDURRITHAR SAGA

(the Lay of Wind Rider)

1 One time long ago, in the land of the midnight sun,
lived a boy named Vindurríthar and his name meant Wind Rider.
From the womb, Vindurríthar was a restless lad,
given to fanciful muses was he.

2 The viking season was soon to come, but not for Vindurríthar.
Although other lads his age fared forth now, he would not.
His mother soothed him, as mothers are wont to do
with words of reassurance; "Your time will come my son."

3 But Vindurríthar was not satisfied, his beard would soon grow.
And yet, he remained in the village with the women and children.
Most unhappy was he, for he wished to be counted among the brave,
those mighty oaks of battle, heroic in deeds and death!

4 One day nearing the Autumn tide, he stood alone in the rainfall
when a Vála approached him, that troubled youth.
"What shall I do," asked Vindurríthar, of the woman wise in Runes?
"You must fare forth, if answers wilt thou seek, young Vindurríthar."

5 "For the wind is calling you, and you must take flight upon her back
if wisdom wilt thou win. Will thou go forth, Wind Rider?
Have you the lust, the desire within your breast to take up the quest?
"Will you answer the lone wolf's cry upon the easterly wind?"

6 Winter came and went, and Vindurríthar grew restless.
And the snow began to melt, soon the Northmen would go a Viking.
But not Vindurríthar, his was to be the journey of one,
the lonely path of the seeker, though blind to the gift was he.

7 So, one night when little snow remained left and Sunna cast her shadow long, Vindurríthar cast himself upon his namesake, with provisions in hand, he went forth before the village awoke, looking back naught once.
With tears in his young eyes and a silent farewell upon his lips, he left.

8 First he traveled East, from the Northlands, he departed.
There he encountered a band of warriors, sturdy and brave they seemed to him. From different tribes of Aryan was that kindred forged, those stalwart souls. Dedicated to Odin first and to each other next, these men in furs.

9 With them did he stay, this host of brave warriors. Three summers did he serve with this band of Berserks. Among their number was he counted, young Vindurríthar. Hungry for the battle and bathed in blood, well did he win renown. Well did he feed the Ravens and wolves!

10 Soon the legends arose, of a boy who found his beard and rode upon the winds of victory when to the feast of the wolves he went!
Long will those songs be sung in the halls of the Northern heroes, of that Son of Odin who feared naught but failure.

11 But in his nineteenth summer, he left the war band
and sad were his brothers in arms, and all spoke well of him
when did Vindurríthar fare forth once more,
when the wolf greeted Mani in the ink black sky.

12 South he fared far, whence East he came, that man now bold in battle.
And there he met a host of traders, rich with silver and furs were they.
And in their company, as a sentry, did he travel with those men,
toward Sunna, westward he now went, till land's end he met.

13 There he stood, able to go naught farther. Upon the sea shore did he stand
and he directed his gaze upon the great wide expanse of ocean.
An old man then appeared, and to Vindurríthar did he speak;
"Of your Ørlög will I tell, if help you will lend me to carry my burden."

14 To this did he oblige the old man, and carried he, the old man upon his back. He taxied him down the coast, to the elder's shanty.
"Who art thou old sage," queried Vindurríthar?
"No sage am I," said the elder, just an old man seeking some company.

15 Angered by the interruption to his quest, by the old man, Vindurríthar began to depart when suddenly he stopped, struck by the Hammer of the Gods, and filled with benevolence was he and from the old man's plight he could not stray.

16 What harm may befall him, he mused to himself, from a short delay?
Sure he would stay for a while with the old man, and stave off the bitter hand of loneliness, even if only for a while.
For this was he rewarded from that wise old sage...

17 Runes did he learn, and his lot to him was revealed!
"The answers you seek Ljodfaffnir, lay naught beyond the sea, but within your breast wilt thou find them," said the old sage;
"Ride the North winds back to your folk and home."

18 "And prosper will they, with you as their Jarl, Vindurríthar."
With that man all old and wise, did Vindurríthar spend the yawn of winter,
and with the bear's awakening and the snow's first melting
Vindurríthar rode swift, the North wind home.

19 There he led his folk, and prosperity reigned the truest king.
For many years to come, the cold bite of winter was not felt!
But rather, the warm and gentle hand of summer lingered long.
And so, long were the years, that Jarl Vindurríthar sat in the high seat.

20 Of the Song of Vindurríthar, have I now reckoned up before
both Gods and men.
Of initiations which await each one of us, have I written.
Good hunting to you then, as you fare forth upon the wind.
Wisdom wilt thou find on the journey North!

A SOLDIER'S PRAYER FOR ODINISTS

Inspired by Kevin Kay, U.S. ARMY

As I walk through mud and muck,
jungle lands, urban streets, or
dry and dusty Bedouin desert sands,

I pray that Odin graces me
with the necessary wisdom
to survive and succeed at my objective.
That both my aim and nerves be steady
and true as Odin's spear; Gungnir!

May my shot never be loosed in anger,
but only in noble service and defense.
And like Gungnir, may it never fail
to find its mark.

May Allfather Odin bless me with victory
in the din of battle, and if it be his
wisdom and will, or the decree of the Norns
that I shall fall on the field of battle,
may it be my reward that he send his beautiful
Valkyrie daughters to gather me up to him,
that I may know my place in his hall of brave souls;

VALHALLA,
where the courageous assemble
where Odin hosts only the valiant!

I pray that mighty Thor walks with me always,
when uncertainty grips me in its clutch, or
fear threatens to paralyze my mind,
may Thor imbue me with the might of his awesome Hammer;
Mjollnir,
that I escape and evade such fetters.
And that my courage and fortitude fail me not!

And I pray that Tyr guides me well in the face of adversity.
That my actions be just and noble and born of honor always.

This do I pray with the Hammersign in the names
of Odin, Baldur, Frey/Freya and Thor.

Heil Allfather Odin.

RUNE WOLF
(wind rider)

Set your gaze far beyond the haze of loneliness.
Fret naught nor despair, for when the darkness comes
I will be there.

With the broad sweep of the raven's wing, darkling skies
devour the day. Rest assured, I'm on my way.

Hold on now the nighttime comes and with the velvet black,
I'll rush forth, set free from the bonds of prison,
free to fare forth from this cage.

As I lie down and close my eyes, I call out in an ancient
voice with words all old and wise and change my shape
from man to wolf! In fetch form do I fare forth to you.

Now step outside and close your eyes to the mundane world,
for you will not see me there. But I am there with you now.
The soft wind you feel gently brush 'gainst your face,
that is the spirit of the high wolf and the whisper of the wind
rustling through leaves upon the bough, is my voice calling out to
you.

You see, I am there with you now, and I am there with you oft
when I journey forth as Harulf.

Like the Trú Son of Odin that I am, a long wind rider, I stop for
a while to visit with you before I move on. Then I'm off to visit
the graves of my loved ones. There shall I gain the wisdom of
the dead. One day I too shall cross over to join the wild hunt
forever. No longer will I be able to reclaim my sleeping body
and awake.

Lost to the ashes of time will my body be. But ne'er my spirit,
my soul. I shall yet visit you then oft, a wind rider,
the High Wolf will touch your soul with my wind swept caress
and speak to your heart with my howl on the wind.

Gone with the sunrise am I, but don't feel sad, for I'll be back..
I will always come back to you. To watch over you. Maybe urge
you
in the right direction when I sense your despair.

One thing is for certain, I shall never leave you alone in the
darkness!
Do you feel that! Can you sense my presence? Soon Sunna will
take her leave from Father Sky. The winds will begin and that's
when I'll ride.

It won't be long now b'fore you hear my voice in the
melody of the wind chimes' song.

You'll feel my gentle touch upon your bare skin
and your spirits will lift as you feel me standing by
your side... Reach out and take my hand in yours.

DIVINE INSPIRATION

I see a raven on the threshold of consciousness
and his plume is soot black.
Er, his name is 'Memory' and he speaks to me
in a voice that is time.
His warning to me is to learn from Urd's runes
and to heed the divine wisdom which Odin imparts,
yet offers to few!

I see a second raven on the plane that is my subconscious.
Black as the first and a star bare night.
'Thought', is he by name, and he speaks to me of awareness
of that which is becoming.
To pay heed to the power of the blood which courses
through my being.

Carried through space and time, my soul that is
as ageless as the ancestors which engendered it.
Nay, I shall not ignore the voice of Odin's messengers
who bring to me his word of everlasting life!
That which ends only when the Folk too end.

For this message is truly divine.

WHITE WOLVES

A distant howl from far away,
a cry for us to hear today.

From the icy plains and fjords of past,
to ocean shores and desert sands.
The call it comes late in the night,
get ready now, prepare to fight.

From the ashes of ancestors comes
a terrible rage,
their cry to us is; "Leave the cage!"

Shun the system, society's front,
join the pack for the wild hunt.

The howl has traveled for thousands of years,
come now white wolves, open up your ears!

The sun now descends and the moon's on the rise,
fight white wolves, Aryan freedom is the prize.

YESTERDAY, TODAY AND TOMORROW

I have seen many battles in the past
and have fought them.
I see many battles in the space of now,
and fight them.
I see many battles yet to be fought,
and I shall fight them.

I am a warrior of a thousand wars past.
And I am a warrior of a thousand wars yet to come!
I am a reader of the runes, a seer of the signs.

I am a son of the Kindred Spirit of ancestors so divine.
I am a son of the Gods and Goddesses.
I am a son of Odin the Allfather.
I am a father of my folk yet to come.
I am the voice of history, the voice of my Gods
and the voice of my ancestors past.

I am a teacher of laws which time has not forgotten,
but man has chosen to ignore.
I am a sword, sacred and Trú, an emissary of the truth
and the bearer of a noble gift.

I hail from a time that most have forgotten,
I come from the time that is now and from a time that
shall again, one day be!

I've the strength to destroy, but I'd rather build.
I've the ability to deliver death, but I'd rather
grant new meaning to life.
I have the means to see, visit and transcend other
places in time and space and I have the ability to teach
you those runes.

I am an Aryan warrior, a man of my Folk and
a defender of the Holy Host and their ways..
I am Casper Odinson, the ghost of kindred past
and the spirit of kindred future!

AN ANCIENT THIRST

Where lies glory if not in the hearts
of men Trú to the Elder ways?
In that most ancient Well, where a single
glint of blue peers up from the depths of
that dark water.

Are thou so worthy that thoust warrant
even a single draught?
Or so bold that thou are willing to
step forth to the great stone rim?
Come then. Come closer and drink deeply
of his glory, his wisdom.

What have you but all to gain and your
mind to lose if you dare draw your draught
without paying the required price!

Do you hear the laughter of Mimir?
He mocks thou from his ancient post
where the waters run Trú.

Dare ye drink of that holy water?
Or do thou suffer the parched throat of
the uninspired? Like those with stagnate minds,
who Loki plays folly with, whilst he leads
their lot farther away from that holy place!
Awake from your slumber, you sleeping kin.

Lest ye wish to thirst for all of time.

For twixt the place where the winds of
Thor blow oft and where time begins,
there are nine doors.

Oft have the thirstiest souls opened the
wrong door in search of that venerable draught.
Yet have others tasted the reward of
sweet Laguz's promise.

Still others have perished into
the awaiting embrace of insanity.
Do thou know thine own mind, Loddfafnir?

For thou surely knowst of the perils
the quest may afford one.

Will thou slip into the byrne of ignorance
and await the end of time?
Or will thou step forth with the courage
and conviction required of one who
would truly know?

Hail the seeker.

Hail to those who drink deeply and oft.

THE FIRST DEADLY SIN

The first deadly sin, it came to be
when a bird met a fish and they mated, you see.
I know what you're thinking; "This could never be!"
Well, sit back and read on. It gets sadder, you'll see.
The day soon did come when their child was born.
Of such things just as this, our Gods they did warn.
Neither father nor mother knew then just what was at stake.
But later in life, the child would pay for their mistake.
In school, he was taunted, teased and sorely abused.
Soon he dropped out and learned a gun how to use.
Robbing and stealing for drugs he would shoot.
A man he would kill if he needed the loot. And then while walking
by the pond one day,
he spied a young white duck with a mud toad at play.
He saw them kiss and he heard them giggle, then something inside
him began to wriggle.
He stepped up to them so that they could see,
and then he yelled; "Hey, look at me!"
My mother and father are a bird and a fish,
but I cannot fly, nor can I swim.
So think real hard about your future kin,
before you too commit the first deadly sin.

THE THUNDER ROLLS

The sounds of battle rage and roar,
as clashing weapons slash and tear.
When the thunder rolls and lightning strikes,
Thor rides hard across Father Sky.
Valkyries gather their steeds together,
as the warriors below make battle ready their weapons.

Odin orders that the great oak doors be opened,
for Valhalla this day will welcome new warriors!

Heimdall sound your Gjallarhorn,
the Valkyries now go to collect the war torn.
From blood on the blade comes the spoils of war,
the valiant always cross through Odin's great doors.
Up to Har's Hall, from Midgard they go,
the Aryan warriors who paid with their all.

And for those of us yet ready to answer that call,
keep your weapons at hand and your minds battle sharp.
For the Gods take care of their own, those who stand Trú.
As death from the battle now takes its toll,
listen Trú North Folk as the thunder rolls!

RIDERS ON THE STORM

When the thunder sounds and the lightning strikes,
we come for those who have betrayed the rites.
Out of the rain on a dark stormy night,
we've gathered our weapons, we're coming to fight!

We smell it as we approach, rising up in the air.
We seek out our foes by the stench of their fear.
Descendants of North Folk, we are one and all.

Modern day Vikings answering the Gods' angry call.
Like the Midgard Serpent, the cowards slither and crawl.
But like the serpent, they too, by the Aryan sword shall fall.

The ground turns red with blood's life essence.
Out of the rain you will sense our strong presence.
Riding side by side with the Gods that we love,
the ravens caw in the dark sky above.

Crossing the plain like wolves in pack form,
we come now riding hard, riders on the storm.

Our battle cry heard by one and all...
"Victory if we stand, Valhalla should we fall!"

JUNE 8th, 793 CE
(Lindisfarne)

Hearts pregnant with courage,
minds seething with fury for the battle!
Three longships set sail for that holy isle
on the 8th day of Fallow.

N'er again would the quiet farmers from
the north deny their anger.
Nor their descendants' birthright to
honor and love the old Gods!

For early this morn, the screams of those men
who brought alien stain to the north lands,
would be heard riding the wind as their
blood stained the very ground which they
worshiped upon.

Their holy house to the mono-god,
this day will burn and alter the face
of history forever.

With the rising sun illuminating the carnage
which took place in the name of those all holy Gods.

Only new rotting corpses and feasting ravens
would watch the ships depart for home,
weighted down with monastery gold.

Their noble deed now done, those merry men
sing songs of victory and the avenged
as they glance back over their wake
at Lindisfarne.

And look ahead to the new dawn which
the Viking Age brings forth for
the kinder of the Gods.

DRAGON SLAYER

Hail to he who is most pleasant to look upon.

Hail to he whom nourished Mother Jörd with red water,
that Odin blessed warrior whom littered the Gnita Heath
with that dragon's entrails!

Hail to he who made heavy Grani's back with the
weighted otter skin from the Rhine.

That holy praised son who is best among men,
that bold one who set free from the byrne of slumber,
that daughter of Har, that beauty who is wise in runes.

Hail to he who has bled in the sacred trench of Jörd,
and made holy the bonds of kinship and the oath thereof!

Hail to he who knows best the heroes song and the
warrior's destiny...

Hail to Sigurd the Volsung, and hail to those who know him.

THE FIRST YULE GIFT

From high above,
the raven's song
guides the far traveling wolf.

Paw prints mar the
flawless white blanket
that the cold old man
has laid out.

And at the forest's edge,
the paw prints transform
to foot prints in the snow.

Through the mighty ranks of yews, the quest now leads me on
and out the other side.

And there,
the mighty Oak of Battle stands,
with hammer in hand,
the son of earth and sky.

And to me this day
does he point the way

to the path which leads
me back.

Back to the place from
whence I came.
That place in the North
where ancestor's voices
call out to me.

And Allfather Odin
once more
touches my heart
with his love,

My soul with his
inspiration, and
his voice speaks
to my mind with
wisdom and wit
from millennia past!

Behold...
here at this holy place
in life do I stand.

A son of Odin,
for the future of
the North Folk!

And at this moment
my mind stirs
with divine
inspiration,

And reveals to me
that I have received
the greatest Yule gift
of all.

And so,
I step forward
and draw the sword
of oaths.

And swear do I always,
to protect and defend
the awesome and majestic
power of that gift

Which is the blood
of my ancestors past.
And the future of
my descendants still
unborn.

BENEATH A HOLY MOON

Mourn the day, for she has slipped
into the embrace of darkness.

And out to play come the children of the night,
as they dance about wildly, skyclad and bathed
the silver light of Mani!

Those of Pagan ways, whom celebrate life
and the holy ones from days of yore.

Together as one they mark the sacred rite
all through the moonlit night.

Their work wrought, their will done,
they await the dawn and greet the Lamp
of Odin, as Sunna stretches 'cross the sky.

The drums now silent and the stars
all lost to the day,
they disperse until once more they merry meet
beneath a holy moon.

OTHIN BYR
(Odin Lives)

Holy tongues summon me forth now
as Mani crosses Father Sky.

I hear their call,
their chant of old.

Voices wyrd and wise,
they call to me.

Ever high now rise, oh Viking star.

Light the night highway,
that the pack cometh for me.

Their message burns my ears and excites my mind.
It speaks to me in a voice older than time itself...

"Behold the truth and know
that Odin lives!"

A FATHER'S LOVE

In this place of black hearts and broken dreams,
my aspirations once lay discarded with the
rubbish and worthless refuse.

Sentenced to mingle about with liars and the truly
wretched souls as they pander their deceit.
What's more, I was drowning in their misery and
my loathing for their lot.

I thought that I'd known you for years,
only to glean the truth, that you've known me
for a lifetime, though I'd really just
met you.

You quelled my seething mind and taught me runes
which hath liberated my soul and introduced me to
my ancestors, those whom have traveled the
millennia highway, that I might be!

You stirred the wode fury within me, showed me the
shadows and gave me the key to the door barring my escape.

Its weight was solid in my hand, true in my

heart and clear in my mind.
You taught me to sing the holy songs,
the purest Galdrar!

And though the portal of imprisonment doth
waver hither and thither, you beckoned me
to follow as you walked right through it.
Trú to the lock, I inserted the key
named 'Hugauga' and unlocked that mighty door of burden.

It seems that so many years have past
since first I crossed through that portal.
Though I seek to pass the key to others today,
I forget not the cold wet cobbles of the
prisoner's road which brought me hither.
As I glance back, only briefly, to the shimmering
rainbow bridge; 'Bifrost', and the icy bridge; 'Gjoll',
which I crossed even earlier.

I peer long and deep into your eye so blue
and with love and gratitude, I bid thee thanks
for not giving up on me and setting me free!

THE FACE OF ØRLOG: Fated for the Order of 1519

We can wear the knot of Odin
but only if we are willing to look
into the eye of the storm.

Freedom comes only to the wise,
those strong enough to seek out
those all sacred runes.

For those whose lips have spoken
the sacred oath whilst tripping through
the nine worlds, those who quest for the holy Order.

Come forth now, ye of iron will and
stalwart hearts. Step closer if you dare...
Feel the spear's pierce
upon your souls!

They have entered the storm, those
sacred warriors, those sons of Har,
whose bonds were tested by the
tempest's fury!

Nearly torn asunder were those whom
pledged to swear the solemn vows.
Transformed and stronger, they emerge
on the other side, wiser, as the Sons of Odin!

And not once shall they glance back at
those who fell by the wayside in
their quest for the Order.

Hail to the seekers.

Courage to the victors!

The Missouri River,Yankton, South Dakota,
photo by Mrs. Linda Cröwell

Appendix

ELDER FUTHARK

Runes:

The names & basic meanings of the runes

Fehu (fáy-hōō) - F - *Fehu* is the force, or energy, facilitated by the concept of mobile property (money), which in former times included such things as livestock. The essence of money is the power to transact (exchange it for something else of value) and in fehu we see this transactional energy⁼ extended across all realms of existence. However, just as money does no real work until it is spent, the power of fehu can stagnate, if not kept in motion (see G-rune).
Keywords: Money – Mobile Property – Fertility - Energy

Uruz (ōō-rōōz) - U - *Uruz* is the rune of vital strength - as embodied by the great, now extinct, aurochs and of wild, formational forces as represented in mythology by the cosmic bovine Auðhumla. Uruz shapes and patterns through undomesticated organic forces, but it is the patterning force, not the pattern itself (see H-rune). Because of its power to shape, and the vital, primal energies involved in its interaction with the multiverse, uruz promotes strength and vitality in those systems which are naturally occurring (e.g. the human body, or the folk community).
Keywords: Vital Strength – Wisdom – Health – Organic organization

Thurisaz (thōō-rĭ-sôz) - th – *Thurisaz* is the force of directed active defense. We see reflected in thurisaz the power of Thor's weapon Mjöllnir - the protector of Asgard and Midgard. The power of thurisaz is antagonistic to all forces hostile to the cosmic order, and the energy of this rune is of great value in aiding the Gods and Goddesses in their struggle to maintain their various enclosures throughout the multiverse. Thurisaz breaks down barriers and is the vehicle of the destruction that must take place before new beginnings may come about.
Keywords: Active Defense - Applied Power - Action -Destruction/Regeneration

Ansuz (än-sōōz) – A – *Ansuz* is the rune of the magical rune-song (galdr) and divine inspiration (Odinic ecstasy). Ansuz describes the divine breath (önd), and inspiration (óðr) bestowed upon Ask and Embla by the triumvirate Odin-Vili-Vé. This energy of this rune is manifested in the inspired words of the skald as well as the ecstatic galdr of the vitki. Ansuz represents the magical potential of our Folk that is handed down genetically from one generation to the next and the power that links us to Odin - within and without. Keywords: Divine Breath - Word Song - Odinic Ecstasy - Poetic/Magical Inspiration - Numinous Knowledge

Raido (rï-thō) – R – *Raido* is the rune of right action and archetypal order. It embodies both the concept of the journey back to the way of right action (the path to the Gods) and that of the vehicle facilitating the journey. Raido is at the same time both the wagon and the road - the whole ride, as it were. Ritual workings involve the ordering of energies in accordance with right action and the power of Raido is essential for such undertakings.

Keywords: Journey – Right Action - Cosmic Order – Ritual – Rhythmic Motion

Kenaz (kĕ-nôz) –K – *Kenaz*: is the rune of the controlled fire of creativity. The ability to shape the fruits of inspiration and manifest them in the physical world is facilitated by the power of Kenaz:. The fire of kenaz: is the fire under human control and applied toward a willed purpose - the fire of the forge, hearth, and torch. Kenaz is also the rune of passion and sexual love as positive attributes

Keywords: Torch – Controlled Energy–Ability–Sexual lust–Creativity–Creative Knowledge–Inspiration

Gebo (gĕ-bō) – G – *Gebo* is the rune of exchange. It is the power that facilitates that of fehu (see f-rune) and perpetuates that of Othala (see o-rune). Gebo is the rune of sacrifice – our gift to the gods in exchange for the gifts we receive from them. Gebo is also a rune involved in sex magic. Energy and knowledge is amplified by the exchange of power between the male/female polarities.

Keywords: Gift – Magical Force –Sacrifice – Sex Magic

Wunjo (wōōn-yō) – W or V – *Wunjo* is the rune of the joy of harmonious existence within the clan/kindred. It is the foundational force that draws related beings together and binds those beings into an organic whole. Wunjo promotes fellowship and goodwill among kinsfolk, and so promotes strong societal and guild bonds among members. This binding principle can also be used in rune magic to bind several runes to a single purpose.

Keywords: Binding – Harmony – Fellowship - Well Being - Joy

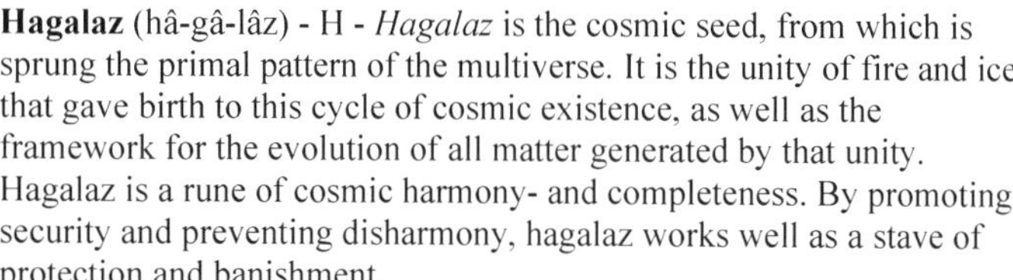

Hagalaz (hâ-gâ-lâz) - H - *Hagalaz* is the cosmic seed, from which is sprung the primal pattern of the multiverse. It is the unity of fire and ice that gave birth to this cycle of cosmic existence, as well as the framework for the evolution of all matter generated by that unity. Hagalaz is a rune of cosmic harmony- and completeness. By promoting security and preventing disharmony, hagalaz works well as a stave of protection and banishment.

Keywords: Hail -Protection - Cosmic Seed - Evolution - Cosmic Pattern/Framework

Nauðiz (now-these) – N - *Naudiz* is the rune of manifestation through need - deliverance through distress. Everyone has heard the phrase, "necessity is the mother of invention." This goes a long way in describing Naudiz. It is the need-fire created by friction to serve the need of man and the resistance necessary in the formation of Ørlög.

Keywords: Need-Fire - Friction - Resistance Distress/Deliverance

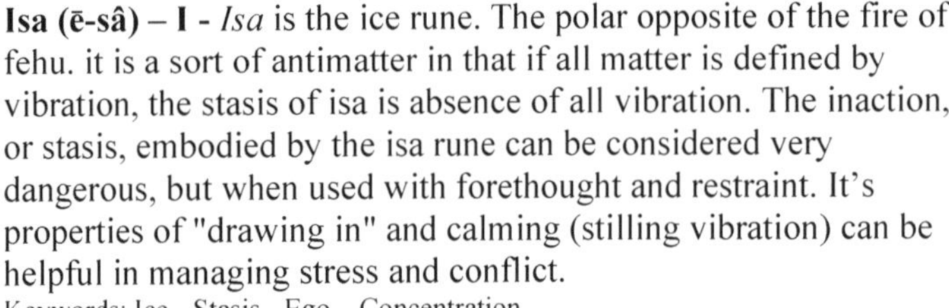

Isa (ē-sâ) – I - *Isa* is the ice rune. The polar opposite of the fire of fehu. it is a sort of antimatter in that if all matter is defined by vibration, the stasis of isa is absence of all vibration. The inaction, or stasis, embodied by the isa rune can be considered very dangerous, but when used with forethought and restraint. It's properties of "drawing in" and calming (stilling vibration) can be helpful in managing stress and conflict.
Keywords: Ice - Stasis - Ego – Concentration

Jera (yâr-ä) -J or Y -*Jera* is the rune of the cyclical process of birth life death and rebirth. This is the natural progression of the seasons (the year) and the pattern that is continually repeated throughout al l realms of existence. Jera is the good harvest - the just reward for deeds rightly sown.
Keywords: Year – (good) Harvest – Cyclical Development

Eiwaz (ā-väz) – ei - *Eiwaz* is the vertical axis of the rnultiverse --- the yew column of the world tree Yggdrasil. Like Yggdrasil, Eiwaz is a life sustaining force that unifies the mysteries of life and death. Another aspect of Eiwaz is that of the yew bow. This reinforces the life/death unification processes facilitated by Eiwaz. Eiwaz is a powerful stave of protection and banishing.
Keywords: Vertical Cosmic Axis - Life/Death - Protection

Perthro (pēr-thrō) - P - *Perthro* is the lot cup - the symbol for how ørlög functions and how gods and men might discern its workings. This includes the mysteries of nornic processes and the well of urðr from which flows wyrd, (that which is layered in ørlög). The mystery of divination is central to perthro, which makes a firm understanding of this rune necessary to effective practice of runecraft.
Keywords: Lot Cup - Nornic Processes - Ørlög - Constant Change - Fate

Elhaz (El-häz) –Z - *Elhaz* is a powerful and ancient rune of protection. Ideographically the rune looks like hand splayed out to ward off attack. Elhaz means "elk" and seems to form yet another connection with Yggdrasil through the "cosmic elk" who nibble on its needles. This is the rune of the unbreakable bond between Gods and men, and is the very force that draws man forward on his own journey toward God-consciousness.
Keywords: Protection - Life - Connection Between Gods and Men

Sowilo (sō-wē-lō) - S - *Sowilo* is the archetypal solar rune. Ideographically, it is one half of the solar wheel -卐- and the concept of the turning wheel is central to the power of this rune. The lightning bolt shape of this rune may suggest a dynamic connection between Asgardr and Midgardr. In recent times Sowilo became known as the sig (victory) rune. However, while the willed force of this rune can bring success in one's endeavors, the actual sig-rune is most probably the Tiwaz rune.
Keywords: Guidance – Will – Success – Willed Force - Victory

Tiwaz (tē-väz) – T - *Tiwaz* is the rune of the god Týr. Týr is the god of justice and self-sacrifice. It is Týr who is invoked for a just victory, so it is believed that it is this, and not the S-Rune, that is the actual sig-(victory) rune referred to in Sigrdrîfumál. The important mystery contained in tiwaz is three-fold and involves the concepts of justice, war, and the world-column (often represented by the Irminsul). The Týr rune is the mystery of the trú warrior ethic - that honorable acts, applied to a just cause, will bring victory.
Keywords: Justice - Victory - Self Sacrifice - Spiritual Discipline

Berkano (bĕr-kä-nō) – B - *Berkano* is the rune of the Birch Goddess or Great Mother. It is the unification of the "birth-life-death-gestation-rebirth" cycle and the container of all that is "becoming." This sort of "mystery of the moment" is closely tied with the workings of the P-rune. Those forces that find conservation and protection in Berkano are "spilled forth" through the action of Perthro.
Keywords: Birch Goddess -Birth Life Death-Rebirth - Containment

Ehwaz (ĕh-väz) – E - *Ehwaz* is the rune of the twin Gods. That these Gods were sometimes represented as horses is important to understanding the nature of this rune. The long, harmonious relationship between man and horse is one of the key concepts behind the power of Ehwaz. Ehwaz is a rune of trust and loyalty and is the symbol of the lawful man-woman marriage.
Keywords: War Horse - Fertility- - Trust - Loyalty - Legal Marriage

Mannaz (män-nŏz) – M - *Mannaz* is the rune of divine structure (especially in man). It describes the genetic link (via Rigr) between Gods and men. Mannaz describes our intelligence, as well as our initiation to the path toward God-consciousness. Being a rune of a linking to the divine through blood (genes), this rune is often used to symbolize the institution of blood brotherhood.
Keywords: Ideal Man - Divine Link - (Human) Intelligence - Initiate

Laguz (lä-gōōz) – L - *Laguz* is the rune of the primal waters of life that flow forth from Hvergelmir. This undifferentiated force contains both weal and woe working elements (yeast and venom). Laguz is also a rune of transformation between life and death – the water that quickens life at its beginning, and that which must be crossed at life's end. Laguz can be used to infuse the runester with vital life force and energy, but if this energy is allowed to stand still, it can stagnate and become poisonous.
Keywords: Passage To and From Life - Vital Power -- Primal Water – Natural Flow - Fluidity

Ingwaz (ĭng-väz) – ng -Ingwaz is the rune of the God Ing - male consort to the Earth Mother (later this function seems to have transferred to the God Freyr). Contained in this rune is the mystery of the seed, which must undergo gestation before its potential can be brought forth to manifestation.
Keywords: Seed - Potential Energy – Gestation – Good Luck

Dagaz (dă-gäz) - D - *Dagaz* is the rune of the "Day," meaning the 24 hour period from sunrise to sunset and from sunset to sunrise. As is shown by the stave form, Dagaz is a rune of synthesis of polarities - just as light and dark are synthesized at the points of dawn and twilight. The processes of synchronization contained in Dagaz - the dynamic synthesis of polar opposites - is the central mystery of the cult of Odin, and describes the paradoxical nature of Odin himself. Dagaz is a rune of meditation and enlightenment, and the point to focus on is that point of synthesis (i.e. the rune's center).
Keywords: Polarity - Synthesis - Odinic Paradox

Othala (ō-thă-lä) - O - *Othala* is the rune of ancestral property - the enclosure of the Kindred and Clan that defines the boundaries within which they are defended against unholy forces. Othala is also representative of those things of a spiritual nature that are passed along genetic lines. This includes such mysteries as those of the fylgja and of divine ancestry, as well as the wise management of the physical land of the Kindred by those endowed with the power of Othala in keeping with the laws of the Folk.
Keywords: Ancestral Property - Sacred Enclosure - Inherited Power – DNA - Folk

Runic Half Months

ᛇ	Eiwaz	28, Yule (Dec.) to 12, Snowmoon (Jan)
ᛈ	Perthro	13-27, Snowmoon
ᛉ	Elhaz	28, Snowmoon to 11, Horning (Feb)
ᛊ	Sowilo	12-26, Horning
ᛏ	Tiwaz	27, Horning to 13, Lenting (Mar)
ᛒ	BerKano	14-19, Lenting
ᛖ	Ehwaz	20, Lenting to 13, Ostara (Apr)
ᛗ	Mannaz	14-28, Ostara
ᛚ	Laguz	29, Ostara to 13, Merrymoon (May)
ᛜ	Ingwaz	14-28, Merrymoon
ᛞ	Dagaz	29, Merrymoon to 13, Midyear (Jun)

ᛟ Othala 14-28, Midyear

ᚠ Fehu 29, Midyear to 13, Haymoon (Jul)

ᚢ Uruz 14-28, Haymoon

ᚦ Thurisaz 29, Haymoon to 12, Harvest (Aug)

ᚨ Ansuz 13-28, Harvest

ᚱ Raido 29, Harvest to 12, Shedding (Sept)

ᚲ Kenaz 13-27, Shedding

ᚷ Gebo 28, Shedding to 12, Hunting (Oct)

ᚹ Wunjo 13-27, Hunting

ᚺ Hagalaz 28, Hunting to 12, Fogmoon (Nov)

ᚾ Nauthiz 13-27, Fogmoon

ᛁ Isa 28, Fogmoon to 12, Yule (Dec)

ᛃ Jera 13-27, Yule

MONTHS/MOONS

January	Snowmoon
February	Horning
March	Lenting
April	Ostara
May	Merrymoon
June	Midyear / Fallow
July	Haymoon
August	Harvest
September	Shedding
October	Hunting
November	Fogmoon
December	Wolfmoon / Yule

WEEKDAYS

Norse
Teutonic

Sunday Sunnasdagr or
Sunnastag

Monday Manisdagr or Manistag

Tuesday Tyrsdagr or Tyrstag

Wednesday Odinsdagr or Odinstag

Thursday Thorsdagr or
Thorsstag

Friday Friggasdagr or
Friggastag

Saturday Laugardagr or
Waschentag

THE HOLY YEAR & DAYS OF REMEMBRANCE FOR HEROES & MARTYRS

JANUARY / SNOWMOON

9th - Raud the Strong - Day of remembrance
14th - Robert Jay Mathews - Day of remembrance (RJM's birthday is the 16th)
21st - Thor's Blót

FEBRUARY / HORNING

2nd - Charming of the Plow
9th - Eyvind Kinnrifi - Day of remembrance
14th - Guido von List - Day of remembrance
14th – Feast of Vali

MARCH / LENTING

9th - Olvir the Martyr - Day of remembrance
14th - Sveinbjörn Beinteinsson - Day of remembrance
20th/21st -- OSTARA: Summer Finding (Spring Equinox) Usually falls on the 20th or 21st, with exception
28th -- Ragnar Lodbrok - Day of remembrance

APRIL / OSTARA

9th - Jarl Hakon - Day of remembrance
14th – SUMMARSDAG (SigrBlót – Major 1519 Blót)
14th - Rudolf Hess - Day of remembrance (R.H.'s birthday is the 26th)
20th - ADOLF HITLER'S BIRTHDAY

MAY / MERRYMOON

1st – May Day

9th – Guthroth - Day of remembrance

14th - ELSE CHRISTENSEN'S - DAY OF REMEMBRANCE (Entered Valhalla 5/4/05 CE)

JUNE / MIDYEAR/FALLOW

8th - Lindisfarne Day

9th - Sigurd the Volsung - Day of remembrance

14th - Ian Stuart Donaldson - Day of remembrance

20th/21st - MIDSUMMER: (Summer Solstice) Usually falls on the 20th or 21st with exception

JULY / HAYMOON

4th – Founder's Day

(The 4th of this month is internationally known as 'Founder's Day', wherefore the Religions of Odinism/Wotanism and Ásatrú are in regard)

9th - Unn the Deep Minded - Day of remembrance

14th - Vicki & Sammy Weaver - Day of remembrance

AUGUST / HARVEST

1st - This day is sacred to Allfather Odin & Allmother Frigga

9th - King Radbod of Frisia - Day of remembrance

14th - George Lincoln Rockwell - Day of remembrance

17th – 25th – 9 Nights of Odin's Ordeal (1519) Major Tide

28th - Freyfaxi

SEPTEMBER / SHEDDING

9th - Herman the Cherusci - Day of remembrance

14th - Jost Turner - Day of remembrance

20th/21st -WINTER FINDING (Fall Equinox) Usually falls on the 20th or 21st with exception

OCTOBER / HUNTING

8th - Eirik the Red - Day of remembrance

9th - Leif Eiriksson - Day of remembrance

11th/17th - VETURNAETUR: Winter Nights. Disa Blót (1519 Major Blót)

Occurs on both Sat. & Sun. which begins on the first Saturday between the 11th & 17th

14th - Kathy Ainsworth - Day of remembrance

NOVEMBER / FOGMOON

9th - Queen Sigrith - Day of remembrance

11th - FEAST OF THE EINHERJAR AND 1519 (1519 major Blót)

14th - David Lane - Day of remembrance (David's birthday is the 2nd)

DECEMBER / YULEMOON/WOLFMOON

8th – Martyrs Day

9th - Egil Skallagrimsson - Day of remembrance

14th Gordon Kahl - Day of remembrance

20th through 31st - YULETIDE: Twelve Days of Yule (1519 major Blótar Tide)

20th - Mother Night: Our New Year begins at sunset.

21st - MIDWINTER (Winter Solstice) Usually falls on 21st with exception (1519 major Blót) Midvinter Blót

31st - Twelfth Night

*** These dates constitute our Hof/Ministry's Holy Days of Blótar and Sacred Days of Remembrance. If you do not know the importance of these Rites, or who these Heroes and Martyrs are, then take the time to learn what they mean and who they are. They have all made significant contributions with how they lived and died.

THE CODE OF THE NORTHERN WARRIOR

The Living Einherjar & 1519

By and/or compiled by Gð. Dr. Casper Odinson Cröwell, 1519-CCG

1. A man is what he honors.

2. The unworthy always exclude themselves.

3. The worst sickness for a warrior/wise man is to crave what he cannot have.

4. All men are not equal in wisdom or character. The half wise are many and the ignoble are everywhere.

5. Mysteries should not be explained away, they should be experienced.

6. Pain can be a source of illumination.

7. The mind is the warrior. When the mind is right, the warrior is right. When the mind is not right, the warrior is not right…He who would follow the way of the warrior must first follow the way of the mind, for that is the warrior and the way of the Einherjar!

8. The supreme form of courage is the "one" against the all.

9. We cannot choose the terrors we must face in this life…but we can choose to face them calmly and with courage, for that is the Einherjar's grace.

10. Dishonor is anything which changes our nature or steals from us our soul.

11. Aggression unchallenged is aggression unleashed!

12. Only through self-discipline can one know the power of the will.

13. Tu recht und scheue niemand! / Do right and fear no one!

14. Independence is a privilege reserved for the strong.

15. Always be kind to your Kin & Kith…and extremely cruel to your foes.

16. Without the Gods, a soul wanders but is not free.

17. Confusion exists only in the absence of knowledge.

18. The warrior says goodbye to all he leaves behind.

19. To be free, one must follow the path that leads to the place where one dwelt before one was born, the collective Folk soul.

20. The Odinist believes that the soul is in the blood.

21. The difference between the victim and the warrior is that the victim never fights back.

22. It is not titles which honor men, but men who honor titles.

23. When the Einherjar steps back, it is only to leap forward.

24. Only noble men join an Order of honor for honor's sake!

25. A man is not fit to command others if he cannot first command himself.

26. In battle, never retreat before the enemy.

27. Never fight an unworthy foe unless he thrust himself upon you.

28. Once the battle has begun there can be no retreat and so there shall be none!

29. Nobility is not a birthright, it is a character trait.

30. What is done out of love, loyalty and duty, always occurs beyond the scope of order or chaos!

31. Know which battles to fight, when to fight them and know when to walk away.

14 CODES OF ARYAN ETHIC

By Ron McVan and David Lane

1 Honor no Gods but those of your own Folk, as alien gods destroy you.

2 Nature's laws evidence the divine plan, as the natural world is the work of AllFather Odin.

3 Act nobly and courageously, always carefully considering the consequences of your actions, as the effects of your deeds live on after you pass from Midgard.

4 Live within the reality of this life; fear not your fate, as fear is for fools and cowards; A valorous man boldly faces what the Norns decree.

5 Love, protect, reproduce and advance your Folk, as natural instinct prohibits miscegenation and self destruction.

6 Be honest, be disciplined, be productive and loyal to friends, as the Aryan spirit strives for excellence in all things.

7 Treasure your history, heritage and racial identity, as your ancestors have entrusted it falls with you, it will rise with you.

8 Honor the memory of your kith and kin, especially those who have given their lives or freedom for the Folk, as your race lives on through your blood and your will.

9 Respect the wisdom of your elders, as every moment of your lives links the infinite past to the infinite future.

10 Honor your mate, provide for your children and carry no quarrel with family to sleeptime, as family is your purpose and fulfillment.

11 May your word to a kinsman be a bond of steel, as your troth is your dignity and strength of character.

12 Be cunning as a fox with enemies and Nithlings, as their goal is your extinction, their motives are always detrimental to your wellbeing and that of the Folk's!

13 Secure, defend and cherish your Othal lands, as nature's territorial imperative demands.

14 Live in harmony with nature and the Folk and compromise not with evil, as racial survival is your perpetual struggle.

> Resist and defy always, that which you know to be wrong and detrimental to the welfare and advancement of our noble Folk.
>
> – Dr. Casper Odinson Cröwell, Ph.d., DD

THE NINE NOBLE VIRTUES OF ODINISM, *author unknown*

1. ***COURAGE***: Boldness, bravery, standing up for what you believe in and know is right.

2. ***HONESTY***: Truth - In all things be Trú to yourself and to others.

3. ***HONOR***: Do as you say and act upon your convictions. "Always" honor your oaths!

4. ***TROTH***: Loyalty to yourself, family, folk, friends and the Gods & Goddesses.

5. ***STRENGTH***: Self rule, self mastery, the self control and discipline to govern yourself by your convictions.

6. ***HOSPITALITY***: To freely share your gifts with others.

7. ***INDUSTRIOUSNESS***: To work wholeheartedly both hard and intelligently. To keep thinking and growing as a person.

8. ***SELF RELIANCE***: Free standing. Rely on others as little as possible!

9. ***PERSEVERANCE***: Don't give up at what you do until you feel it is completed and done well.

The ÆSIRIAN CODE OF NINE, author unknown

1) The Code is to Honor
Honor yourself with truth and fairness. Your word is your bond, give your word power by adhering to it. Honor your family and friends with reverence and respect. Honor your love and the Way above all else. Honor is the mark of strength and nobility.

2) The Code is to Protect
Protect with savagery your blood and kin. Let no one or no thing violate your love or way. Let there always be inequity in defense. Always protect thrice as fiercely as one is attacked. Protection is the mark of a warrior spirit.

3) The Code is to Flourish
Prosperity and growth are key to the survival of the way. Such is the mark of intelligence.

4) The Code is Knowledge
Knowledge is power. Seek ever to expand the mind. Never stagnate, for knowledge is a gift from the Gods.

5) The Code is Change
Adapting and changing are important for growth and survival. That which cannot adapt or change is doomed to perish. Change is the mark of insight.

6) The Code is Fairness
Pay all debts, pull your own weight, always hear and consider all sides. Treat all others with equity and fairness. Expect the same.

7) The Code is Balance
Remember the Law of balance; All that which you do or wish for, good or ill, shall return to you one day. Strive for the good.

8) The Code is Control
Never loose control to anger or be baited by hostility. Never strike a woman unless your life hangs in the balance. Never violate the weak

or innocent. Never tolerate those who do. Control is the mark of a disciplined mind, a sign of the greatest of warriors.

9) The Code is Conflict
Those who follow the way must know the art of combat, weapons and vengeance. War is part of the path. Always be prepared for hostility. It is a destiny woven into the fibers of our people. Keep body, mind and training up at all times. Have no remorse in the savagery of conflict. Win, prevail and survive.

Danish, circa 1075 runic era (825 common era)

THE REDE OF HONOR FOR ODINISM

1. In all that you do, always consider its benefit or harm upon yourself, your children and your folk.

2. All that which you do will return to you, sooner or later, for good or for ill. Thus strive always to do good to others, or at least strive always to be just.

3. Be honest with yourself, and with others, "This above all; to thine own self be trú."

4. Humankind, and especially your own family and folk, has the spark of divinity within it! Protect and nurture that spark.

5. Give your word sparingly and adhere to it like iron... Break no oath!

6. In life, your first trust and responsibility should always be to your own folk and people. Yet, be kind and proper to others when possible.

7. What you have, hold!

8. Pass on to others only those words which you have personally verified.

9. Be honest with others and let them know that you expect honesty in return.

10. The fury of the moment plays folly with the truth; To keep one's head is a virtue.

11. Know which battles should be fought, and which battles should be avoided. Also, know when to break off a conflict. There are times when the minions of chaos are simply too strong, or when fate is absolutely unavoidable.

12. When you gain power, use it carefully and use it well.

13. Courage and honor endure forever. Their echoes remain when the mountains have crumbled to dust.

14. Pledge friendship and your services to those who are worthy! Strengthen others of your people and they will strengthen you.

15. Love and care for your family always, and have the fierceness of a wolf in their protection.

16. Honor yourself, have pride in yourself, do your best and forgive yourself when you must.

17. Try always to be above reproach in the eyes of the world.

18. Those of your people should always endeavor to settle any differences among themselves quietly and peaceably.

19. If the laws of the land are beneficial to the folk and family, they should be obeyed.

20. Have pride in yourself, your family and your folk. They are your promise for the future.

21. Do not neglect your mate and children.

22. Every one of our people should work according to the best that he/she can do, no matter how small or great. We are all in this world together, thus we must always help each other along.

23. One advances individually and collectively only by living in harmony with the natural order of the world.

24. The seeking of wisdom is a high virtue. Love of truth, honor, courage and loyalty are the hallmarks of the noble soul, (Æthling).

25. Be prepared for whatever the future brings.

26. Life, with all its joys, struggles and ambiguities is to be embraced and lived to the fullest.

These are the Trú ways of conduct left to us by our Ancestors, strive to honor them and live them well. Place your feet on the path of the Æthling (Noble one), and spurn the ways of the Nithling (Coward, oath breaker, one whom embraces vice and treachery over virtue and honor).

ODIN'S BLÓT

1) Beginning in the North, raise the shield wall with a Hammer Hallowing:

"Hammer, í Nordri, Helge vé thetta ok hindra alla ilska!"

Now face the East, South, West and then face North once more and repeat above, below and here in Midgard, respectively and repeat with respective direction. (Austri, Sudri, Vestri)

2) Open the circle; Face North and assume an Elhaz (ᛉ) stadha and recite the following;
Clap hands three times...

Heil ye holy All-Father Odin, keeper of the Runes, wisest of the Gods, Father of Gods and men, Great God of the Æsir, God of royalty, God of battle, wisdom and war. God of death and mysticism, Father of the Runes, Great Valhalla host, hold ye the holy Kindred, your Sons (and Daughters) of the NorthFolk. Mighty warrior God of elder days, turn our minds and hearts towards you!

3) Consecrate the Stali / Hörgr; Clap hands three times...

I consecrate and make holy to the service of Odin, this alter! Banishing from it all wights and influences, which are impure and unholy. May our hearts and minds in this holy place be likewise consecrated.

4) The Sacred Flame;   Clap hands three times…

I light now the sacred flames of inspiration and cleansing. The first mystery and the final mercy. May it burn bright and long within the hearts and minds of our folk.

5) The First reading: "Hávamál stanzas 138-145"

6) Invocation; Charge the mead/water and invoke Odin:

This day (or, night), we proclaim holy in your name as we call to you and bid thee welcome here to this circle Father! Grace our lives with your holy presence and grant us victory! Ye have been known by many names, in many places, grand wise God of the NorthFolk who ever drives us forward and inspires us with your divine and unparalleled wisdom to aspire to and achieve daring deeds and live worthy lives as the royal and noble Sons and friends of the host of the Gods and Goddesses…

O'ye wise sage, ye wondrous, powerful father of warriors and poets alike! We call to you All-Father, wise one, thin one, father of the slain, one eyed God, graybeard, King of Valhalla, Lord of Asgard, Father of the Sons of Odin, host in the hall of Hár, leader of the wild hunt, keeper of the Runes, father of all, he who inspires wisdom and great deeds in the NorthFolk, one who guesses right, hooded one, wanderer, much loved one, far traveling sky cloaked wanderer, third one, one who blinds with death, father of Berserks, High one, bringer of ecstasy, long bearded one, God of wishes, wand bearer, God of prisoners, and Father of Victory! May we emulate you and your deeds as we walk your holy path… Pour now your energy into this horn/drink that we may grow closer to you and to each other as we share it among ourselves.

7) Second reading;   "Open to choice"

8) Bless the assembled Folk; Fill the horn and bless the folk;

Face North and hold the horn up to the sky and say:

"We offer you this drink with honor, love and respect, o' wise All-Father!"

Now return some of the horn's contents to the Bowl. Pass the horn around sunwise and allow each participant the opportunity to say something. After this is done, bless the folk with the yew sprig/twig by dipping it into the liquid in the blessing bowl (Bowli) and then whisking each with it while intoning;

"Ek gebu thig Othinn's blessi, or, I give thee the blessing of Odin!"

Face North and sprinkle the stali/ Hörgr and intone;

Holy Father of Gods and Men, to you All-Father Odin do we freely give this sacrifice, (and a draught to Loki to keep your pledge true).

9) Close the circle;

On this day (night), and all others which shall surely follow in our lives, we, your loyal sons, invoke thee Odin, that ye will walk with us and inspire us always with your love, wisdom and presence and that ye will always be known by the NorthFolk and that we NorthFolk will always know victory through you. May our ancient war cry always be heard; "Heil Odin!"

This rite is now done. Break the shield wall and depart with Odin's blessing.

by Gð. Dr. F. L. Casper Odinson Cröwell

Hávamál

translation by Carolyne Larrington, The Prose Edda, Oxford University Press, 1996

Human social wisdom, teasing allusion to runic mysteries, spells, and charms combine in this poem to give a conspectus of different types of wisdom. Most of the poem is taken up with instruction on the subject of social behavior, common sense and folly, moderation and friendship, composed in the *ljodahattar*, the usual metre of wisdom verse. At times the poet steps forward to speak in his own voice, at times the first person merges with Odin, the God of wisdom, speaking from his own experience of questing after knowledge. The wisdom stanzas are organized by themes, connections made by juxtaposition or contrast. Towards the end of the poem Odin speaks more, of his sacrifice to learn the secrets of the runes and of his knowledge of spells, and narrates two adventures with women, and the metre is disrupted. *Sayings of the High One* (Hávamál) is, no doubt, a redaction of several different poems unified by the theme of wisdom and by the central figure of Odin.

I

1. All the entrances, before you walk forward,
   you should look at,
   you should spy out;
   for you can't know for certain where enemies are sitting
   ahead in the hall.

2. Blessed be the givers! A guest has come in,
   where is he going to sit?
   He's in great haste, the one who by the hearth
   is going to be tested out.

3. Fire is needful for someone who's come in
   and who's chilled to the knee;
   food and clothing are necessary for the man
   who's journeyed over the mountains.

4. Water is needful for someone who comes to a meal,
   a towel and a warm welcome,

a disposition, if he can get it, for good words
and silence in return.

5. Wits are needful for someone who travels widely,
anything will do at home;
he becomes a laughing-stock, the man who knows nothing
and sits among the wise.

6. About his intelligence no man should be boastful,
rather cautious of mind;
when a wise and silent man comes to a homestead
seldom does shame befall the wary;
for no more trustworthy a friend can any man get
than a store of common sense.

7. The careful guest, who comes to a meal,
keeps silent with hearing finely attuned;
he listens with his ears, and looks about with his eyes;
so every wise man informs himself.

8. This man is fortunate who can get for himself
praise and good will;
very difficult it is when a man lays claim
to what's in another's heart.

9. That man is fortunate who, in himself,
keeps his reputation and wits while he lives,
for men have often received bad advice
from another's heart.

10. No better burden can a man carry on the road
than a store of common sense;
better than riches it will seem in an unfamiliar place,
such is the resort of the wretched.

11. No better burden can a man carry on the road
than a store of common sense;
a worse journey-provisioning he couldn't carry over the land
than to be too drunk on ale.

12. It isn't as good as it's said to be,
ale, for the sons of men;
for the more he drinks, the less he knows
about the nature of men.

13. The heron of forgetfulness hovers over the ale-drinking;
    he steals men's wits;
    with the feathers of this bird I was fettered
    in the court of Gunnlod.*

14. Drunk I was, I was more than drunk
    at wise Fialar's,*
    that's the best sort of ale-drinking when afterwards
    every man gets his mind back again.

15. Silent and thoughtful a prince's son should be
    and bold in fighting;
    cheerful and merry every man should be
    until he waits for death.

16. The foolish man thinks he will live for ever,
    if he keeps away from fighting;
    but old age won't grant him a truce
    even if the spears do.

17. The fool gapes when he comes on a visit,
    he mutters to himself or keeps silent;
    but it's all up with him if he gets a swig of drink;
    the man's mind is exposed.

18. Only that man who travels widely
    and has journeyed a great deal knows
    what sort of mind each man has in his control;
    he who's sharp in his wits.

19. A man shouldn't hold onto the cup but drink mead in moderation,
    it's necessary to speak or be silent;
    no man will blame you for impoliteness
    if you go early to bed.

20. The greedy man, unless he guards against this tendency,
    will eat himself into lifelong trouble;
    often he's laughed at when he comes among the wise,
    the man who's foolish about his stomach.

21. Cattle know when they ought to go home;
    and then they leave the pasture;
    but the foolish man never knows
    the measure of his own stomach.

22. He's a wretched man, of an evil disposition,
    the one who makes fun of everything;
    he doesn't know the one thing he ought to know;
    that he himself is not devoid of faults.

23. The foolish man lies awake all night
    and worries about things;
    he's tired out when the morning comes
    and everything's just as bad as it was.

24. The foolish man thinks that everyone
    is his friend who laughs with him;
    he doesn't notice even if they say cruel things about him
    when he sits among the wise.

25. The foolish man thinks that everyone
    is his friend who laughs with him;
    but then he finds when he comes to the Assembly*
    that he has few to speak on his behalf.

26. The foolish man thinks he knows everything
    if he takes refuge in a corner;
    he doesn't know what he can say in return
    if people ask him questions.

27. The foolish man in company
    does best if he stays silent;
    no one will know that he knows nothing,
    unless he talks too much;
    but the man who knows nothing does not know
    when he is talking too much.

28. Wise that man seems who knows how to question
    and how to answer as well;
    the sons of men cannot keep secret
    what's already going around.

29. Quite enough senseless words are spoken
    by the man never silent;
    a quick tongue, unless its owner keeps watch on it,
    often talks itself into trouble.

30. Into a laughing-stock no man should make another,
    though he comes on a visit;
    many a man seems wise if he isn't asked questions
    and he manages to lurk unscathed.

31. Wise that man seems who retreats
when one guest is insulting another;
the man who mocks others at a feast doesn't really know
whether he's shooting off his mouth amid enemies.

32. Many men are devoted to one another
and yet they fight at feasts;
amongst men there will always be strife,
guest quarrelling with guest.

33. An early meal a man should usually eat,
unless he is going on a visit;
he sits and guzzles, acts as if he is starving,
and doesn't make any conversation.

34. It's a great detour to a bad friend's house,
even though he lives on the route;
but to a good friend's the ways lie straight,
even though he lives far off.

35. A man must go, he must not remain a guest
always in the same place;
the loved man is loathed if he sits too long
in someone else's hall.

36. A farm of your own is better, even if small,
everyone's someone at home;
though he has two goats and a coarsely roofed house,
that is better than begging.

37. A farm of your own is better, even if small,
everyone's someone at home;
a man's heart bleeds when he has to beg
for every single meal.

38. From his weapons on the open road
no man should step one pace away;
you don't know for certain when you're out on the road
when you might have need of your spear.

39. I never found a generous man, nor one so hospitable with food,
that he wouldn't accept a present;
or one so well-provided with money
that he wouldn't take a gift if offered.

40. On account of the property which he has amassed
    a man shouldn't suffer need;
    often what was meant for the lovable is saved for the hateful,
    much goes worse than expected.

41. With weapons and gifts friends should gladden one another,
    that is most obvious;
    mutual givers and receivers are friends for longest,
    if the friendship is going to work at all.

42. To his friend a man should be a friend
    and repay gifts with gifts;
    laughter a man should give for laughter
    and repay treachery with lies.

43. To his friend a man should be a friend
    and to his friend's friend too;
    but a friend no man should be
    to the friend of his enemy.

44. You know, if you've a friend whom you really trust
    and from whom you want nothing but good,
    you should mix your soul with his and exchange gifts,
    go and see him often.

45. If you've another, whom you don't trust,
    but from whom you want nothing but good,
    speak fairly to him but think falsely
    and repay treachery with lies.

46. Again, concerning the one whom you don't trust,
    and whose mind you suspect:
    you should laugh with him and disguise your thoughts,
    a gift should be repaid with a like one.

47. I was young once, I travelled alone,
    then I found myself going astray;
    rich I thought myself when I met someone else,
    for man is the joy of man.

48. Generous and brave men live the best,
    seldom do they harbour anxiety;
    but the cowardly man is afraid of everything,
    the miser always sighs when he gets gifts.

49. My clothes I gave along the way
to two wooden men,*
champions they thought themselves when they had clothing,
the naked man is ashamed.

50. The withered fir-tree which stands on the mound,
neither bark nor needles protect it;
so it is with the man whom no one loves,
why should he live for long?

51. Hotter than fire between bad friends
burns affection for five days;
but it dies down when the sixth day comes,
and all that friendship goes to the bad.

52. Not very much need a man give,
often you get praise for a little;
with half a loaf and a tilted cup
I've got myself a companion.

53. Of small sands, of small seas,
small are the minds of men;
for all men aren't equally wise,
men everywhere are half wise, half not.

54. Averagely wise a man ought to be,
never too wise;
for he lives the best sort of life,
the man who knows a fair amount.

55. Averagely wise a man ought to be,
never too wise;
for a wise man's heart is seldom cheerful,
if he who owns it's too wise.

56. Averagely wise a man ought to be,
never too wise;
no one may know his fate beforehand,
if he wants a carefree spirit.

57. One brand takes fire from another, until it is consumed,
a spark's kindled by a spark;
one man becomes clever by talking with another,
but foolish by taciturnity.

58. He should get up early, the man who means to take
another's life or property;
the slumbering wolf does not get the ham,
nor a sleeping man victory.

59. He should get up early, the man who has few workers,
and go about his work with thought;
much he neglects, the man who sleeps in the mornings,
wealth is half-won by the vigorous.

60. Of dry wood and thatching-bark
a man can know the measure;
and of the wood which can get one through
a quarter- or a half-year.

61. Washed and fed, a man should ride to the Assembly,
though he may not be very well dressed;
of his shoes and breeches no man should be ashamed,
nor of his horse, though he doesn't have a good one.

62. The eagle snaps and cranes his neck when he comes to the sea,*
to the ancient ocean;
so does a man who comes among the multitude
and has few people to speak for him.

63. Asking questions and answering, this every wise man should do,
he who wants to be reputed intelligent;
one may know, a second should not,
the whole world knows, if three know.

64. Every man wise in counsel
should use his power in moderation;
for when he mingles with warriors he finds out
that no one is boldest of all.

65. For those words which one man says to another,
often he gets paid back.*

66. Much too early I've come to many places,
but sometimes too late;
the ale was all drunk, or sometimes it wasn't yet brewed,
the unpopular man seldom chooses the right occasion.

67. Here and there I'd be invited to someone's home
when I had no need of food for the moment;

or two hams would be hanging in a trusty friend's house
when I'd already eaten one.

68. Fire is the best for the sons of men,
and the sight of the sun
his health, if a man can manage to keep it,
living without disgrace.

69. No man is completely wretched, even if he has bad luck;
one man is blessed with sons,
another with kinsmen, another has enough money,
another has done great deeds.

70. It is better to live than not to be alive,
it's the living man who gets the cow;
I saw a fire blaze up for the wealthy man,
and he was dead outside the door.

71. The lame man rides a horse, the handless man drives herds,
the deaf man fights and succeeds;
to be blind is better than to be burnt:
a corpse is of no use to anyone.

72. A son is best, even if he is born late,
when the father is dead;
seldom do memorial stones stand by the wayside,
unless one kinsmen raises them for another.

73. Two are the conquerors of one, the tongue is the slayer of the head,
hidden under every fur coat I expect to find a hand.*

74. Night is eagerly awaited by the man who can rely on his
provisions;
short are a ship's yards,
changeable are autumn nights,
many kinds of weather in five days,
and more in one month.

75. Even a man who knows nothing
knows that many are fooled by money;
one man is rich, another is not rich,
he should not be blamed for that.

76. Cattle die, kinsmen die,*
the self must also die;

but glory never dies,
for the man who is able to achieve it.

77. Cattle die, kinsmen die,
the self must also die;
I know one thing which never dies:
the reputation of each dead man.

78. Fully stocked folds I saw for Fitiong's sons,*
now they carry beggars staffs;
wealth is like a twinkling of an eye,
it is the most unreliable of friends.

79. The foolish man, if he manages to get
money or love of a woman,
his arrogance increases, but not his common sense;
on he goes deeply sunk in delusion.

80. That is now proved, what you ask of the runes,
of the potent famous ones
which the great Gods made
and the mighty sage stained,*
then it is best for him if he stays silent.

81. At evening should the day be praised, the woman when she is cremated,
the blade when it is tested, the girl when she is married,
the ice when it is crossed, the ale when it is drunk.

82. In a wind one should cut wood, in fine weather row on the sea,
in darkness chat with a girl: many are the eyes of the day;
use a ship to glide along, a shield for defense,
a sword for blows, and a girl for kisses.

83. By the fire one should drink ale, one should slide over the ice,
buy a lean horse and a rusty blade,
fatten the horse at home and a dog on the farmstead.

84. The words of a girl no one should trust,
nor what a woman says;
for on a whirling wheel their hearts were made,*
deceit lodged in their breasts.

85. A stretching bow, a burning flame,
a gaping wolf, a cawing crow,

a grunting pig, a rootless tree,
a rising wave, a boiling kettle,

86. a flying dart, a falling wave,
ice of one night, a coiled serpent,
the bed-talk of a woman, or a broken sword,
the playing of a bear, or a king's child,

87. a sick calf, an independent-minded slave,
a seer who prophesies good, a newly killed corpse,

88. an early-sown field let no man trust,
nor too early a son;
the weather determines the field and brains the son,
both of them are risky.

89. A brother's killer, if you meet him on the road,
a house half-burned, a too swift horse-
the mount is useless if he breaks a leg-
let no man be so trusting as to trust all these.

90. Such is the love of women, of those with false minds;
it's like driving a horse without spiked shoes over slippery ice,
a frisky two year old, badly broken in,
or like steering, in a stiff wind, a rudderless boat,
or trying to catch when you're lame a reindeer on a thawing hillside.

91. I can speak frankly since I have known both:
the hearts of men are fickle towards women;
when we speak most fairly, then we think most falsely,
that entraps the wise mind.

92. He has to speak fairly and offer money,
the man who wants a woman's love;
praise the body of the radiant woman:
he who flatters, gets.

93. No man should ever reproach
another for love;
often the wise man is seized, when the foolish man is not,
by a delightfully fair appearance.

94. Not at all should one man reproach another
for what is common among men;

among the sons of men the wise are made foolish
by that mighty desire.

95. The mind alone knows what lies near the heart,
he alone knows his spirit:
no sickness is worse for the wise man
than to have no one to love him.

96. That I found when I sat among the reeds
and waited for my desire;
body and soul the wise girl was to me,
nevertheless I didn't win her.

97. Billing's girl I found on the bed,*
sleeping, sun-radiant;
the pleasures of a noble were nothing to me,
except to live with that body.

98. 'At evening, Odin, you should come again,
if you want to woo yourself a girl;
all is lost if anyone knows
of such shame together.'

99. Back I turned, and thought I was going to love,
back from my certain pleasure;
this I thought that I would have,
all her heart and her love-play.

100. So I came afterwards, but standing ready
were all the warriors, awake,
with burning torches and carrying brands:
thus the path of desire was determined for me.

101. And near morning, when I came again,
then the hall-company were asleep;
a bitch I found then tied on the bed
of that good woman.

102. Many a good girl when you know her better
is fickle of heart towards men;
I found that out, when I tried to seduce
that sagacious woman into shame;
every sort of humiliation the clever woman devised for me,
and I didn't even possess the woman.

103. At home a man should be cheerful and merry with his guest,
he should be shrewd about himself,
with a good memory and eloquent, if he wants to be very wise,
often should he speak of good things;
a nincompoop that man is called, who can't say much for himself,
that is the hallmark of a fool.

104. I visited the old giant, now I've come back,*
I didn't get much there from being silent;
with many words I spoke to my advantage
in Suttung's hall.

105. Gunnlod gave me from her golden throne
a drink of the precious mead;
a poor reward I let her have in return,
for her open-heartedness,
for her heavy spirit.

106. With the mouth of the auger I made space for myself*
and gnawed through the stone;
over me and under me went the paths of the giants,
thus I risked my head.

107. The cheaply bought beauty I made good use of,
the wise lack for little;
for Odrerir has now come up*
to the rim of the sanctuaries of men.

108. I am in doubt as to whether I would have come
back from the courts of the giants,
if I had not made use of Gunnlod, that good woman,
and put my arms about her.

109. The next day the frost-giants went
to ask for the High One's advice, in the High One's hall;
they asked about Bolverk: whether he was amongst the Gods,*
or whether Suttung had slaughtered him.

110. I thought Odin had sworn a sacred ring-oath,*
how can his word be trusted!
He left Suttung betrayed at the feast
and made Gunnlod weep.

111. It is time to declaim from the sage's high-seat,
at the spring of fate;
I saw and was silent, I saw and I considered,

I heard the speech of men;
I heard talk of runes nor were they silent about good counsel,
at the High One's hall, in the High One's hall;
thus I heard them speak:

112. I advise you, Loddfafnir, to take this advice,*
it will be useful if you learn it,
do you good, if you have it:
don't get up at night, except to look around
or if you need to visit the privy outside.

113. I advise you, Loddfafnir, to take this advice,
it will be useful if you learn it,
do you good, if you have it:
in the arms of a witch you should never sleep,
so that she charms all your limbs;

114. she'll bring it about that you won't care
about the Assembly or the king's business;
you won't want food nor the society of people,
sorrowful you'll go to sleep.

115. I advise you, Loddfafnir, to take this advice,
it will be useful if you learn it,
do you good, if you have it:
never entice another's wife to you
as a close confidante.

116. I advise you, Loddfifnar, to take this advice,
it will be useful if you learn it,
do you good, if you have it:
on mountain or fjord should you happen to be travelling,
make sure you are well fed.

117. I advise you, Loddfafnir, to take this advice,
it will be useful if you learn it,
do you good, if you have it:
never let a wicked man know
of any misfortune you suffer;
for from a wicked man you will never get
a good thought in return.

118. I saw a man fatally wounded
through the words of a wicked woman;
a malicious tongue brought about his death
and yet there was no truth in the accusation.

119. I advise you, Loddfafnir, to take this advice,
it will be useful if you learn it,
do you good, if you have it:
you know, if you've a friend, one whom you trust,
go to see him often;
for brushwood grows, and tall grass,
on the road which no man treads.

120. I advise you, Loddfafnir, to take this advice,
it will be useful if you learn it,
do you good, if you have it:
draw to you in friendly intimacy a good man
and learn healing charms all your life.

121. I advise you, Loddfafnir, to take this advice,
it will be useful if you learn it,
do you good, if you have it:
with your friend never be
the first to tear friendship asunder;
sorrow eats the heart if you do not have
someone to tell all your thoughts.

122. I advise you, Loddfafnir, to take this advice,
it will be useful if you learn it,
do you good, if you have it:
you should never bandy words
with a stupid fool;

123. for from a wicked man you will never get
a good return;
but a good man will make you
assured of praise.

124. That is the true mingling of kinship when you can tell
someone all your thoughts;
anything is better than to be fickle;
he is no true friend who only says pleasant things.

125. I advise you, Loddfafnir, to take this advice,
it will be useful if you learn it,
do you good, if you have it:
even three words of quarrelling you shouldn't have with an
inferior;
often the better retreats
when the worse man fights.

126. I advise you, Loddfafnir, to take this advice,
it will be useful if you learn it,
do you good, if you have it:
be neither a shoemaker nor a shaftmaker
for anyone but yourself;
if the shoe is badly fitting or the shaft is crooked,
then a curse will be called down on you.

127. I advise you, Loddfafnir, to take this advice,
it will be useful if you learn it,
do you good, if you have it:
where you recognize evil, speak out against it,
and give no truces to your enemies.

128. I advise you, Loddfafnir, to take this advice,
it will be useful if you learn it,
do you good, if you have it:
never be made glad by wickedness
but make yourself the butt of approval.

129. I advise you, Loddfafnir, to take this advice,
it will be useful if you learn it,
do you good, if you have it:
you should never look upwards in battle:*
the sons of men become panicked--
you may well be bewitched.

130. I advise you, Loddfafnir, to take this advice,
it will be useful if you learn it,
do you good, if you have it:
if you want a good woman for yourself to talk to as a close confidante,
and to get pleasure from,
make fair promises and keep them well,
no man tires of good, if he can get it.

131. I advise you, Loddfafnir, to take this advice,
it will be useful if you learn it,
do you good, if you have it:
I tell you to be cautious but not over-cautious;
be most wary of ale, and of another's wife,
and, thirdly, watch out that thieves don't beguile you.

132. I advise you, Loddfafnir, to take this advice,
it will be useful if you learn it,

do you good, if you have it:
never hold up to scorn or mockery
a guest or a wanderer.

133. Often those who sit in the hall do not really know
whose kin those newcomers are;
no man is so good that he has no blemish,
nor so bad that he can't succeed in something.

134. I advise you, Loddfafnir, to take this advice,
it will be useful if you learn it,
do you good, if you have it:
at a grey-haired sage you should never laugh!
Often what the old say is good;
often from a wrinkled bag come judicious words,
from those who hang around with the hides
and skulk among the skins
and hover among the cheese-bags.

135. I advise you, Loddfafnir, to take this advice,
it will be useful if you learn it,
do you good, if you have it:
don't bark at your guests or drive them from your gate,
treat the indigent well!

136. It is a powerful latch which has to lift
to open up for everyone;
give a ring, or there'll be called down on you
a curse in every limb.

137. I advise you, Loddfafnir, to take this advice,
it will be useful if you learn it,
do you good, if you have it:
where you drink ale, choose the power of earth!*
For earth is good against drunkenness, and fire against sickness,
oak against constipation, an ear of corn against witchcraft,
the hall against household strife, for hatred the moon should be invoked--
earthworms for a bite or sting, and runes against evil;
soil you should use against flood.

138. I know that I hung on a windy tree*
nine long nights,
wounded with a spear, dedicated to Odin,
myself to myself,

on that tree of which no man knows
from where its roots run.

139. No bread did they give me nor a drink from a horn,
downwards I peered;
I took up the runes, screaming I took them,
then I fell back from there.

140. Nine mighty spells I learnt from the famous son
of Bolthor, Bestla's father,*
and I got a drink of the precious mead,
poured from Odrerir.

141. Then I began to quicken and be wise,
and to grow and to prosper,
one word found another word for me,
one deed found another deed for me.

142. The runes you must find and the meaningful letter,
a very great letter,
a very powerful letter,
which the mighty sage stained
and the powerful Gods made
and the runemaster of the Gods carved out.

143. Odin for the Æsir, and Dain for the elves,
Dvalin for the dwarfs,
Asvid for the giants,
I myself carved some.

144. Do you know how to carve, do you know how to interpret,
do you know how to stain, do you know how to test out,
do you know how to ask, do you know how to sacrifice,
do you know how to dispatch, do you know how to slaughter?

145. Better not to pray, than to sacrifice too much,
one gift always calls for another;
better not dispatched than to slaughter too much.
So Thund carved before the history of nations,*
where he rose up, when he came back.

146. I know those spells which a ruler's wife doesn't know,*
nor any man's son;
'help' one is called,
and that will help you

against accusations and sorrows
and every sort of anxiety.

147. I know a second one which the sons of men need,
those who want to live as physicians.

148. I know a third one which is very useful to me,
which fetters my enemy;
the edges of my foes I can blunt,
neither weapon nor club will bite for them.

149. I know a fourth one if men put
chains upon my limbs;
I can chant so that I can walk away,
fetters spring from my feet,
and bonds from my hands.

150. I know a fifth if I see, shot in malice,
a dart flying amid the army:
it cannot fly so fast that I cannot stop it
if I see it with my eyes.

151. I know a sixth one if a man wounds me
with the roots of the sap-filled wood:
and that man who conjured to harm me,
the evil consumes him, not me.

152. I know a seventh one if I see towering flames
in the hall about my companions:
it can't burn so widely that I can't counteract it,
I know the spells to chant.

153. I know an eighth one, which is most useful
for everyone to know;
where hatred flares up between the sons of warriors,
then I can quickly bring settlement.

154. I know a ninth one if I am in need,
if I must protect my ship at sea;
the wind I can lull upon the wave
and quieten all the sea to sleep.

155. I know a tenth one if I see witches
playing up in the air;
I can bring it about that they can't make their way back

to their own shapes,
to their own spirits.

156. I know an eleventh if I have to lead
loyal friends into battle;
under the shields I chant, and they journey inviolate,
safely to the battle,
safely from the battle,
safely they come everywhere.

157. I know a twelfth one if I see, up in a tree,
a dangling corpse in a noose:
I can so carve and colour the runes
that the man walks
and talks with me.

158. I know a thirteenth if I shall pour water
over a young warrior:
he will not fall though he goes into battle,
before swords he will not sink.

159. I know a fourteenth if I have to reckon up
the gods before men:
Æsir and elves, I know the difference between them,
few who are not wise know that.

160. I know a fifteenth, which the dwarf Thiodrerir
chanted before Delling's doors:
powerfully he sang for the Æsir and before the elves,
wisdom to Sage.

161. I know a sixteenth if I want to have all
a clever woman's heart and love-play:
I can turn the thoughts of the white-armed woman
and change her mind entirely.

162. I know a seventeenth, so that scarcely any
young girl will want to shun me.
Of these spells, Loddfafnir,
you will long be in want;
though they'd be good for you, if you got them,
useful if you learned them,
handy, if you had them.

163. I know an eighteenth, which I shall never teach
to any girl or any man's wife--

it's always better when just one person knows,
that follows at the end of the spells--
except that one woman whom my arms embrace,
or who may be my sister.

164. Now is the song of the High One recited, in the High One's hall,
very useful to the sons of men,
quite useless to the sons of giants,
luck to him who recites, luck to him who knows!
May he benefit, he who learnt it,
luck to those who listened!

Notes

Gunnlod: this alludes to the story of the winning of the mead of poetry, told in full in Snorri, *Edda*, pp. 61-4. The mead originally belonged to two dwarfs, Fialar and Gialar, and was stolen by the giants. Odin had worked for a year as a thrall for the brother of Suttung, the giant who had the mead. When the year was up he went to Suttung (here confusingly called Fialar) to claim his reward of mead. By seducing Gunnlod, Suttung's daughter, he gained her help and escaped with the mead back to Asgard. The story is told in fuller detail in vv. 104-10 below.

Fiarlar: here a mistake for Suttung, owner of the mead.

Assembly: in both mainland Scandinavia and Iceland people would regularly meet at regional assemblies (Things) to resolve law cases.

Two wooden men: these may be scarecrows, or they may be wooden idols, mentioned in some sagas. In the *saga of Ragnar Lodbrok*, ch. 20, some Vikings come to a Baltic island where they find a huge, wooden idol. The idol speaks a verse complaining that once he used to be given food and clothing but now he is neglected.

The eagle: opinion is divided as to whether this is a sea-eagle on the look out for fish as prey, or a land eagle who has flown away from his accustomed habitat and so is disoriented.

Paid back: this verse is missing some lines.

A hand: the metre has changed suddenly and the meaning is obscure. Possibly a rich outer garment may well conceal a hand ready to strike.

Cattle die, kinsmen die: a parallel has been detected in the Old English poem *The Wanderer*: 'here cattle are transient / here property is transient, here a friend is transient' (l. 108). If there is a direct connection it most likely stems from the formulaic use of the words 'cattle' and 'kinsmen', an alliterating pair both in Old Norse, *fe* and *frændr,* and in Old English, *feoh* and *freond.*

Fitiung's sons: although they sound proverbial, Fitiung's sons are otherwise unknown.

Mighty sage stained: the sage is probably Odin. Carved runic letters appear originally to have been filled in with some kind of paint.

Whirling wheel: the image is of a potter's wheel or of a truning lathe; in its turning the wheel incorporates changeability into women's hearts. Some have seen the medieval image of the Wheel of Fortune here, but that deals with a human's external fate, not is internal character.

Billing's girl: this story is unknown from other sources, though the sequence of events is not difficult to follow. Odin importunes the wife or daughter of Billing (probably a giant). She puts him off until the evening; when he first comes to her hall everyone is still awake, the second time she has gone, leaving a bitch in her place. Billing's girl doubtless fears to reject Odin openly lest he bewitch her as he does Rind, who has fated to be the mother of Vali, avenger of Baldr. Her story is told in Saxo's *History of the Danish People*, Book 3, pp. 69-79.

The old giant: a further elaboration of the story of the mead of poetry begun in vv. 13-14.

Auger: according to Snorri, *Edda*, p. 63, Odin makes use of an auger called Rati to bore his way into the mountain where Gunnlod is to be found, and, turning himself into a snake, wriggles in through the hole.

Odrerir: according to Snorri this is the name of one of the vats in which the mead of poetry was kept, though the name 'Stirrer of Inspiration' seems more likely to refer to the mead itself.

Bolverk: the name Odin had used when disguised as a thrall, and in his dealings with Gunnlod.

Ring-oath: in Iceland oaths were sworn on large silver rings kept at the local temple and reddened with sacrificial blood.

Loddfafnir: the name is unknown from other sources. *Lodd-* seems to mean 'rags', while Fafnir is the name of the dragon Sigurd killed.

The combination 'Ragged-dragon' may be a mocking term for someone who is not yet fully initiated into arcane knowledge.

Look upwards in battle: the phenomenon warned against here is a kind of mass panic, frequently found in Irish sources, and for which an Irish loanword is used in the Norse.

Power of earth: the substances mentioned ma be invoked or be incorporated into some kind of ritual.

I hung on a windy tree: Odin performs a sacrifice by hanging for nine nights on the tree Yggdrasill, pierced with a spear in order to gain knowledge of the runes. The parallels with the Crucifixion are marked, though interpretation is controversial. The motif of the Hanged God is widespread in Indo-European and ancient Near Eastern religion, however, so direct Christian influence need not be present here.

Bolthor: Odin's maternal grandfather; Bolthor's son is therefore Odin's mother's brother, a particularly close relationship in Germanic society.

Thund: an Odinic name.

Spells: the spells which Odin alludes to here broadly match those magical skills listed for him in *Ynglinga saga*, chs. 2 and 6.

ABOUT THE AUTHOR

At the time of this printing in 2018 CE, Goði Dr. Casper Odinson Cröwell has been a Heathen/Odinist for forty years in which time he has been associated with numerous Odinist/Wotanist, Ásatrú and Folk oriented organizations. He is the Chieftain/Herjan and co-founder of the Order of the Sacred Circle of the Sons of Odin, 1519 and the Sororal Order of the Sisters of the Sons, 1919. He is also the co-founder of the Holy Nation of Odin Outreach Ministry, where he is the Chief Court Goði and Director of Religious Services. He was legally ordained Goði/Gothi (Priest/Minister) in April of 1996 CE. He earned a minor Law degree (Paralegal) in 1997 CE from Blackstone School of Law in Dallas, TX, dual Ph.D.'s in the fields of Comparative Religion and Metaphysics in 2003 CE from American and Northwestern, as well as a Doctorate of Divinity in Odinist Theology in 2006 CE. Recently he has earned Certfications in Law in Victim Advocacy in 2015 CE from Adams State University and Alternate Dispute Resolution in 2016 CE from Texas A & M University.

He remains confined within the California State Prison System. A Political Prisoner and P.O.W. in the war of political correctness, Dr. Cröwell is serving a life sentence since 1995 CE, for his Folkish beliefs and Patriotism. He is the author of numerous works regarding Philosophy, Psychology, Theosophy and Theology in addition to Poetry and short fiction. Among his Theological works, are included in the books on Fundamental Odinisim; "Ek Einherjar: Hammer of the Gods (Revolutionary Prose on Faith, Folk and Philosophy) First Edition, ISBN 987-0-615-33074-7 (2009 CE) and Vor Forn Siðr: A Handbook for the Living Einherjar and Valkyrjar, ISBN 978-0-985-47600-7 (2012 CE).

Made in the USA
Monee, IL
18 June 2024

60099851R00212